The United Nations

THE
UNITED
NATIONS

A View from Within

Ralph Townley

CHARLES SCRIBNER'S SONS
NEW YORK

PRINTED IN THE UNITED STATES OF AMERICA

LIBRARY OF CONGRESS CATALOG CARD NUMBER 68–17357

The author is a member of the United Nations
Secretariat, but the views expressed here are en-
tirely his own and not necessarily those of the
United Nations Organization.

Map by Veit-Martin Associates

TO THE MEMORY OF MY FATHER
FRANCIS HARRY TOWNLEY

ACKNOWLEDGMENTS

It is impossible to give recognition to everyone who has helped to create this book. Of those friends and mentors to whom I am particularly indebted, mention should be made of the following: Mr. P. F. Stewart, M.C., who first introduced me to scholarship; Professor R. Fryer and Mr. J. Lees who helped me so much when I was an undergraduate at the University of Nottingham; Professors C. A. W. Manning, Geoffrey L. Goodwin, Martin Wight and the late Sir Charles Webster who, in my day, taught at the London School of Economics and Political Science; and Professor Henry Steele Commager who, at the Seminar in American Studies at Salzburg, introduced me to American studies. Also, my thanks are due to many of my colleagues in the United Nations and the Specialized Agencies. But, perhaps, most of all I am grateful to the staff and students of the Graduate School of Public and International Affairs in the University of Pittsburgh and of the New School for Social Research in New York, who were sometimes surprised but always courteous in the seminars and lectures that gave rise to the present text.

Mr. John McMahon, Fellow and Lecturer in Law at Hertford College, Oxford, kindly read the manuscript and had many helpful suggestions to make on its revision. I am deeply obligated to Mrs. Robert Sheets and Mrs. Colin Brathwaite for preparing the manuscript and to Mrs. Phyllis L. Collins for making the index. My thanks are due to the University of Nottingham for permitting me to use in Chapters X and XII material contained in the Montague

Burton Lecture which I gave in March 1965 under the title of *International Assistance Comes of Age*. I am grateful to Mr. H. G. Nicholas and the Oxford University Press for permission to quote from *The United Nations as a Political Institution*. The passage from "Pogo" is reprinted by permission of Walt Kelly and the Hall Syndicate, Inc.

I also wish to express my warmest thanks to the publisher's staff for their assistance and guidance in preparing this work for publication.

PREFACE

This book has been written for the general reader wishing to inform himself about how the United Nations family has developed, for the official entering his country's or the international services and for the student requiring a supplementary textbook on international organizations. In the interest of all three, I have tried not to confuse seriousness with solemnity.

As this is the first book dealing broadly with international organizations to be written by a serving member of the United Nations Secretariat, a word of explanation is called for. Most books about international organizations are written by scholars who seldom, if ever, have had experience in public affairs. This is as it should be. But I think there is a place for a book which gives an occasional insight into the practical problems, inherent in the daily tasks of the international public servant. I should also add here that my experience has been almost entirely in economic and social developments, and not in the political field. Finally, I should state that as a serving member of the United Nations I have been given permission to have this book published, but the United Nations accepts no responsibility for its contents.

In writing about the evolution of the United Nations system, I have tried to avoid overwhelming the reader with a vast array of facts. Instead I have concentrated on the development of an awareness of the nature of our international society, and the organizations that have been devised to further its integration and development. In so doing, I have limited the study to the United Nations and the Specialized Agencies which, for the most part, are world-wide in scope.

Although it has resulted in some departure from United Nations practice, in the interest of stylistic consistency American usage has been observed in this volume.

R. T.

CONTENTS

TABLES

The United Nations

Chapter I

THE WAR YEARS

The weekend sailor, when he brings his boat in to pick up her mooring, may misjudge the wind or the tide and slip by, in which case he goes round the buoy again hoping not to muff it a second time. Although the procedure will be almost identical to that followed during the first attempt, he may, to cover his embarrassment before the assembled onlookers, affect an attitude to convey the impression that this is really the first time he has ever done it.

The process by which the United Nations was brought into being was very similar to that by which the League of Nations had been created. But in establishing the United Nations, there was a deliberate attempt on the part of the negotiators and drafters to disassociate themselves from the League, so much so that there was a determination, which, in retrospect, may seem to have been almost excessive, to avoid using the language of the Covenant even when the drafters were preparing sections of the Charter almost identical to those of the Covenant.

The reason for this sprang, for the most part, from a respect for Russian and American sensitivities. The League, as one of its last acts, had evicted the U. S. S. R. for its attack on Finland in 1939. In setting up the United Nations, the U. S. S. R., as a Great Power, was to play a major role. It would complicate matters considerably if the work went forward in such a way that the United Nations assumed the mantle of the League.

The spirit of the United States is one that abhors failure. It is instead one that is adventurous and forward-looking and is more given to leaving the wreck behind and moving on to start afresh rather than spending time tinkering with whatever it was that has

broken down. Psychologically, therefore, it was considered imprudent to attempt to revive and refurbish the League, particularly
since in the United States there were guilt feelings over its failure
to join the League after having done so much to bring it into being.
The United States considered that it had problems enough without
having to find a seat for President Wilson's ghost at the conference
table.

While the other Allies understood this and were themselves for
the most part only too happy to start afresh, the League was never
far from their minds. After all, the League had been the only world
organization with broad responsibilities ever created. It had accumulated twenty years experience, albeit sometimes unfortunate,
and the body of competence it had built up could not be disregarded. It will come as no surprise, therefore, to find that the
Charter (which can be found in Appendix 1) was modeled closely
on the Covenant although the terminology used is, in almost every
case, new.

Genesis.   In this chapter we will trace the origins of the Charter
and how it came to be adopted during World War II. We will then
examine a constitutional theory for the Charter which may, at first
sight, seem somewhat unconventional.

However critical we may be of the founders, we should always
bear in mind that the making of the Charter represents a remarkable achievement. Even now, in times of relative peace, international commitment on a major matter—even when everyone agrees
on what should be agreed, and the best minds are available to
assist in the negotiations—is a highly difficult and often protracted
process calling for all the patience, understanding and professional
skill that can be mustered.

The Charter was created during the greatest international conflict ever. When work started, the German armies were approaching Moscow. When it was completed at San Francisco in 1945, the
end of the war with Japan was not yet in sight. In the terrible years
of war, when every effort was made to defeat common enemies, it
is something to be wondered at that governments could find time
and resources to devote to considering how best to fashion the

world after the conflict, the outcome of which was still in the balance.

The most unsordid act. When did the process begin? Perhaps the starting point was the Lend-Lease Act of 23 February 1941, as it represented the final departure of the United States from the watershed of isolation. By this act, Great Britain could make dollar purchases for her war effort without having to worry about repayment arrangements. It also represented a major step in the direction of postwar cooperation because, in carrying out the provisions of the act, the Allies had to establish a major interallied economic organization for the purchase of foodstuffs and raw materials in Latin America and elsewhere. The systematization of working relationships in these matters was to prove as useful a lesson in the postwar world as that furnished by the experience during World War I of pooling of Allied shipping and providing joint purchasing missions during the inter-war period in the League.

On 12 June 1941, the countries then at war with the Axis adopted the London Declaration. Although mainly concerned with the common struggle, the Declaration contained a statement of intention to create a world where "relieved of the menace of aggression, all may enjoy economic and social security." It should be noted that in this earliest of wartime pronouncements on Allied intentions after the war, prominence was given to global economic and social goals.

Argentia Bay. Under dramatic circumstances, President Roosevelt and Winston Churchill, the British Prime Minister, met for a series of meetings from 9 to 12 August 1941 on board the United States cruiser *Augusta* and H.M.S. *Prince of Wales* off the coast of Newfoundland. On 14 August, they both issued the Joint Declaration by the President and the Prime Minister or, as it came to be known, the "Atlantic Charter." The terms of Articles 5, 6 and 8 provided for full collaboration between nations on economic matters after the war; the future peace would ensure freedom from want and fear; and aggressor nations would be disarmed pending the establishment of a general security system.

Washington and Moscow. With the entry of the United States into the war, the twenty-six nations then fighting the Axis powers signed, on 1 January 1942, in Washington, the United Nations Protocol. This instrument, which was concerned with the prosecution of the war more than with the war's aftermath, endorsed the provisions of the Atlantic Charter. Its name was coined by President Roosevelt, to give expression to the common endeavor of the nations, then sorely pressed, in the struggle against the Axis, many being at war with Japan as well.

The Treaty of Alliance signed by Great Britain and the U. S. S. R. in Moscow on 26 May 1942 associated the U. S. S. R. with the Atlantic Charter and stated that both parties would cooperate closely with one another and the United Nations after the war.

Taking soundings: 1942. All these statements and declarations had so far given no precise indication of what form postwar cooperation would take and what institutional framework should give effect to it. The principal Allies have often been criticized for their lack of precision in these matters. But it is not possible to be precise when there is nothing to be precise about. Also, as Wilson saw in 1918, the adoption of general principles furthered the unification of the war effort. To descend into details would be an invitation to divide and debate, and thus distract the Allies from the more pressing business of winning the war. Nevertheless, Roosevelt saw the need to move ahead during the war, when the nations were held together by the presence of a common enemy, to reach agreement on the postwar institutions and for such agreement to be embodied in instruments which would *not* form part of the peace treaties. The shaping of the League had been difficult because the Covenant was drawn up after the war ended and lived always under the stigma of being part of the Treaty of Versailles. These mistakes were to be avoided at all costs when next the time came to establish a world organization.

The year 1942 began with the Grand Alliance everywhere on the defensive, but later in the year the tide of war turned with the great victories of El Alamein and Guadalcanal and, at the end of the year, of the battle on the Volga. It was during this period that the Allies took soundings on the sort of "United Nations" organization which might be established. There was almost unanimous consent not to attempt to revive the League, which continued to maintain a skeleton secretariat in Geneva and Princeton (New Jersey) on contributions from the United States and the British Commonwealth. If not the League, then what new organization should succeed it?

Between the Great Powers there existed common ground on one point. As at the Congress of Vienna in 1815 and again at the Paris Peace Conference in 1919, the continuation of Great Power unity after the war would have to form the hard core of any international setup concerned with the maintenance of security. But American and British opinion (both official and unofficial) rejected the naked assumption of authority by the Great Powers along the lines of the Great Power Alliance that gave rise to the Concert of Europe.

The smaller powers, some of which had made major sacrifices in the war, were adamantly opposed to the assumption of exclusive responsibility by the Great Powers and wanted a global organization in which they would be able to play a full part. The differences between the great and small powers became noticeable. They were to increase as the negotiations opened up and, when the United Nations came into existence, the lineup of the small versus the great gave rise to one of the three main sources of difference between the members.

At the same time as the Great Power Alliance was being canvassed, a related proposal by Churchill was also being advanced. The organization would have a framework in which authority would be exercised on a regional basis. Various regions of the world would be identified, and in each a great power would hold responsibility for the maintenance of peace and security. The separate regions would then be linked together through treaty arrangements. This idea harked back to the Pan-American Pact, promoted by the United States in the years immediately prior to 1914. Perhaps, also, it reflected a fading echo of the Grand Design, outlined by the Duc de

Sully in his letters to Henry IV in the seventeenth century, in which he saw the need to reinforce his proposed European security system with regional arrangements.

The importance that decentralized activities within the United Nations and regional arrangements outside it came to have will be discussed later. But the Churchill idea was destined to fall apart on closer examination. First, the tide of the war had turned in favor of the Allies at least in Africa and Europe, and it became increasingly difficult to define without an embarrassing amount of overlapping which Great Power would be responsible for what region. Second, the Commonwealth could not agree to regional arrangements which cut across its community of interest. Third, events were overtaking the airing of the proposal as global agencies were already being created or planned. For these reasons the international canvassing of ideas resulted in at least an awareness, if not an understanding, that in any organization the Great Powers would have special responsibilities; it would be a global organization, but one that permitted regional security arrangements.

The Great Debate: 1943. In the United States where the technique of the great debate is from time to time practiced as a basis for policy-making, major statements by political leaders, the press, radio—and today television—give full rein to an open-ended discussion of the issues. Through a continental airing of views of public and private persons and groups, there can be established a substratum of public awareness upon which policy, with some assurance, can be developed.

At this time the Democratic administration took steps to insure that there should be a thorough ventilation of the many points of view and proposals concerning international cooperation after the war and, at the same time, to avoid the fatal division between the two political parties that blighted Wilson's attempts in 1919. The bitter opposition of Senator Lodge to the Treaty of Versailles, and with it to the League, ended United States leadership and participation in world affairs for a generation.

The major step to establish collaboration between Congress and the State Department was taken by Republican leaders when they met on Mackinac Island in Michigan. Without those Republicans who supported Willkie's positive approach to world cooperation, the Republican leadership adopted, in August 1943, the Mackinac Declaration. Thanks largely to Senator Vandenberg, common ground was found among the leadership, cautiously committing the Republican party to a policy of postwar international cooperation. The party was put on record as favoring "responsible participation by the United States in a postwar cooperative organization among sovereign nations to prevent military aggression and to attain permanent peace with organized justice in a free world."

Connally Resolution. After long debate in the Committee on Foreign Relations, the Senate passed a resolution favoring a just peace and the establishment of an authority that would be able to preserve it. This historic resolution named after Senator Tom Connally, the Committee's chairman, insured American participation in the United Nations and this, in turn, assured the world that in all likelihood there would be such an organization. The final adoption of the resolution did not take place until after the Moscow Conference, but its passage was assured before the conference, so the United States negotiators could move ahead in confidence.

Quebec, Moscow, and Teheran. With bipartisan support guaranteed, the forward movement began. In September 1943, at the Quebec Conference, it was agreed that a draft to provide the basis for discussion should be put forward at the forthcoming Foreign Ministers' Conference in Moscow.

The United States prepared the draft which, with a few changes proposed by Great Britain and the U. S. S. R., was adopted. The governments represented in Moscow were China, Great Britain, the United States and the U. S. S. R. Article 4 of the Moscow Declaration of 30 October 1943 recognized "the necessity of establishing at the earliest practicable date a general international organization, based on the principle of the Sovereign equality of all peace-loving states, and open to membership by all such states, large and small, for the maintenance of international peace and security."

Churchill, Roosevelt and Stalin met at Teheran later in 1943. On 1 December, they issued the Declaration of Teheran which recognized fully the responsibility of every peace-loving state, great or small, to make the peace and work together in keeping it. But even at Teheran, there were lingering traces of the Churchill proposal for a Great Power Alliance working through regional councils. The concept of the "Four Policemen"—China, Great Britain, the United States and the U. S. S. R.—still held an attraction. While the leaders continued to toy with this idea, however, the drafters and diplomats in the United States and Great Britain were already moving firmly in the direction of a global organization in which all could participate.

Dumbarton Oaks. The four powers met at Dumbarton Oaks from August to October 1944 for exploratory conversations. The U. S. S. R. did not participate throughout the meetings, for (although later at San Francisco no objection was raised at the presence of China) at Dumbarton Oaks the U. S. S. R. was not prepared to sit with the Chinese delegation. After one month, therefore, the U. S. S. R. withdrew, and the Chinese delegation moved in. An agreed document, *The Dumbarton Oaks Proposals for the Establishment of a General International Organization* was released simultaneously by the four governments in October 1944. This draft was intended by the Great Powers to serve as a basis for discussion with other states (future members) of the United Nations.

Twenty years later, little is still known of the discussions that took place, for such records of the Conference and state papers as do exist have still to be made public. The meetings were attended, for the most part, by statesmen of the second rank (although many subsequently rose to positions of eminence as international civil servants or as diplomats). This, after all, is not always a bad thing: specialists working together can often produce better work than their masters, if only because they are not likely to be quite so bemused about the possibility that they may be writing their names in history. (The intransigence of Gorchakov and Beaconsfield at the Congress of Berlin in 1878 had to be bridged by the painstaking efforts of Peter Shuvalov and Salisbury; in 1919, at the Paris Peace Conference, Hurst, Cecil, House and others, when preparing the Covenant of the League, brought together Wilson and Lloyd George.)

Be that as it may, the Dumbarton Oaks proposals made dry reading and were lacking in appeal. They also lacked clarity and polish. This was partly due to an error in the conference procedure which prevented the proposals from receiving the scrutiny of the legal committee. All this is relatively unimportant: what is important is that the proposals were agreed to by the four powers after a successful attempt to reconcile different attitudes.

Four viewpoints. The United Kingdom was anxious to have a text which could be agreed to by the four powers so that they would, in concert, confront the smaller powers when it was exposed to wider scrutiny. This attitude also featured in the British position on the nature of the international organization. It should have as its central pillar, they considered, a council concerned with peace and security, with the four powers, to be joined in due course by France, carrying the main burden as its permanent members. Thus there would be enshrined in the Council the Grand Alliance which, successful in war, would be "institutionalized" to maintain the peace.

On colonial questions and the arrangements to transfer to the new organization the mandates responsibilities of the League there was, by mutual agreement, silence.

Neither the British nor the Russians attached importance, as the Americans did, to the creation of a special body to deal with economic and social problems. While the British recognized the importance of the problems, they considered for two reasons that the Security Council (as it came to be called) should have general responsibility for them. In the first place, the British believed that there was such a close relationship between problems of peace and security and economic and social questions that they should not be artificially separated by being dealt with in two separate organs. Also, if the Security Council were restricted to settling international squabbles, its functions would be exercised in an arid and negative atmosphere and, lacking in constructive purpose, it would not have the opportunity to be a positive instrument of international cooperation.

It is not surprising that the U. S. S. R., with casualties already approaching the twenty million mark, should have been preoccupied

almost exclusively with security. It wanted maximum security provisions and was anxious to see that these preoccupations were not
obfuscated by discussion of what it considered ancillary responsibilities, such as furthering economic and social cooperation, which
might divert the members' attention from the vital issues with which
the new organization would have to contend.

At Dumbarton Oaks, the Chinese delegation was as anxious as
the Russians to see that the new organization had increased responsibilities for maintaining peace and security and had powers
commensurate with those responsibilities. In 1931, the League,
when appealed to by China, had failed to prevent Japan from taking
over Manchuria. This time China wanted to see established an international organization whose security provisions had real teeth.

The United States Department of State acted as host to the
Conference. A large staff had been set up to handle the negotiations
for the establishment of an international organization. The United
States wished to see an international secretariat with greater re-
sponsibilities than the staff of the League. It wanted a General
Assembly and a Security Council based on the League pattern. In
giving the Security Council "teeth," it joined with the British in
calling for a military staff committee to serve the Security Council.
Such a body would be selected from the military staffs of the Great
Powers. Based on the experience of the Anglo-American Combined
Chiefs of Staff, which in the later stages of the war had organized
the strategy of victory, the military staff committee would, it was
hoped, in case of aggression play a similar role under the political
direction of the Security Council as the chiefs of staff were playing
vis-à-vis the Allied governments.

Agreement. At Dumbarton Oaks, the four Great Powers
reached agreement on the broad framework of an international organization. Basically, it reflected the League setup. There would be
four principal organs: a Security Council, a General Assembly, an
international court and an international secretariat.

Decisions would be taken in the Council and Assembly by majority vote instead of by unanimous agreement as in the League.
The Security Council would have five permanent members: China,

France, the United Kingdom, the U. S. S. R. and the United States.

Decisions of the Security Council would be by majority vote but included in that majority must be the affirmative votes of the five Great Powers. For one of them to vote against a resolution would constitute a veto and thus prevent action by the Security Council. The veto, legally the prerogative of every member of the Council under the Covenant, would, under the new management, be the exclusive right of the Great Powers.

With a Security Council meeting in permanent session, with broad powers to deal not only with acts of aggression but with situations likely to lead to a breach of the peace, and underpinned by a military staff drawn from the great powers, a formidable instrument to deter aggression seemed to have been forged. The General Assembly, composed of all members of the organization, would have as its broad concern the general welfare of the international community, but it could not deal with a matter relating to peace and security when the matter in question was before the Security Council.

Without reference to the League's Permanent Court of International Justice, the Dumbarton Oaks proposals briefly recommended that there should be an international court. The Economic and Social Council was not to be a principal organ as the United States had hoped, and there was no reference to colonial or mandates matters.

The international Secretariat, it was agreed, should be headed by a Secretary-General as its chief administrative officer. His responsibilities were to be greater than those of the Secretary-General of the League. He was to be charged with the task of bringing to the attention of the Security Council "any matter which in his opinion may threaten international peace and security."

Agreement to disagree. On one matter and a crucial one the conference could not agree. It related to the extent to which a Great Power could fall back on the veto when it was a party to the dispute in question. If a Great Power, by virtue of the provision that required the unanimous and affirmative votes of the Great Powers in any majority vote before the Security Council, could act by a negative vote to forestall such action, should it continue to enjoy this privilege when it was itself a party to the dispute?

The United Kingdom representatives saw little to commend such an arrangement by which the cards would always be stacked on the side of the Great Powers. The U. S. S. R., with acute political foresight, saw little to condemn in such an arrangement. How could an international organization, whose very existence was based on the assumption of Great Power unity, be given such authority that might permit it to marshall the forces of its membership against one or more of the Great Powers? The United States at first was undecided on this issue and then veered to the British position. The decision was held for the Crimean Conference which was then being convened for early in the following year.

Yalta: 1945. Churchill, Stalin and Roosevelt met in the Crimea with their staffs in early February 1945 to review the military situation and make plans for the final phase of the war and its aftermath. Part of the discussions dealt with the vexing matter of voting procedure in the Security Council left unresolved at Dumbarton Oaks and the next steps to be taken to bring an international organization into being.

In the form of amendments to the Dumbarton Oaks proposals, the four powers made known the compromise they had reached on voting. (China, not represented at Yalta, agreed subsequent to the meeting, and the amendments were circulated on 5 May 1945).

The compromise distinguished between situations on the one hand, where the Security Council made recommendations concerning the peaceful settlement of disputes, and on the other, where the Security Council called for enforcement measures. On the former, recommendations would be made by a majority vote, and on those occasions a member of the Security Council, be it great or small, if a party to the dispute, would have no vote. On the latter, there could be a veto as decisions would require the concurring vote of the five permanent members. The veto would apply whether or not a Great Power was a party to the dispute in question. This seemed prudent. If a Great Power had no veto, it might find its armed forces committed to fight in a collective action. If the wording of the

Charter had permitted this, it is unlikely that the Charter would have ever been ratified by the United States Senate. If a Great Power were likely to find itself confronted by the collective forces of the other members through not having a veto to prevent such action, then the U. S. S. R. would probably never have been prepared to participate. That this would have been a disaster was stated by Field Marshal Smuts who wrote to Churchill: "Should a World Organization be formed which does not include Russia, she will become the power centre of another group. We shall then be heading towards a third World War."

At Yalta, Stalin also put forward his claim to have all sixteen Soviet Socialist Republics given individual membership in the United Nations. Roosevelt countered by stating that in that case, all forty-eight states of the United States should be admitted on the same basis. Churchill was more cautious in his response. Possibly he saw the dangers in the spectacle of a Great Power being in a perpetual voting minority. Other institutions were being set up as a result of the meetings at Bretton Woods where voting was proportionate to financial power, so why not in a political organization according to political power? This is surmise. But caution may have been dictated by possible opposition from the U. S. S. R. to the admission of India to membership, for although India had been a member of the League, in 1945 it still had to attain full independence. The compromise reached was that in addition to the U. S. S. R., two republics, the Byelorussian S. S. R. and the Ukrainian S. S. R., were to be given full membership.

Roosevelt, anxious to bring the United Nations into being before the war ended and while there remained unity of purpose on participation in an international organization in the United States, prevailed on the others to agree to an early meeting to conclude the negotiations to establish the new organization. Consequently on 5 March, in the names of China, France, the U. S. S. R. and the United Kingdom and itself, the United States issued invitations to a United Nations Conference on International Organization which was convened on 25 April 1945 in San Francisco. The states invited were those that had declared war on one or more of the Axis powers before 1 March 1945, and had signed the 1942 declaration by the United Nations. There was a marked increase in the number of belligerents before the 1 March deadline. Forty-six governments were invited; all accepted.

San Francisco: 1945.   When discussions began in 1941 on what sort of international organization should be established, the German armies were within commuting distance of Moscow. On 25 April 1945, the day the San Francisco Conference opened, the Russian forces laid siege to Berlin. The end of the war was in sight in the west although no one could foresee when hostilities in the east would conclude.

Invitations to the United Nations Conference asked governments to send representatives to San Francisco "to prepare a charter for a general international organization for the maintenance of peace and security." The invitation ended by stating that the Dumbarton Oaks draft would, with some amendments tabled by the Great Powers, serve as a basis for discussion.

Facts and information abound about the negotiations in the San Francisco Opera House, but there is still little knowledge of exactly what went on. No writer present there has come forward to give an account of the proceedings as, say, David Hunter Miller, Paul Mantoux or Harold Nicolson did of the Paris Peace Conference. But in many respects the conference may be viewed as having been an excellent one. After all, it succeeded in doing what it set out to do, which was to "prepare a charter." This was due to the existence of the Dumbarton Oaks proposals which served a purpose similar to that of the draft of the Covenant in 1919. As then, the work of the Conference had largely been completed before the Conference itself had been convened. But this time there was a difference. At Paris, the draft of the Covenant had been railroaded by the American and British delegations. At San Francisco, the Dumbarton Oaks proposals were hammered out clause by clause by all delegations fully participating and they were adopted, by a two-thirds majority vote, to form an agreed text.

The Great Powers, armed with their own draft from Dumbarton Oaks, which had been sharpened up on a number of critical issues by the Yalta decisions, tried to maintain a semblance of unity in the face of the criticisms of the smaller powers. The latter were led by H. V. Evatt, Australian Minister of External Affairs, who was a thorn in the side of the sponsors of the Conference. But the attacks leveled against the Great Powers inadvertently brought them together again on crucial issues. Nevertheless, signs of strain between the sponsors were apparent from the beginning. Molotov, at the commencement the chief delegate of the U. S. S. R., objected to the conference being chaired by Edward R. Stettinius, Jr., the United States Secretary of State. The U. S. S. R. considered that the four sponsoring powers, in whose names the United States had issued the invitation, should chair the conference in turn. The United States maintained that, in accordance with diplomatic practice, the host to the conference should preside over it.

The smaller powers were principally concerned with the veto provisions which the Great Powers had reserved for themselves in the Security Council. Armed with the veto, the Great Powers had collectively placed themselves in a position of almost absolute authority over the other members, and individually each had carefully removed itself from any possibility of being the object of enforcement action by the United Nations. While there was no chance of forcing the Great Powers to abandon their positions, Evatt and his colleagues succeeded in making them yield on a number of points, which resulted in a strengthening of the hands of the smaller powers.

Matters came to a head on 22 May due to the submission to the sponsoring powers of a *Questionnaire on Exercise of Veto in Security Council.* Twenty-three questions were forwarded by a subcommittee comprising the smaller nations, in an attempt to confront the Great Powers with a demand for clarification and, if possible, for a concession on the exercise of the veto power.

Holding the line. In diplomacy, questions are not always answered. But the Great Powers acknowledged the need for clarification and adjustment of the Yalta formula and this they attempted to do, on 7 June, through a *Statement by the Delegations of the Four Sponsoring Governments on Voting Procedure in the Security*

Council. The statement recalled that at Yalta a distinction was made between decisions of the Security Council calling for direct measures relating to the "settlement of disputes, adjustment of situations likely to lead to disputes, determination of threats to the peace, of removal of threats to the peace, and suppression of breaches of the peace;" and secondly, decisions which did not involve the taking of direct measures. In the first category the veto could apply; in the second it could not.

The occasions when the veto would not apply were clarified. On procedural matters, there would be no veto. But in a discussion on whether or not a matter was procedural or substantive in character, the issue was a substantive matter and therefore the veto would apply.

The Security Council by a simple majority of seven out of its eleven members could alter its rules of procedure; determine the method of selecting its President; organize its work and meetings so that it could function continuously; establish bodies or agencies to assist it in its work; invite members not on the Security Council to participate in discussions; and invite a party to a dispute, whether it was a member of the United Nations or not, to join in the Security Council's deliberations. The veto was not designed to prevent consideration by the Security Council of disputes brought to its attention, nor could parties to such a dispute be prevented from being heard by a negative vote cast by a permanent member. In related matters, the smaller powers had greater success. Under Article 44 of the Charter, any member supplying troops to enforce the peace would be permitted to participate and vote in the Security Council on the use of such forces.

That was about as far as the Great Powers jointly were prepared to go. On matters calling for action, the Great Powers considered that their concurrence should always be obtained. This meant not only action calling for, say, armed intervention, but also for taking such seemingly modest steps as sending, for example, a fact-finding mission to a trouble spot. Although there would be little in such a step itself to worry the Great Powers, they saw such action as the beginning of a chain of events. Initial preliminary action of this kind might well (as, in fact, it subsequently did) lead to further involvement of the United Nations in a situation, ending up with the Great Powers carrying the main burdens involved. Therefore, the concurring vote of the permanent members would need to feature in any majority vote involving action by the Security Council at any stage of its handling of a dispute.

The veto could be applied, then, all along the line even at the initial stage when the Security Council was called upon to determine the "existence of any threat to the peace, breach of the peace, or act of aggression." The outer limits of the veto extended to recommendations addressed to states to settle their disputes peacefully, and to making recommendations to the parties even when they had specifically asked the Security Council to make them. In other matters also the veto could apply. These included the election of the Secretary-General, admission of new members and the suspension of members.

At Dumbarton Oaks, the right of self-defense was specifically stated in the proposals (it had only been implicit in the Covenant). By the time the San Francisco Conference took place, regional security arrangements, such as those entered into by the American States through the Act of Chapultepec (early 1945), had been established. To take into account such arrangements, Article 51 was inserted in the Charter to extend the right of self-defense to collective self-defense against an armed attack until the Security Council could move into action.

Widening the scope. In other matters the San Francisco Conference added to or elaborated on the somewhat bald proposals of Dumbarton Oaks. These changes were reflected in the United Nations Charter subsequently adopted by the Conference.

The Economic and Social Council, dear to the heart of the United States Department of State, was promoted to being a Principal Organ of the United Nations, with wide responsibilities concerning economic and social advancement and the furtherance and protection of human rights.

The mandates responsibilities of the League, not referred to at Dumbarton Oaks but touched on at Yalta, were, with more emphatic terms of reference, vested in the General Assembly and the Trusteeship Council. A seemingly more modest statement on the future of colonies was contained in the Charter's *Declaration. Regarding Non-Self-Governing Territories.*

The Secretariat was strengthened, and the proposals at Dumbarton Oaks concerning an international court of justice took the form of continuing, with a face-lifting and a change in name the Permanent Court of International Justice. Finally, the role and responsibilities of the General Assembly were enhanced.

The Great Powers had included amendment of the Charter in the list of items subject to a veto. There was little the smaller powers could do about that. The rigidities this imposed on the new Organization, however, must have been obvious to everyone and, perhaps, for that reason, it was agreed to include a provision for Charter review after ten years.

Cautious optimism. Thus may be described the mood in which President Truman closed the conference. By then great power unity, which had been preserved only with the greatest difficulty at Yalta, was more apparent than real. The conference nearly broke down over voting rights in the Security Council, and only direct appeal by British and United States diplomats in Moscow resulted in agreement again being secured between the Great Powers.

More than two hundred delegates, on 26 June 1945, took over eight hours to sign the five documents that represented the culmination of three years' work and many conferences. Six days later the United States Senate received the Charter of the United Nations and, with great promptitude, on 28 July approved it. Article 110 of the Charter demanded ratification of the Charter by the five Great Powers (which now included France in their number), together with a majority of the signatories to bring the Charter into effect. By 24 October, the necessary number of ratifications had been deposited with the Department of State in Washington, and the United Nations came into being.

Opening up the shop. The United Nations was at last officially in business, and it did not wait for formal ceremonies before opening shop. In 1919, it will be recalled, Sir Eric Drummond, when appointed Secretary-General of the League by the Paris Peace Conference, proceeded at once to undertake the preparatory arrangements for the League before it formally came into existence in 1920.

In 1945, the United Nations had no Secretary-General because the machinery involved in his appointment did not exist except on paper. The responsibility for the preliminary arrangements, therefore, was vested in the Preparatory Commission which met in London from August into November. The commission was composed of all signatories to the Charter. (An active member of the United States delegation was Adlai Stevenson.)

The Preparatory Commission, which was assisted by a fourteen-member Executive Committee whose Executive Secretary was Gladwyn Jebb (now Lord Gladwyn), had many housekeeping tasks to perform, and most of them hurriedly. Basically, they were to call into being the various United Nations organs and subsidiary bodies and to find a home for the United Nations.

The General Assembly was convened in London for its first session in January 1946. So that it could function immediately, rules of procedure had to be prepared and other housekeeping matters looked after. The Economic and Social Council had to be established, and with it its galaxy of subsidiary and associated bodies such as the Commission on Narcotic Drugs, the Statistical Commission and, perhaps of greatest significance, the Commission on Human Rights.

All this was relatively plain sailing, but snags were encountered over the establishment of the Trusteeship Council and the Secretariat. The composition of the Trusteeship Council was relatively complicated. It was to comprise those members who were Administering Authorities, i.e., those that were responsible for administering Trust Territories. These were to be joined by those permanent members of the Security Council which were not Administering Authorities. Finally, the balance between Administering Authorities and members without such responsibilities was to be made up by the election of a sufficient number of other members. (For example, if there were six Administering Authorities and two permanent members of the Security Council without trusteeship responsibility, then four other members of the United Nations would be elected to balance the two groups.) It was not possible to hold elections until the number of Administering Authorities was known, and that could not be determined until those members who continued to hold mandates responsibilities from the League had concluded an agreement to come under the United Nations trusteeship provisions. Eventually, all but South Africa did; but the transfer agreements were not concluded during the period the Preparatory Commission was at work.

The functions of the Secretary-General and of the Secretariat were outlined in the Charter but not the distribution of responsibilities between them. The United States and the United Kingdom delegations considered that a monolithic structure with the Secretary-General as the head was not only desirable, but ineluctable. The U. S. S. R. delegation wanted to see more of a commonwealth arrangement with the Secretary-General *primus inter pares*. The other equals would be chiefs of servicing units responsible for the functioning of the major divisions. There would be a secretariat for the Economic and Social Council, another for the Trusteeship Council and another for the General Assembly.

We shall see later how, throughout the life of the Secretariat, constant adjustment has been necessary to accommodate these different approaches to its organization. The Preparatory Commission, however, plumped for a Secretary-General with a unified secretariat.

Greatest difficulty of all was encountered in arriving at a decision on where the headquarters of the United Nations should be established. There was a natural nostalgia on the part of many for Geneva on whose outskirts the *Palais des Nations*, built to house the League, remained only partly in use. But the associations were the wrong ones. Besides, Switzerland was not a signatory to the Charter, and her neutrality which was not compromised by acting as host to the League might not so easily remain intact with the United Nations.

Paris, London and The Hague were other European sites offered. But here again members from other continents preferred to look elsewhere so that the United Nations did not revert to being —as the League basically was—a European institution. More exotic sites were offered: Tangier with its quasi-international status and Jerusalem with its significance for many faiths.

The new world loomed large in everyone's reckoning. The first contender was Chicago whose mayor presented in person to the Preparatory Commission the "Windy City's" invitation. San Francisco extended a welcome, and even a corner of Wyoming was set aside to provide a magnificent site for the United Nations.

The Preparatory Commission was somewhat bewildered, and as far as invitations from the United States were concerned, the State Department appeared to vacillate. Successive missions were appointed and were sent on their luckless rounds by the Preparatory Commission. Eventually, it was made known that the State Department favored a site somewhere on the eastern seaboard of the United States. Washington would not have been appropriate. The United Kingdom favored Philadelphia. Other locations when visited did not welcome the prospect of intrusion by the United Nations and made their views emphatically clear.

Finally, the Rockefeller brothers resolved the problem by their timely offer of twenty-six acres (then slum and slaughterhouse property) on Manhattan's East Side overlooking Turtle Bay. This was a straw and it was grasped. The General Assembly accepted the offer, and decided to house the United Nations in New York. The United Nations had moved first to Hunter College in the Bronx, then to a factory at Lake Success on Long Island. Finally, when it had been partly constructed, it came to the towering glass structure on the East River.

Harold Nicolson, writing after his experiences in Paris in 1919, urged that international problems should be considered in an oasis of calm and tranquillity where diplomats would not be exposed to the daily pressures of news media, and the hurry and bustle of big city life. There is much to be said for this kind of withdrawal. But, on the other hand, a removal from the world when negotiating on the world's problems has its own dangers. There is much to be

said for having the United Nations set bang in the middle of the
bustle of a big city with reasonable communications and where
the very turbulence of the atmosphere generates its own infectious
enthusiasm and, in the case of New York, the stimulation of a place
in which all things are possible if you just work hard enough.

It is doubtful whether the Preparatory Commission had these
present thoughts in mind: rather it was jaded by the conflicting
claims, and the ready-made solution was greeted with relief. But
that the United Nations should be housed somewhere in the United
States was generally agreed, if only for the reason that without the
spirited leadership of the United States, the United Nations would
never have become a living reality. Moods can change quickly in
the United States, and to have the United Nations in its midst
could do more than anything else to halt any incipient retreat into
isolation.

Some comparisons.   We have now reviewed how the Charter
was prepared and the United Nations established. Before examining the structure of the United Nations, we will consider the Charter
in theoretical terms bearing in mind the spirit of the times of a
generation ago. It may make our examination of the Charter more
meaningful if we compare it with its precursor, the Covenant of the
League of Nations.

In the years immediately after World War II, before the United
Nations had accumulated much experience of its own, some authorities on international organization compared the Charter unfavorably with the Covenant. In spite of the failure of the League
to be an effective instrument of international peace and security,
there were many defenders of the Covenant as a great political
document. They considered that the League failed primarily because the Great Powers did not attempt seriously, in concert with
one another, to make it work.

Moreover, one Great Power—the United States—was never a
member of the League. This was a great blow to the organization,
particularly as, having renounced all claims to reparations, the
United States stood alone as a Great Power with immense moral
authority and political prestige. Another Great Power—the U. S. S. R.

—was not admitted to membership until the League had already begun to decline after the invasion of Manchuria by Japan.

In the League itself, however, a disproportionate amount of time was devoted to the examination of the Covenant's theoretical weakness. Time was spent in attempts to "plug the gaps" in the Covenant, rather than in efforts to make the Covenant work. No sooner had the League been established than the Anglo-Saxon perfectionists, who were disappointed in the Covenant, joined forces with the continental critics who wished to introduce into the document stringent security provisions which were prevented from being incorporated in 1919. Their attempts were centered on the draft Treaty of Mutual Assistance (1923), the Geneva Protocol (1924), the Optional Clause to the Statute of the Permanent Court of International Justice and the General Act of Pacific Settlement (1928). For many reasons, these attempts to improve the international machinery for taking collective action against aggression and for offering alternative arrangements by which disputes could be settled peacefully, failed.

In Chapter VI, we shall refer again to the fruitless quest for cast iron security guarantees in the inter-war period. For those members who considered the League machinery woefully inadequate, the principal weakness of the Covenant was in Article 16. While in Article 10 the Covenant commits members to respect and preserve against external aggression the territorial integrity and existing political independence of all Members of the League, the intentions of Article 16 were more apparent than real since it was left to the judgment of individual members to decide whether a *casus foederis* had arisen.

Finally, the Covenant was based upon three related principles. Members of the League were, as sovereign states, merely induced to cooperate with one another in the interests of certain objectives laid down in the Covenant. If, as sovereign states, they did not enjoy equal status with one another, then their sovereignty could not be fully exercised. Legal equality was respected by the provisions of Article 5.1 which required that most decisions should be taken unanimously.

The Charter, on the other hand, sought to avoid these weaknesses. All the Great Powers were signatories. Their special status was assured by their position as permanent members of the Security Council. In a certain sense, this arrangement presupposed the continuation into peacetime of the Grand Alliance of the Allies which had defeated the Axis in World War II. (The mistaken assumption was that wartime alliances continue in peacetime when the danger which has brought nations together has been removed. The same mistake was made at the Congress of Vienna after the defeat of Napoleon. Just as after the battle of Leipzig in 1813 the Allies began to draw apart, so did the Allies after the Battle on the Volga in 1943.)

The Charter, in this respect, may be considered as an incipient blueprint for a world state. The keystones are Articles 24.1, 25 and 48. Article 24.1 makes the Security Council the executive arm of the United Nations. In Article 25, the members of the United Nations agree to carry out the decisions of the Security Council and in Article 48, the Security Council determines which members shall do what to carry out its decisions.

The concentration of authority is in the five permanent members. These numbers are set by the Charter and, unlike the League of Nations Council, cannot be increased except by Charter amendment. On all matters of substance, and a vote on whether a matter is procedural or substantive is a matter of substance, the concurring vote of each of the five permanent members is required.

The Charter is much less flexible in structure than the Covenant. Amendment of its provisions is more difficult than revision of the Covenant. Also, there is no provision for withdrawal from membership of the United Nations, while under the Covenant this was possible and, indeed, not uncommon. There is, therefore, much less incentive to attempt to amend the Charter and, in the light of the League experience, every reason to try to make the Charter work, however imperfect its provisions are, rather than to tamper with the substantive content.

The power to take action regarding threats to the peace, breaches of the peace and acts of aggression was vested in the Security Council. The Charter in theory gave the Security Council the power to make decisions binding on the members of the United Nations.

Furthermore, the Charter is drafted to prevent sanctions being applied by the United Nations against a permanent Security Council member, for such action would be frustrated by the veto exercised by the power in question. This is a deliberately inserted safety valve so that the United Nations would never find itself arrayed against a Great Power.

The position of the Great Powers in the Charter could hardly have come as a surprise. Article 5 of the Moscow Declaration of October 1943 gives statutory recognition of their role, stating that they could consult together on matters of peace and security. Such a role was confirmed in the Yalta Declaration in 1945 and subsequently in the provision in the Potsdam Agreement of August 1945 providing for the establishment of a Conference of Foreign Ministers (similar, in fact, to the old Supreme Council, which was continued alongside the League of Nations Council after the First World War). As with the statesmen of 1815 at Vienna and again in 1919 at Paris, the representatives of the Great Powers, having fought the war victoriously, accepted the responsibility for making and keeping the peace.

The United Nations is a prolongation of the wartime alliance into peace. The bridge between the Grand Alliance and the Charter can be found in Article 106 relating to transitional security arrangements. Pending the entry into force of the security provisions of the Charter, the parties to the 1943 Moscow Declaration and France were to consult with one another (and, as appropriate, with other members of the United Nations) on any matters requiring joint action.

Unlike the Covenant of the League, the Charter was not part of the peace settlement. At the Dumbarton Oaks Conference the outcome of the war was still in some doubt. When the Charter was signed in San Francisco, the war had not ended. The assumption, at least at Dumbarton Oaks, was that aggression would come only from the ex-enemy states should there be a recrudescence of their power.

Enemy states could be deprived of rights. Such enemies are defined, in Article 53.2, as any state which, during the Second World War, was an enemy of any signatory of the present Charter. Under Article 107 of the Charter, no provision was made to invalidate any action taken or authorized, as a result of actions during the war, against an enemy state.

The original members of the Organization were those states which had signed or adhered to the United Nations Protocol of 1 January 1942. On the same basis it was argued that a qualification required for the admission of new members was that they had been belligerents during the Second World War on the side of the Allies. This qualification was not pursued when Afghanistan, Thailand and Sweden were admitted in 1946 and Yemen in 1947. In fact, the position of the Great Powers was modified at Potsdam in August 1945, by agreeing to support for admission new members which had been neutral during the war or, if they had been supporters of the Axis powers, had concluded peace treaties with the Allies.

The extensive powers of the Security Council are modified by the statement of purposes and principles in Articles 1 and 2 of the Charter. Article 24.2 states that the Security Council must observe them. The principles relate to the rule of law, sovereign equality of members and reservations concerning domestic jurisdiction.

There is no decisive judicial machinery to circumscribe the power of the Security Council. Under Article 96 of the Charter, there is an option to invoke the jurisdiction of the International Court of Justice and request an advisory opinion, which would not be legally binding on the Organization. This may be compared with the jurisdiction of the Court of the European Communities (Common Market) which is both compulsory and decisive. Although the Charter is not precise in this matter, there is, nevertheless, an assumption that international law does place a limitation on the powers of the Security Council.

Sovereign equality also finds its place in the Charter in Articles 2.1 and 78 particularly. Recognition of this concept is shown specifically in the provisions relating to the General Assembly. In that

Principal Organ, all members are represe.
18.1, each member of the General Assembly

The rights which the Greek city-states r
they formed to preserve their exclusive right
domestic affairs are acknowledged in the Chart
2.7 begins "Nothing contained in the present Cha
the United Nations to intervene in matters wh
within the domestic jurisdiction of any State . . .
preambular paragraph ends ". . . but this principl   prejudice the application of enforcement measures unde ̣napter VII,"
thus qualifying substantially the domestic jurisdiction clause.

The Covenant may have been more idealistic than the Charter
which reflects the harsh political realities as they seemed to the
Charter makers in 1945. With twenty years of League experience,
the Charter makers went to considerable lengths to avoid the shortcomings of the Covenant and to fashion an instrument which could,
with goodwill and an awareness of a common interest, contribute
significantly to the establishment of world order. However, the
stringent security arrangements of Chapter VII of the Charter—
perhaps fortunately—did not work out in practice as it was assumed, in theory, they would. This, as we have seen, was basically
because wartime great power unity did not continue into peacetime. Also, the atomic bombing of Hiroshima and Nagasaki in
August 1945 presaged a new world of insecurity, which could not
have been foreseen by the Charter makers, who had completed their
labors at San Francisco only a few weeks earlier.

THE SIX PILLARS OF COLLECTIVE WISDOM

The United Nations structure is built around six pillars or Principal Organs. These are: the General Assembly, the Security Council, the Economic and Social Council, the Trusteeship Council, the International Court of Justice and the Secretariat.

In what order should we study them? The popularity rating of each changes constantly. Over twenty-one years of United Nations activity it is possible to identify an almost seesaw relationship between the Security Council, for example, and the General Assembly. When one is up, the other is down. The Secretariat, which in other times has only merited merely a perfunctory mention, has on occasion loomed so large as to almost dwarf the other organs. There seems to be an almost constant process of adjustment taking place between them. That this should happen is healthy and is a demonstration of a degree of flexibility in the structure, without which the whole edifice might well have cracked.

The General Assembly. Composed of all members of the United Nations, each of which is allowed to designate five representatives, the General Assembly meets in *regular session* once a year under a President elected from among the representatives. The opening is usually set for the third Tuesday in September.

Special sessions of the General Assembly may be convened at the request of the Security Council, by a majority of members, or by one member with concurrence of a majority of the members. *Special emergency sessions* may be called within twenty-four hours at the request of the Security Council, voting by simple majority.

Each member has one vote. Voting on important questions is by a two-thirds majority. Important questions include recommendations on peace and security, elections, admission and disciplining of members and adopting the budget. Otherwise, voting is by simple majority.

Peacekeeping . . . The General Assembly's functions are of a broad and general nature. The General Assembly can discuss almost anything it wishes. In its broadest terms, the General Assembly may consider and make recommendations on the principles of international cooperation in the maintenance of peace and security, including principles governing disarmament and the regulations of armaments. In more specific terms, the General Assembly can discuss any problem affecting peace and security and, except when a dispute is before the Security Council, can make recommendations on it. Similarly, it can make recommendations for the peaceful settlement of a situation which might impair friendly relations.

Its mandates enable the General Assembly to discuss any questions within the scope of the Charter. It can initiate studies and make recommendations to promote international political cooperation, the development of international law and its codification, the realization of human rights and fundamental freedoms, and to further international economic, social, cultural, educational and health cooperation. The General Assembly also receives and considers reports from the other Principal Organs. It supervises through the Trusteeship Council the carrying-out of trusteeship agreements.

. . . and housekeeping. In addition to these more general responsibilities, the General Assembly votes the budget of the United Nations and determines the burden-sharing of each member. It also examines the budget of the specialized agencies that make up the wider United Nations family.

Finally, the General Assembly elects the non-permanent members of the Security Council; the members of the Economic and Social Council; and those members of the Trusteeship Council which are elected. It also shares in the election of judges to the International Court, and, on the recommendation of the Security Council, appoints the Secretary-General.

De facto amendment?   The responsibilities of the General Assembly were considerably increased in November 1950 when the General Assembly, on the initiative of the United States, adopted a resolution called "Uniting for Peace." The effect of this resolution was to introduce a *de facto* amendment to the Charter. Under this resolution, if the Security Council, because of the lack of unanimity of the five permanent members, fails to act on an apparent threat to the peace, breach of the peace, or act of aggression, the General Assembly itself may take the matter up. This can be done within twenty-four hours in special emergency session. The General Assembly may recommend collective measures, including the use of force, if the matter involves a breach of the peace or an act of aggression.

Committees.   During World War II, when Churchill, expostulating about committees, said that "We are over-run by them, like the Australians were by rabbits," he was giving voice to the natural intemperance felt by men-of-action for men-of-committees. But as an old parliamentarian he would have been the first to recognize that any collective group decision or action first requires deliberation in committee. The General Assembly is well-endowed with committees, and although their deliberations seem sometimes to be unnecessarily protracted, each one has its function.

At the hub of the General Assembly's work is the General Committee. It is composed of the President, the seventeen Vice-Presidents, and the chairmen of the seven main committees. It meets to allocate agenda items among the various committees and supervises the work of the Assembly. It is a committee to administer. The Credentials Committee appointed by the President at each session is responsible for verifying the credentials of representatives. It is a committee to scrutinize and control.

The work of the General Assembly is for the most part conducted through seven main committees on which all members may be represented. At present these are the:

> *First Committee,* concerned with political and security questions, including disarmament and arms control;
> *Special Political Committee,* a sort of overflow committee

to take over part of the work which otherwise would go to the
First Committee;

Second Committee, dealing with economic and financial
questions;

Third Committee, a companion to the Second, concerned
with social, humanitarian and cultural questions but principally
those relating to human rights;

Fourth Committee, concerned with trusteeship and colonial
matters;

Fifth Committee, voting the budget and general responsibility for administrative and budgetary questions;

Sixth Committee, concerned with legal questions.

Of these main committees, the First, Special, Second, Third and
Sixth are bodies to enquire and to recommend. The Fourth has, in
addition to that function, administrative responsibilities regarding
Trust Territories. The Fifth is a committee to administer.

To assist the General Assembly in its housekeeping tasks, two
standing committees have been set up—the Advisory Committee on
Administrative and Budgetary Questions and the Committee on
Contributions. Both are committees to inquire and to recommend.

The Advisory Committee is composed now of twelve members
elected as individuals for three-year terms on a basis of personal
qualification and geographical distribution. It eases much of the
main burden of the Fifth Committee by first examining administrative and budgetary proposals put forward by the Secretary-General
and then by forwarding the proposals to the Fifth Committee with
its own comments and recommendations on them.

The Committee on Contributions is composed of ten members
elected in the same way as the members of the Advisory Committee. It is responsible for allocating the share each member of
the United Nations will be called upon to pay for the regular budget
of the Organization.

Finally, the General Assembly has set up four other standing
bodies. Three are the Board of Auditors, the Investments Committee and the United Nations Staff Pension Committee, which
scrutinize and control. The fourth, the International Law Commission, is a committee to enquire and to recommend.

Agenda items are handled by the main committees assisted by the standing committees, standing bodies and such other bodies as may be set up from time to time. Items once dealt with are referred back to the Plenary Session where the General Assembly is expected to confirm the work done in committee. Items not referred to committee are dealt with by the General Assembly in Plenary.

The Security Council. China, France, the U. S. S. R., the United Kingdom and the United States are the five permanent members of the Security Council. Until 1965, six non-permanent members were elected by the General Assembly to serve two-year terms. By an amendment to the Charter that entered into force in 1965, the number of non-permanent members increased to ten in 1966. Where two candidates have equal support for a seat, an accommodation has become customary by which the two contenders split the term. Czechoslovakia and Malaysia are examples for 1964–1965 and Jordan and Mali for 1965–1966. Non-permanent members are not eligible for immediate reelection. The presidency is held monthly in turn by each member rotating in English alphabetical order.

The Security Council is organized to function continuously. The representatives of the members of the Security Council, therefore, must at all times be present at United Nations Headquarters. While it has rarely done so, the Security Council may, if it wishes, meet elsewhere than at United Nations Headquarters in New York. The voting procedure of the Security Council was described in Chapter I, and there is no need to repeat it here. With the exception of the provisions of the Charter which affect Security Council procedure, the Security Council is master of its own procedure.

The functions of the Security Council are generally to maintain international peace and security in accordance with the purposes and principles of the United Nations. These may be found in Chapter I of the Charter. Provisions relating to the Security Council may be found in Chapters V, VI and VII of the Charter (Appendix 1).

It will be seen from these chapters of the Charter that the Security Council can:

investigate any dispute or situation which might lead to international friction or give rise to a dispute;

recommend methods of adjusting such disputes or the terms of settlement;

formulate plans for the establishment of a system to regulate armaments;

determine the existence of a threat to the peace or act of aggression and recommend what action should be taken;

call on members of the United Nations to apply economic sanctions and other measures short of war in order to prevent or stop aggression; and

take military action against an aggressor.

In addition, the Security Council recommends the admission of new members and the terms on which states may become parties to the Statute of the International Court of Justice. It may exercise in what are termed "strategic areas" the trusteeship functions of the Organization. The Security Council also recommends to the General Assembly the appointment of the Secretary-General and, together with the General Assembly, elects judges to the International Court. Finally, the Security Council submits annual and, on occasion, special reports to the General Assembly.

In view of the striking nature of the obligations of the Security Council and the considerable powers that go with them, Chapter IV is devoted to a more detailed study of the provisions of the Charter on these matters. In discussing the structure of the Security Council we need now merely to refer to its subsidiary bodies and to its relationship with the other Principal Organs.

Modern major-generals. The Military Staff Committee of the Security Council is composed of the Chiefs of Staff of the five permanent members or their representatives. It was set up to advise and assist the Security Council on such questions as the Council's military requirements and the strategic direction of the armed forces which would be placed at its disposal. It is also concerned with the regulation of armaments and possible disarmament. To date the provisions of the Charter relating to the Military Staff Committee have remained a dead letter.

At present there are only two standing committees of the Security Council, the Committee of Experts which enquires and recommends on rules of procedure and other technical matters to the Council, and the Committee on Admission of New Members which enquires and recommends to the Security Council on such matters. Each committee is composed of all members of the Security Council.

Two bodies, although not established by the Security Council, have duties that impinge upon its work. The General Assembly in 1952 replaced the Atomic Energy Commission and the Commission for Conventional Armaments with the Disarmament Commission. In making recommendations for the regulation, limitation and balanced reduction of armaments, this Commission was to formulate plans establishing an international control organ within the framework of the Security Council to insure implementation of the measures agreed upon as a result of its work.

The other body whose work impinges on that of the Security Council is the Collective Measures Committee, also set up by the General Assembly. The Uniting for Peace Resolution of 1950 provided for this committee to inquire and recommend on methods to maintain and strengthen international peace and security.

The Security Council, because of its special responsibilities to maintain peace and security, may request assistance from the Economic and Social Council and the Trusteeship Council. In addition to its other responsibilities vis-à-vis the International Court, the Security Council may intervene in a situation in which a party fails to respond to the judgment of the Court and the aggrieved party appeals to the Security Council.

The Economic and Social Council.   Until 1965, eighteen members of the United Nations formed the Economic and Social Council, one-third of which was elected by the General Assembly each year for a three-year term. Its membership, in 1966, was enlarged to twenty-seven by an amendment to the Charter. Unlike the Security Council, retiring members are eligible for reelection. Like the General Assembly, the President is elected for a one-year term. The Council meets usually twice a year. It has followed a general pattern of meetings by which the Spring Session is held in New York and the Summer Session in Geneva. Each member has one vote and voting is by simple majority.

Castor and Pollux. It will be seen from Chapters IX and X of the Charter that the Economic and Social Council has certain *substantive* responsibilities of its own to carry out. At the same time it is charged with the task of *coordinating* the substantive activities of the many technical agencies which make up the United Nations system. These are the twin responsibilities of the Economic and Social Council.

Under the first heading, the Economic and Social Council:

makes or initiates studies, reports and recommendations on international economic, social, cultural, educational, health and related matters;

promotes respect for and observance of human rights and fundamental freedoms;

calls international conferences; and

prepares draft conventions for submission to the General Assembly on matters within the purview of the Economic and Social Council.

In its twin function, the Economic and Social Council is required to *negotiate* agreements with the specialized agencies, defining their relationship with the United Nations. Following that it is required to *coordinate* their activities by means of consultation with them and recommendations to them, as well as by means of recommendations to the General Assembly and members of the United Nations.

Commissions functional . . . The pattern of work of the Economic and Social Council is broken down functionally and regionally. Some of the functional commissions, such as the Fiscal Commission and the Transport and Communications Commission, have been discontinued when they have served their purpose.

In 1967 the following functional commissions were in existence: the Statistical Commission, Population Commission, Social Commission, Commission on Human Rights, Commission on the Status of Women and the Commission on Narcotic Drugs. Members elected to the commissions usually nominate their representatives after consultation with the Secretary-General. These nominations are subsequently confirmed by the Council. This procedure is designed to insure that experts rather than laymen find their way on to these bodies, and together they bring from various allied disciplines a collective body of competence.

Of several subcommissions created at one time or another in the life of the Council one remains: the Subcommission on Prevention of Discrimination and Protection of Minorities. This subsidiary group of the Commission on Human Rights has now been joined by an *ad hoc* Committee on Periodic Reports on Human Rights.

. . . and regional.   In addition to a functional breakdown of much of the work of the Economic and Social Council, there are four regional commissions serviced by regional secretariats.

The Economic Commission for Europe based in Geneva and the Economic Commission for Asia and the Far East, eventually established in Bangkok, were both created by the Council in 1947. The Economic Commission for Latin America located in Santiago, Chile was created in the following year and, in 1958, the Economic Commission for Africa came into being with its main office in Addis Ababa.

Functional and regional commissions usually meet biennially or annually and report to the Economic and Social Council on their work as frequently as the periodicity of their sessions makes desirable.

Committees standing . . .   At present the Council is assisted by several standing committees. These include the Committee on Program and Conferences; the Committee for Development Planning; the Committee on Housing, Building and Planning; and and the Advisory Committee on the Application of Science and Technology to Development. The first is a committee to scrutinize and control, the last three are to inquire and to recommend.

. . . and special.   Of the Special Committees, reference should be made to the following, all of which are committees to administer. The Permanent Central Opium Board and the Drug Supervisory Body, which had residual functions—but important ones—inherited from the League of Nations will, in 1968, be replaced by the International Narcotics Control Board under the terms of the 1961 Single Convention on Narcotic Drugs.

Committees that administer major programs with a quasi-autonomous status within the United Nations are the Governing Council of the United Nations Development Program, the Executive Board of the United Nations Children's Fund, the Executive Committee on the Program of the United Nations High Commissioner for Refugees and, since 1967, the Industrial Development Board of the United Nations Industrial Development Organization.

Two major committees are the Administrative Committee on Coordination and the Inter-Agency Consultative Board of the United Nations Development Program. These are composed exclusively of international civil servants, membership consisting of the Secretary-General of the United Nations and the directors-general or heads of the specialized agencies and economic and social programs of the United Nations.

The constellation of the United Nations. Having as the second of its major responsibilities the coordination of the work of the specialized agencies, the Economic and Social Council has relationships with all of them. We shall meet them again later in our study, but for reference purposes they are mentioned here.

The doyen of them all is the International Labor Organization. The other major specialized agencies are the International Monetary Fund and the International Bank for Reconstruction and Development, both created as a result of the Bretton Woods Conference in 1944. The Bank now has two affiliates: the International Finance Corporation and the International Development Association. The World Health Organization, the Food and Agriculture Organization of the United Nations and the United Nations Educational, Scientific and Cultural Organization are also specialized agencies.

Smaller technical agencies are the International Civil Aviation Organization, the World Meteorological Organization, the Intergovernmental Maritime Consultative Organization and the oldest agencies—the Universal Postal Union and the International Telecommunications Union.

Strictly speaking, the International Atomic Energy Agency is not a specialized agency, but it has entered into relations with the Economic and Social Council. One agency, the International Refugee Organization, was created in 1946 and wound up in 1951. The International Trade Organization never came into existence, but some of its functions were rescued by the General Agreement on Tariffs and Trade. This agreement, serviced by a small secretariat, has a special, if informal, relationship with the United Nations.

Different totems. The Council establishes relationships not only with intergovernmental bodies but with *non*-governmental organizations for consultative purposes. The latter form three groups. Category A is comprised of about ten major international groups such as the International Federation of Trade Unions. Category B lists a score of those with a special competence and consequently concerned with a limited range of the Council's activities, e.g., the International Federation of University Women. A register is compiled for the rest, numbering about 200. Many are medical associations such as the International Leprosy Association.

The Trusteeship Council. As we gathered from the end of the previous chapter, seating members of the Trusteeship Council appears trickier than that of the other bodies. This Council is composed of members administering Trust Territories; permanent members of the Security Council without such responsibilities; and enough other members to strike a balance between members which administer trust territories and those which do not. This latter group is elected for a three-year term by the General Assembly and is eligible for immediate reelection.

The Trusteeship Council, on behalf of the General Assembly, is responsible for the International Trusteeship System set up by the Charter. This system is described in Chapter XII of the Charter and the framework of the Council itself in Chapter XIII. The objectives of the system are, among other things, to promote advancement of the inhabitants of the Trust Territories toward self-government or independence, to encourage respect for human rights and to ensure equal treatment in the trust territories for all members of the United Nations and equal treatment for their nationals.

When appropriate, the Trusteeship Council may avail itself of the assistance of the Economic and Social Council and the specialized agencies. In strategic areas, the functions of the trusteeship system are performed by the Security Council which, in effect, carries out its tasks through the Trusteeship Council.

The International Court of Justice. The Court is the principal judicial organ of the United Nations. It is composed of fifteen judges elected by the Security Council and the General Assembly voting independently. Those elected represent the principal legal systems of the world. No two judges can be nationals of the same state. Judges serve nine-year terms and may be reelected.

The Court sits at The Hague. All questions are decided by a majority of judges present. Nine make up a quorum. In the event of a tie, the President has a casting vote. Parties before the Court may be entitled to choose *ad hoc* or national judges for a particular case. They participate in the same way as other judges of the Court. Assessors may be invited by the Court to sit with it on particular cases but without the right to vote. The Registry of the Court consists of a Registrar, a Deputy Registrar and other officials.

All members of the United Nations are automatically parties to the Statute. Non-members may become parties on conditions determined by the General Assembly on recommendation of the Security Council. States which are not parties to the Statute may also have access to the Court. Parties to the Statute may accept the jurisdiction of the Court with or without reservations. This is permitted by the so-called "optional clause" in Article 36 of the Statute.

The law applied by the Court is derived from four sources: international treaties and conventions; international custom; general principles of law recognized by the principal legal systems; and judicial decisions and the teachings of the most highly qualified publicists as subsidiary means for the determination of the rules of law. The Court may also decide a case according to the principles of equity if the parties involved so agree.

The Court has two functions: to decide cases brought before it and to give advisory opinions. States may seek the judgment of the

Court in the interpretation of a treaty; any question of international law; the existence of any fact which, if established, would constitute a breach of an international obligation; and the nature or extent of the reparation to be made for the breach of an international obligation.

The General Assembly or the Security Council may request the Court to give an advisory opinion on any legal question. Other organs of the United Nations or specialized agencies may request advisory opinions within the scope of their activities when authorized to do so by the General Assembly.

The Court is for states. Individuals do not have access to it except through states acting on their behalf.

The Secretariat. Chapter XV of the Charter deals with the Secretariat, which is comprised of a Secretary-General and "such staff as the Organization may require."

The Secretary-General is appointed by the General Assembly on the recommendation of the Security Council. The first Secretary-General of the United Nations was Trygve Lie of Norway who was appointed on 1 February 1946 for a five-year term. On 1 November 1950 he was reappointed for three more years, and on 10 November 1952 he resigned. Dag Hammarskjöld of Sweden succeeded him. On 26 September 1957, Hammarskjöld was appointed for a further five years beginning 10 April 1958. On 17 September 1961 he was killed in an airplane crash near Ndola in Zambia (then Northern Rhodesia), while on an official assignment.

On 3 November 1961, Ambassador U Thant of Burma became the third Secretary-General, having been appointed to fill Hammarskjöld's unexpired term. U Thant was appointed for a further period on 30 November 1962, and in December 1966, he was reappointed for five years.

The Secretary-General is the chief administrative officer of the Organization. He acts in this capacity in all meetings of the Principal Organs (with the exception of the International Court). He is required to perform such functions as are entrusted to him by these organs. In addition, he submits to the General Assembly an annual report and such supplementary reports on the work of the United Nations as are necessary.

As one of his major responsibilities, the Secretary-General may bring to the attention of the Security Council any matter which in his opinion may threaten the maintenance of international peace and security.

The Secretary-General appoints the staff under regulations established by the General Assembly. The paramount consideration when making appointments and in determining conditions of service is to secure the highest standards of efficiency, competence and integrity. Due regard must also be paid to recruiting on as wide a geographical basis as possible.

Two sides of the medal.   The Charter states that the Secretary-General and his staff shall not seek or receive instructions from any government or any authority external to the United Nations. They also must refrain from any action which might reflect on their position as international officials. Each recruit to the staff swears or affirms to these tenets when he is appointed.

On the other side of the medal, when states become members of the United Nations and thereby assume the obligations laid on them by the Charter, they agree to respect the exclusively international character of the responsibilities of the Secretary-General and the staff and agree not to seek to influence them in the discharge of their responsibilities.

The Secretary-General is assisted by his senior officials, who have the rank of Under-Secretary-General. Others of similar rank are heads of departments within the Secretariat, such as the Department of Economic and Social Affairs, or are heads of quasi-autonomous United Nations agencies such as UNICEF or the United Nations Relief and Works Agency for Palestine Refugees in the Near East (UNRWA).

Admittedly imperfect.   These, then, are the six Principal Organs. The work of some may not now be so important, and their work may have been carried forward by other bodies. This is as inevitable as it is desirable, if an organization is to adapt itself to changing situations and requirements. But gathered round the six is the collective wisdom and the accumulated experience of the whole Organization.

It is this body of international competence that sustains the United Nations, which Hammarskjöld once referred to as an "admittedly imperfect but indispensable instrument of nations in working for a peaceful evolution toward a more just and secure world order." How this instrument became progressively less imperfect and less and less dispensable we shall examine in subsequent chapters.

Chapter III

THE PARTS OF ITS SUM

In the preceding chapters, we have examined the origins, theory and structure of the United Nations. We now begin our study of the United Nations in practice. We start appropriately with the Principal Organ described first in the Charter, the General Assembly. It is also appropriate that we make this the occasion to examine in a wider sense, how, with an increasing and changing membership, the United Nations has assumed some of the characteristics of a diplomatic marketplace for the world.

The student of political philosophy often strikes an awkward patch when confronted by the Hegelian proposition that the state is greater than the sum of its parts. Some bad habits have been derived from such a concept, particularly when it has been enfolded in a mystical Teutonic shroud. But it makes a useful starting point as we begin to discuss the membership in relation to the organization it comprises.

Is the United Nations an "it" or a "them"? The Charter refers to the organization as an "it." The Covenant refers (with one exception) to the membership of the League as a "them" (the co-signatories).

Is the United Nations more than the sum of its parts? In a certain sense: yes, just as a pocket watch is more than the sum of its parts. Each part is different and is clearly identifiable. Collectively assembled and collectively operated, these parts make more than their sum: they make an "it"—a pocket watch. To continue the comparison for a moment: for the watch to have any utility as a timepiece, it needs winding up and setting. Furthermore its user

45

to have some sense of what time is about, otherwise the watch be much less than the sum of its parts, not more.

Bearing this in mind, we should first look at the parts and then examine the whole which, in a non-Hegelian sense, is more than their sum.

The relative decline of Europe. Only European states were represented at the Congress of Vienna in 1815. This limited representation persisted throughout the nineteenth century at the great congresses of Paris in 1856, Berlin in 1878 and elsewhere. The only non-European power represented at Paris was the Sublime Porte but then, although the Ottoman Empire was not European, it did have European possessions. At the Berlin Conference on Tropical Africa in 1885, the United States made its first appearance.

A characteristic of the development of international institutions is the relative decline in European participation. Of the forty-two original members of the League in 1920, sixteen were European; of the original fifty-one members of the United Nations, thirteen were European. By 1950, when total membership rose to sixty, European participation had increased to fifteen. In 1962, membership had risen to ninety-nine with European representation totalling twenty-seven, or all of Europe with the exceptions of Germany, the Holy See and Switzerland. In 1967, membership stood at 122 with European participation unchanged. Of the forty-two original members of the League, 34 per cent was European. In 1967, of the 122 members of the United Nations, the European percentage had lowered to twenty-two.

The growth of international institutions has also been characterized by the increase in African participation. At the beginning of the League there were only three African states as members: Egypt, Liberia and the Union of South Africa. In 1924, they were joined by Ethiopia. This quartet reappeared as founder members of the United Nations. In 1959 the African number rose to ten. By 1960 there were twenty-five and by 1967 thirty-nine.

Moral and political conformity. The preface to *The Book of Common Prayer* refers to "the two extremes, of too much stiffness in refusing and of too much easiness in admitting any variation."

This might not be the worst counsel to follow in adopting a policy on admitting new members to international organizations. Practices veered first in the direction of too much stiffness and now, perhaps, in the direction of too much variation.

How we view what the qualifications for admission should be depends to a large extent on whether we consider membership in an international organization as exclusive or inclusive, homogeneous or heterogeneous.

The League was both more inclusive and at the same time, more exclusive than the United Nations. It was more inclusive in that, under the Covenant, it was prepared to consider for admission "any self-governing state, Dominion or Colony." The United Nations is prepared to consider only states for admission. But the League was more exclusive in that it strove to maintain a high degree of homogeneity in its composition.

Applicants were required: (a) to give effective guarantees of their sincere intentions to observe their international obligations and (b) to accept such obligations as might be prescribed by the League regarding their armaments and armed forces. A state could either apply for admission or be invited to join by the existing membership. Applications were subjected to close scrutiny. Although admission could be secured by a two-thirds majority vote in the League Assembly, courtesy required unanimity.

Those admitted after the League was originally convened were normally ex-enemy states reentering international society, such as Germany, or new states, such as Latvia or the Irish Free State. At its 1923–24 session, however, the League Assembly was faced with the application of Ethiopia. Reaching a decision was difficult, and, after a searching examination, the application was nearly deferred. But upon its representatives' agreement to sign a declaration pledging Ethiopia to end domestic slavery and slave-raiding, it was admitted to the League. The declaration was honored, but in making it, Ethiopia placed itself in a special position vis-à-vis the League, which had important international responsibilities regarding the abolition of slavery and the slave trade.

Mexico and Turkey entered the League on invitation. So did

the U. S. S. R.; but although the resolution inviting it was adopted
by a two-thirds majority in the Assembly, after the invitation had
been accepted there followed an embarrassing debate on the qualifications of the U. S. S. R. for membership.

It was Guiseppe Motta, the President of the Swiss Confederation, whose attitude towards the admission of new members might
be viewed as summing up generally the attitude of the League.
There should be no sacrifice, he considered, of the concept of the
necessary minimum of moral and political conformity. Without that,
the element of cohesion in the League would be lacking.

The exclusiveness of the League did not carry over into the
United Nations except perhaps for its formative period. Heterogeneity rather than homogeneity came to be considered an essential ingredient in a global organization.

Membership in the United Nations is open to all peace-loving
states which accept the obligations of the Charter and, in the judgment of the Organization, are able and willing to carry out these
obligations. Admission is by decision of the General Assembly upon
the recommendation of the Security Council. Depending as it does,
in the first instance, upon the recommendation of the Security
Council, admission to membership has become mainly a political
matter. Admission of a new member is a substantive matter and
must include the concurring vote of the five permanent members in
the affirmative majority vote of the Security Council.

Initially, there was a reluctance to admit those states in Eastern
Europe, such as Bulgaria, with whom peace treaties had been
signed. Doubts were expressed at their willingness to observe the
minority rights clauses that had been featured in those treaties. The
admission of these countries was opposed and, in turn, the U. S. S. R.
effectively blocked the admission of other states which had applied
for membership, such as Japan.

In 1955 the so-called "package deal" between the sponsors of
different states permitted the admission of Albania, Austria, Bulgaria, Cambodia, Ireland, Jordan, Laos and Libya. Some members
could not agree to the admission of Outer Mongolia, and others

were not prepared to admit Japan, so their applications were postponed and they were admitted subsequently.

After 1955, new members began to be admitted more freely. In 1956, Italy, Japan, Morocco, Sudan and Tunisia joined. Two were ex-enemy states; the other three were countries which had acquired independence. Later, with the admission of Ghana in 1957, states were admitted almost automatically as they became independent, sometimes in a matter of hours after independence. In Chapter VI, we will see how the movement towards emancipation gathered strength and more than doubled the membership in ten years.

The admission, in 1965, of Gambia, Maldives and Singapore raised questions in the Security Council, and the Secretary-General cautioned on the need to examine anew the principles upon which the admissions of new members are based. The populations of these members are approximately the same respectively as the cities of Quebec, Oxford and Washington, D.C.

Argentina, in the early days of the League, refused to participate in its work because she considered that a state should decide for itself whether or not it wished to join. If it did, then it should be automatically admitted. The present admissions practice of the United Nations might be considered quite close to what the representatives of the Argentine had in mind forty-odd years ago. The search for universality in a universal organization leads us in that direction.

Not all have applied for membership. Switzerland, although a member of the League, considered that the obligations it would be expected to assume under the Charter would not be consistent with its position of perpetual neutrality. Western Samoa, when the New Zealand trusteeship was withdrawn, decided not to apply for admission but contented herself with participation in certain specialized agencies such as the Food and Agriculture Organization of the United Nations.

One category of states remains outside the Organization. These may be termed "divided" countries. North Korea, the Republic of Korea, North Vietnam, South Vietnam, the Federal Republic of

Germany and Eastern Germany have not been admitted to member-ship. It is not customary for the Secretary-General to accept invita-tions to visit such divided countries.

The Charter makes a clear division between members and non-members. But the early difficulties over admitting new members resulted in a number of steps being taken to draw non-members into association with the United Nations. The General Assembly in a resolution adopted in 1955 listed a number of states which in its opinion were eligible for membership. This gave them a kind of twilight status in the Organization. Also, the regional economic commissions, serving (under the Economic and Social Council) the particular interests of their respective geographical areas, admitted colonies, dependencies and states which were not members of the organization, as associate members or as observers. Finally, practi-cally all states which are not members of the United Nations have become members of the various specialized agencies associated with the United Nations and parties to the Statute of the International Court of Justice. Thus, non-members do not remain "beyond the pale" but participate and contribute to much of the work of the Organization. To give recognition to this and to ensure that the work of the Organization encompasses as many states as possible, it has become customary for the Principal Organs of the United Na-tions to address their recommendations not only to members of the Organization, but also to members of the specialized agencies and, on occasion, to states which are parties to the Statute of the Inter-national Court of Justice as well.

Mini-States. As will be seen in Chapter VI, one of the results of the end of imperialism and the triumph of the anti-colonial move-ment has been the creation of an increasing number of small states, many of which apply for admission to the United Nations. The Secretary-General, in his annual report in 1967, and a number of members of the Security Council (as well as the representatives of some of these small states) have called attention to the problems posed for them in becoming members of the United Nations, partic-ularly where the financial and other obligations might seem too onerous.

The problem is not a new one. In the League, applications from what were termed "diminutive states" were not accepted in some instances. Liechtenstein, San Marino, and Monaco were not admitted into membership of the League. In these cases, it was not merely their small size that was considered as an obstacle, but also the extent to which they exercised independently their functions as sovereign states. A special committee on the position of small states reported to the League Assembly in 1921 at its second session, and made a number of suggestions on how diminutive states might be affiliated with the League without being granted full membership. These suggestions included: the association of such states without full membership; their representation by a state already a member of the League; and, an arrangement by which they would be permitted a limited association. This latter suggestion would have permitted participation of such a state without vote in matters where its interests were involved.

Some of these suggestions met with resistance and at least one of them might have called for amendment of the Covenant. Although no formal action was taken on these proposals, diminutive states collaborated closely in many of the League's activities. Liechtenstein and San Marino, for example, became parties to the Statute of the Permanent Court of International Justice.

It would seem, therefore, that both size and the degree to which a state could be regarded as being independent were significant considerations when diminutive states applied for admission to the League. It might be relevant at this point to bear in mind a definition of "independence." A number of authorities might refer on this matter (which could be subject to many different and perhaps subjective interpretations), to the definition given by Judge Anzilotti in the *Customs Union* case in which he stated that independence ". . . may also be described as sovereignty (*suprema potestas*), or the external sovereignty, by which is meant that the State has over it no other authority than that of international law. The conception of independence, regarded as the normal characteristic of States as subjects of international law, cannot be better defined than by comparing it with the . . . dependent States."

Considerations of this kind were raised in the Security Council regarding the qualifications for membership, prior to their admission, of a number of very small states. With the admission of such states, sometimes referred to as "mini-states," concern has been expressed not so much about their sovereignty as their ability to discharge their obligations under Article 4 of the Charter.

In 1965 and 1966 when a number of very small states were admitted to membership, some of their representatives expressed some hesitation whether the resources of the country would permit them to participate effectively in the activities of the United Nations. In 1966, the general question was raised of the need to recognize that special arrangements should be made for such states and that the Security Council's Committee on Admission of New Members might consider these questions.

When new states, however small, become independent, they become members of the international community. It is to be expected that most of them wish to be associated in some way with the United Nations. But the dilemma they presently face is how to become part of the organic structure of the United Nations without having to carry financial and other responsibilities greater than those they might reasonably be expected to bear. Special arrangements for such states, particularly those that are economically under-developed, could be considered further.

Perhaps some precedent may be found in the arrangements made in certain of the Specialized Agencies for associate membership and also in the regional economic commissions of the United Nations. As will be seen in Chapter XI, the qualifications for admission to most of the Specialized Agencies are neither so exacting nor are the obligations so demanding as in the case of membership in the United Nations. Membership of a state in a Specialized Agency usually qualifies the member for participation in the United Nations Development Program, the work of which is described in Chapter XII, as well as other programs of the United Nations which have been established to assist the economically developing countries.

An irrevocable contract?   Under the League's Covenant members could withdraw by giving two years' notice of their intention to do so. Seventeen members did so; some for reasons that, in retrospect, seem frivolous. Two other members, it may be noted, ceased to be represented as a result of acts of conquest: Albania and Austria. Only one member, the U. S. S. R., was declared by the Council to be no longer a member of the League.

In our comparison of the Charter with the Covenant in Chapter I, it was stated that there is no provision in the Charter for withdrawal from membership. It might be argued that it is implicit in the Charter that, as sovereign states, members have a right to exercise their sovereignty and withdraw should they so wish. Committee reports on this point during the discussions held at San Francisco suggest that this might have been viewed as the case by some representatives.

Nevertheless, although several members have declined to participate in meetings of the Organization at certain times when the proceedings in question were considered as being out of order or simply offensive, no one has withdrawn except Indonesia, which, for two years, from 1964 to 1966, did not participate in the work of the Organization.

Principle, not force.   Any international organization composed of sovereign states is confronted with an institutional dilemma of how, on the one hand, to preserve the concept of equality of its members, and, on the other, by weighted or other systems of voting to give recognition to the more powerful and influential in their midst. In theory if states are sovereign, they are, by this very fact, equal. As a corollary, their collective decision making should be unanimous. In other words, each Member should have a veto.

The Covenant of the League approximated very closely to this theory. The sovereignty of states was implicitly recognized, and their legal equality was made manifest in that they were required to come to unanimous decisions. The present day International Monetary Fund and its twin, the International Bank for Reconstruction and Development both have a system of weighted voting, the strength of each member's vote lying in the size of its financial participation. But, in the United Nations, each member has one vote. Leaving aside the special position enjoyed by Great Powers in the Security Council, the United Nations gives disproportionate weight to members with small populations just as the senatorial system in the United States gives disproportionate weight to the less-populated states in the Union.

At the Dumbarton Oaks Conference Gromyko pleaded for plural voting for the larger and more powerful countries. When the matter was referred to Yalta, Roosevelt was faced with a request to permit the U. S. S. R. to have as many votes as it had Soviet Socialist Republics. He countered by stating that in that case, the United States should have forty-eight votes. The compromise reached was that the U. S. S. R. should be joined in membership by the Byelorussian S. S. R. and the Ukrainian S. S. R., but otherwise each member should have one vote regardless of its size, population or strength. (While the question of plural voting has been touched on in discussions over amending the United Nations Charter, it has not been raised formally. When Syria for a period joined Egypt to form the United Arab Republic, for example, the successor member had one vote, not two. The same applied when Zanzibar joined Tanganyika to form Tanzania.)

The disproportionate weight given to the smaller states has naturally resulted in a marked shift in the work of the General Assembly as the pattern of membership has changed. Those members which now command an absolute majority are for the most part small, economically weak and are not participants in either of the major military alliances.

One member, one vote may, from one point of view, be regarded as a triumph of principle over power. As an historical footnote we might recall, however, how both Benjamin Franklin and Alexander Hamilton argued before the Federal Convention of 1787 against equal representation of the states saying that the method of voting by states was a triumph of power over principle, and was accepted originally by the Continental Congress "under a conviction of its impropriety, inequality and injustice."

Missions. The Constitution of the United States makes no reference to political parties. It has often been said that the United States could better exist without the Constitution than it could without its party system. In much the same way the Charter of the United Nations makes no reference to members maintaining permanent missions to the United Nations nor to the desirability of such arrangements. It might be stated that the United Nations could just as well function without the Charter as without the missions accredited to the Organization.

Each member now maintains a permanent mission to the United Nations. The arrangement stems, perhaps, from the provision in the Charter so organizing the Security Council that it could meet in continuous session. Obviously, members with a seat on the Security Council have to keep their representatives close at hand at all times. The role of the missions, which are probably an outgrowth of the Security Council arrangements, is now vitally important, and it is difficult to see quite how the Organization would function without them.

A permanent mission is an embassy whose ambassador is accredited, not as is normally the case, to a head of state, but to the United Nations. The mission is usually headed by a foreign service official with the rank of "Ambassador Extraordinary and Plenipotentiary." His permanent staff may number as many as forty as in the case of the United States and the U. S. S. R., or it may be very small and run—in the case of a few smaller states—as a kind of branch office of the main embassy in Washington. Mission staff is often quite young, and it is not exceptional to find an ambassador, particularly of a new member, in his mid-thirties.

The mission is swollen by the periodic influx of experts and specialists coming to participate in the large number of technical or highly specialized committees or groups. Also, particularly in the early weeks of the General Assembly, the mission is sometimes taken over by the head of state or the foreign minister and his entourage.

The 128 missions of members and of non-members which maintain observers at the United Nations, are located in New York at a point, as far as this is possible, convenient to the buildings in Turtle Bay. They are never housed, however, on the site of the headquarters itself. Sometimes they share premises with their consulates.

As with embassies elsewhere, a mission reports to and receives instructions from its foreign office. Technical advisers report through these channels to their respective government departments. For example, a United States fishery biologist sitting on an intergovernmental committee negotiating the details of a fishery survey in the Gulf of Guinea would report through the Department of State to his own office in the Bureau of Commercial Fisheries in the Department of the Interior.

The level in the quality of representation has improved generally over the years. The United States and the United Kingdom have taken special steps to insure the highest level of representation. Adlai Stevenson was more than an ambassador; he was a member of the President's cabinet. Lord Caradon is a minister of state and as such a member of the British government. As a result, both were part of the policy-making process although physically somewhat removed from it.

Caucuses, not cabals. Observers have often viewed with reserve the early tendency of missions to group themselves into blocs in order to consult together and, on occasion, to pursue their mutual interests. It is odd that this should be criticized. The United Nations, particularly with its vastly increased membership, could hardly function in an orderly fashion otherwise. There is no party organization, no whips, no division bells. Yet it is as natural as it is desirable that members consult one another on matters of common interest and, if possible, harmonize beforehand their approach to them.

Latin American members make up a natural group. Their common cultural heritage, geographical location and economic problems, and, with the exception of Brazil and Haiti, their common language make it relatively easy for most of them, most of the time, to consult and work together as a group. The socialist countries, led by the U. S. S. R., also work closely; so do the NATO countries. Commonwealth members meet together regularly. The 1955 Bandung Conference resulted in the establishment for the time of a large group of African and Asian members. As interests and policies change, this wider grouping has been replaced by smaller units.

Fairly constant in cooperating as a group are states which are also members of the Arab League.

For the most part such meetings as are held on a regular basis are informal in character. Discussions may sometimes be inconclusive with each representative simply informing the others in advance about his delegation's attitude toward a certain issue. On other occasions, the selection for nomination of members or individuals to serve as officers of different committees and commissions may be decided. Sometimes an agreed line is hammered out in caucus, and a common approach adopted.

Group consultation is facilitated by the fact that there is almost always a participant of one group who is a member of another. This overlapping participation results in private discussions becoming common knowledge and removes any possible stigma that the group is not so much a caucus as a cabal.

This discussion of membership, representation and the group approach to issues before the United Nations leads us naturally back to the General Assembly itself.

The microcosm. Hammarskjöld was fond of quoting T. S. Eliot's phrase about our living in an age where wisdom has given place to knowledge, and knowledge to information. At this point in our study of membership and the General Assembly we could catalogue the main activities of this body over twenty years or so, or discuss current issues which could be out of date as soon as the printer set this type. It is much better to seek an acquaintance with the basic concepts, and the rest will follow as naturally as the daily headlines.

The United Nations is not an ivory tower set apart from the real world. Rather, it is a microcosm of the world. If this is so, and for a while let us assume that it is, we will be immediately aware of the two main forces at work which are frequently at variance: self-interest on the one hand and a sense of common responsibility on the other.

Schopenhauer and hedgehogs. States exist, wrote Schopenhauer, like hedgehogs in a bag—in close and prickly contact. Or, as Alexander Hamilton pointed out in *The Federalist,* proclivity begets enmity. Sovereign states do tend to pursue their own selfish short-term interests.

In the General Assembly, as well as in other Principal Organs, self-interest is pursued, but with restraint. Because certain concepts of international living are expounded, a sense of common obligation is fostered in the United Nations and, where possible, channelled into positive action designed to serve the long-term interests of the world community, rather than the short-term interests of individual members. For example, in 1948, at the height of the Berlin blockade, when the dangers inherent in the situation seemed insurmountable, in an atmosphere hardly less conducive to international harmony, the General Assembly agreed to move forward with a modest program of technical assistance designed to accelerate the growth of the economically underdeveloped countries. Quiet diplomacy behind the façade of public debate subsequently resulted in a reduction of tension concerning Berlin and the acceptance of something approaching a *modus vivendi* by all parties involved.

Areas of conflict. In the General Assembly, there are three related areas of potential conflict: small powers and great powers; underdeveloped countries and developed countries; and socialist economies and private enterprise economies.

The United Nations has grown from a relatively homogeneous instrument of international cooperation based on wartime alliance into a heterogeneous organization of over 120 members, all but a few of which are small powers. The history of the United Nations is characterized by the small powers seeking to restrain the Great Powers, to lessen their own dependence upon them and, when propitious, to exploit the differences which exist between them. The Great Powers in spite of their own differences have sought to preserve their special status, particularly in view of the tendency of the General Assembly to erode their privileged position in the Security Council.

In a different context the basic theme is repeated in the struggle of the underprivileged countries to find an equal place in international society and to persuade what they sometimes consider the overprivileged to assume a greater share of responsibility for their welfare, or at least to enable them to participate in the world economy on more equitable terms. The long drawn out debate on the need to establish a United Nations capital development fund, the establishment of the United Nations Development Program on the successful experience of the Expanded Program of Technical Assistance and the United Nations Special Fund represent a tangible and constructive outcome of the representations of the underdeveloped countries. The creation of the United Nations Conference on Trade and Development (UNCTAD) is an expression of the concern of the developing countries at the increasingly unfavorable terms upon which their products enter international trade. The debates on trade and development permeate practically every discussion in the Organization whatever the subject, be it human rights or disarmament. But the challenge of the underdeveloped countries has found its most dramatic and effective form in the representations and debates designed to bring an end to colonialism.

The third area of conflict of interests lies between the socialist countries of the east and the capitalist countries of the west. In the United Nations we use the clumsy, but perhaps more accurate terms "the centrally planned economies" and "the private enterprise economies." Although there is no evidence that any country since 1939 has planned to wage large scale aggressive war, the deterioration in international relationships between 1945 when the wartime alliance finally disintegrated, and, until recently, when the Great Powers again found points at which their interests converged, has caused continuing anxiety. Countries in the east and in the west consequently remain in a state of armed preparedness.

These then, are the three main areas of conflict. Each plays upon the other and each is affected by developments within each other.

A chamber of reflection. The structure and functions of the General Assembly have been described in Chapter II. From the complexities of its committees and its tedious and time-consuming debates, it is possible to see how the theme of national interest and international responsibility takes two forms: the General Assembly is first of all a chamber of reflection, which is what the Charter expected it to be. It has also become a chamber of second intention for which the Charter made no specific provision.

As a chamber of reflection, the Assembly's hallmark is the general debate. Every year, each head of delegation, often the head of state or foreign minister, mounts the rostrum to place on public record his country's position on international issues. This declaration may range from an expression of fear of a hostile neighbor, or the need to formulate proposals for the next step on arms limitation or the worsening terms of trade to the need to introduce international legislation to codify rights and responsibilities in outer space.

The confrontation technique. The debate may not be so much a debate as a series of monologues. The two antipathetic tendencies in international society confront one another in this way each year. They take different forms in various situations. The process of confrontation enables rival positions, and the dangers inherent in them, to be exposed with great clarity. This is something which was seldom achieved under the old diplomacy where there was no full-scale airing of problems. We may term this process the "confrontation technique." By a full exposure of different and potentially conflicting positions, it is possible to identify the opportunities upon which political compromises can be formulated in committee and private diplomacy.

The spirit that seeks to prevail in the General Assembly is one of tolerance, understanding and good neighborliness. Above all, there is always present the aspiration for a better and more peaceful society. The atmosphere, therefore, encourages mutual adjustment to avoid conflict, reaching through, on occasion, to the harmonization of policies, if not of interests.

Illusory voting victories. It may be difficult to see this pattern of work in the General Assembly's deliberations but it is there as foreseen by the Charter which, in Article 11, permits the Assembly to "consider the general principles of cooperation in the maintenance of international peace and security, including the principles governing disarmament and the regulation of armaments, and may make recommendations with regard to such principles to the Members or to the Security Council or to both."

The debate on a particular problem may give rise to a diplomatic consensus. This is not easily defined, but it can be identified. Unfortunately the process may be confused by the resolutions which are sometimes designed to push the consensus too far or to state in rather abrupt terms exactly what measure of agreement has been reached. The dangers inherent in such a process were hinted at by Hammarskjöld when he wrote: ". . . in an organization of sovereign states, voting victories are likely to be illusory unless there are steps in the direction of winning lasting consent to a peaceful and just settlement of the question at issue." The debate then, is the thing, not the resolutions that punctuate it. The debate is addressed not only to the policy-makers but also to peoples everywhere, "the unseen millions" as Trotsky called them. The mobilization of opinion through debate is not a matter to be dismissed lightly, for the words spoken in the General Assembly penetrate everywhere the spoken word can be heard. The moral weight they carry, however, depends on the probity and integrity of those who utter them.

A chamber of second intention. The General Assembly has assumed, without departing from its constitutional limitations, the task of carrying forward the work of the organization when the Principal Organ properly concerned has been prevented from acting, or has not, in the opinion of the General Assembly, acted vigorously enough.

Its principal role under this new function lies in the realm of peace and security. As Chapters IV and V deal with peace and security in some detail, the developing role of the General Assembly in these matters is also discussed there. In the present chapter a passing reference should suffice.

The General Assembly has been given a broad responsibility under Article 11 to discuss the general political orientation in matters relating to peace and security including the regulation of armaments. The Security Council is given the specific responsibility to act in critical situations and to formulate detailed plans for arms control and disarmament. But the Security Council has had a long history of frustration due to the exercise of the veto by one or another of its permanent members.

As early as 1947, the General Assembly realized that the security provisions of the Charter might become inoperative in a crisis situation unless there was a convergence of Great Power interest toward making the security provisions of the Charter work. In that year, the General Assembly set up the Interim Committee of the General Assembly so that it could, in effect, meet in almost continuous session.

In 1950, the Security Council acted swiftly when the forces of the north invaded South Korea. It was able to do so, however, only because of the absence of the representative of the U. S. S. R. The need to provide for an alternative security system within the framework of the General Assembly, therefore, became urgent. In 1950, the Uniting for Peace Resolution was adopted. It placed the General Assembly in a position where it could meet within twenty-four hours when a critical situation threatened, if the Security Council had failed to act. In such an event, the General Assembly could recommend to the membership what action should be taken. It was this machinery that first proved effective in 1956 in the Suez crisis.

As a chamber of second intention, the General Assembly has now at its disposal the rudiments of an alternative, but not a substitute, security system.

The General Assembly has forced the pace in other areas, which, according to strict interpretation of the Charter, are the responsibilities of other principal organs. In later chapters we shall see how the Assembly used its authority to free territories from their trust status, to make effective the *Declaration Regarding Non-Self-Governing Territories* and to increase economic and social aid to less developed countries.

Paying the piper. The budget of the United Nations is adopted every year by the General Assembly. It is paid for by the contributions of its members. A General Assembly committee apportions the burden which each member should carry. This is worked out on a sliding scale determined by such factors as national income, income per person, any temporary dislocation of national income and ability to secure foreign exchange. The committee is advised in these matters by the Statistical Office of the United Nations. Thus, the regular budget and the funds required to meet it are determined yearly. Contributions from members for extra-budgetary funds, such as the United Nations Development Program, are voluntary and do not fall within this arrangement.

The United Nations was confronted with a difficulty which was political, institutional, and financial, to meet the costs of certain actions authorized by the General Assembly while operating in its capacity as a chamber of second intention. By the first resolution of its first emergency session in 1956, the General Assembly set up the United Nations Emergency Force (UNEF) so that it could physically interpose itself between the forces involved in the Suez crisis and permit the withdrawal of others. It acted under the Uniting for Peace Resolution when the Security Council had failed to act. In so doing it authorized the necessary expenditures involved. In the Congo, while the Security Council acted initially, due to growing political difficulties that were reflected in the various positions taken in the Security Council, the General Assembly acted to authorize the Secretary-General to take certain additional steps.

It was assumed that the expenditures incurred by the General Assembly resolutions constituted "expenses of the Organization" within the meaning of Article 17.2 of the Charter. Some members, opposing the action taken by the General Assembly, considered that as the General Assembly resolutions were recommendations addressed to the membership, it was not mandatory that those who disagreed with the action being taken should pay their apportioned share. Others considered that a refusal to meet such obligations placed in jeopardy the peacekeeping role of the United Nations under the alternative procedure provided for in the Uniting for Peace Resolution.

In 1961 the General Assembly requested the International Court of Justice to give an advisory opinion on whether certain General Assembly resolutions relating to the United Nations operations in the Congo (undertaken in pursuance of earlier Security Council resolutions) and the expenditures authorized by the General Assembly in certain resolutions relating to the operations of the Emergency Force constituted "expenses of the Organization." By a vote of nine to five, the Court in its advisory opinion of 20 July 1962, stated that the expenditures authorized by the General Assembly resolutions constituted "expenses of the Organization." The General Assembly then adopted the advisory opinion. In so doing, it became legally binding on all the members.

The General Assembly subsequently strove to meet the expenses incurred, including the funding of some of the debt arising from some members not paying, by an offer of United Nations bonds. The issues arising from the advisory opinion were then taken up by the General Assembly's Committee on Peacekeeping Operations. The problem may have been a financial one, but the issues were political and constitutional.

The great teach-in.   As we have seen, the General Assembly is the Principal Organ in which the total membership is represented. Through its medium of public debate, vital issues cannot be obfuscated or ignored. Through the confrontation technique, it is possible to formulate compromises and achieve mutual accommodation and adjustment through greater understanding. It also acts as a chamber of second intention capable of springing into action when the Security Council fails, or it may function as a stimulant to other bodies to act more vigorously than they sometimes seem inclined.

Underpinning this is the learning process: worldly wisdom is not something to be acquired by new members alone; it is a continuing process for everyone. Lord Hankey in his essay "Diplomacy by Conference," writes of international conferences—"Perhaps the most important result . . . is the knowledge responsible statesmen acquire of one another." For example, Dean Rusk during the first three weeks of the Seventeenth General Assembly (1966) is reported to have met with fifty foreign ministers.

The General Assembly is not only a great public educator. The occasion of its annual session, as well as the day-to-day routine of the United Nations year, also offer an unrivalled opportunity for an increase in awareness of the problems of members, their policies and aspirations. The daily round also provides an opportunity, in an international setting, for the transacting of the daily business of diplomacy. For those smaller members which have resisted the temptation of saddling their taxpayers with the burden of paying for a large number of embassies abroad, the United Nations offers an excellent setting in which to conduct their diplomacy in a multi-lateral framework which to an increasing extent supplements the traditional pattern of bilateral diplomacy. Such arrangements are facilitated by the presence of the Secretary-General and his staff. His is the special responsibility of bringing members together. To the staff increasingly falls the tasks of assembling information, making facilities available and providing advice within the spirit of the Charter.

Chapter IV

PEACEMAKING

In this and the following chapter we will be concerned with peacemaking and peacekeeping. The first purpose of the United Nations is to maintain international peace and security. In fulfilling these functions there is no real distinction between making and keeping peace, but, given the way the Organization has developed and for the purposes of our study, there is some advantage in creating an artificial distinction.

When examining the United Nations in its peacemaking roles we will deal with three aspects: institutional problems; pacific settlement of disputes; and action with respect to threats to the peace, breaches of the peace and acts of aggression.

Making an international institution. As we have seen, there is a basic problem to be faced by anyone attempting to institutionalize international cooperation in a world inhabited by great powers and small powers. This problem has existed since ancient times. Athens became a dominant power in the Delian League which eventually she converted into an empire with the other city-states falling beneath her sway. In any society where a dominant power emerges, an international institution, even if it does not suffer the same fate, runs the risk of degenerating into an organization where the membership slips into habits whereby its decisions are no more than a cloak of assent placed round the foreign policies of the dominant power.

Early political writers were concerned with this problem. Sully saw the answer in crude political surgery, with some of the smaller states being merged and the larger ones being carved up so that more or less all states would be of approximately equal size and strength in the organization. The proposal was not as bizarre as it seems. Statesmen then, as now, felt no compunction about modifying the frontiers of others.

Other proposals on how to have an organization reflect the power of its membership in the world at large were centered on weighted voting. Larger and stronger states should have more votes than smaller, weaker ones. But great powers do not necessarily remain great, nor small ones weak.

In 1815, at Vienna, the Great Powers felt no hesitation about determining the peace and electing to keep it together. But having made a good peace settlement with difficulty, they found it almost impossible to keep it. The interests of great powers can never be expected to be the same. The most that can be hoped for is that, in moments of crisis, their interests will converge. Then, for different (and possibly opposing) reasons, they may be predisposed to act in concert. Great power interests do converge and modern history abounds with examples where the Concert of Europe did intervene (or agreed not to intervene) decisively.

It was Jan Smuts, a founder of the League, who saw the desirability of the Great Powers having in their midst representatives of the smaller powers to temper the propensities of the great. Thanks to his initiative, the Council of the League of Nations became not the exclusive preserve of the Great Powers but one where small and medium-sized powers were also represented. The Covenant, however, was based on the assumption that action by the Council would be based on the unanimity of its members. Each member, in fact, had a veto.

Votes and vetoes. A radical departure from the constitutional theory upon which the Covenant was based was the introduction into the Charter of the concept of majority voting. The principle of unanimity was abolished, although in practice there has been a constant search in all United Nations organs for a diplomatic consensus, which finds expression in the unanimous adoption of resolutions. The framers of the Charter recognized that demanding unanimity in all things would have paralyzed the future development of any international system based upon collective decisions. Majority voting consequently was introduced as a basis for decision-making in the Security Council as well as elsewhere in the Organization.

The retention of the principle of unanimity would have paralyzed the development of the new Organization. But unless the Great Powers themselves had not been provided with reserved powers in the Security Council, there probably would have been no United Nations at all. Stalin made his position clear at Yalta. "Yugoslavia and Albania and such small countries do not deserve to be at this table," he said. Turning to Roosevelt, Stalin asked: "Do you want Albania to have the same status as the United States?" Stalin saw three Great Powers "protecting" the small powers. Never would he have agreed to submitting Great Power behavior to the judgment of small powers.

Majority voting in the Security Council was thus tempered by the requirements that majority votes on substantive matters must include the concurring vote of the five Great Powers: China, France, the U. S. S. R., the United States and the United Kingdom. This veto power applies to all substantive resolutions. Procedural votes do not call for Great Power unanimity although a resolution to determine whether a matter is substantive or procedural is, in itself, a substantive matter and therefore subject to the veto. The only concession to the small powers in these matters is that a member which is a party to a dispute, cannot vote on the pacific settlement of that dispute whether it be a Great Power or no power at all. In practice the harshness of this requirement has been vitiated by the acceptance by the permanent members of the rule that an abstention on a vote does not constitute a veto (although, strictly speaking, the requirement of a concurring vote would call for a "Yes" rather than an "Abstain").

There is a certain intellectual brutality about this arrangement, but it represents in a rough and ready way something of the pragmatic forces at work in the world at large. What then are the institutional problems, of which there would seem to be two? To see them in sharp relief we should compare briefly the world of the Charter with that of the Covenant.

Two worlds of insecurity. The Charter conceives of a world in which, if the unilateral use of war is threatened, or indeed occurs, there is an Organ—the Security Council—empowered, charged and effectively able to say "Stop that or else. . . ."

The Covenant conceived of a world in which, for many kinds of critical situations, there were available procedures which co-signatories promised to employ, and in which most other co-signatories promised to embarrass them, if they did not. It was a world, incidentally, in which co-signatories promised that territorial integrity and political independence were not to be tampered with from the outside.

Neither the Charter nor the Covenant speaks of "collective security" as such. Each is a compromise set of arrangements negotiated between diverse schools of policy and doctrine arrived at partly under the impulsion of a widespread belief that "collective security" was a possibility much to be desired. In the Covenant, there was a firm promise to do certain things in certain circumstances and to do them on the theory that resort to war against one would be tantamount to war against all.

In the Charter there is a promise that, when certain fuller arrangements to place adequate armed forces at the disposal of the Security Council have been negotiated, collective resistance to aggression would take place if the Security Council could give a timely directive to the Organization's membership to act as it determined.

At the risk of oversimplifying, we might sum up the security provisions of the Covenant as a check for a modest amount but with the details sufficiently written in and signed. On presentation it could be honored. The security provisions of the Charter by contrast might be considered to be a blank check, postdated and, as yet, with only a pencilled "X" showing where the signature is eventually to go. The check will be signed if and when the agreements on making available military forces and related matters have been concluded. But the Military Staff Committee which is charged under the Charter with special tasks regarding these matters, owing primarily to Great Power disunity, has not been able to make any tangible progress in the drafting, let alone the negotiating of the agreements by which the necessary forces would be placed at the disposal of the Security Council. Now that there is a greater convergence of interest on the part of the Great Powers within the United Nations, than perhaps at any point within the past twenty years, any meeting of minds on these matters would probably find expression in arrangements considerably different from those envisaged under the Charter.

The first institutional problem, therefore, is that there is no built-in apparatus, no automatic machinery which would place promptly at the disposal of the Security Council the necessary forces with the logistical and general staff support to deploy a deterrent to any state likely to indulge in a breach of the peace or to commit an act of aggression. This does not mean, however, that states may not be deterred by action taken by the Security Council.

Under the Covenant, the potential victim of aggression might logically fear lest:

> (a) co-signatories misread the situation, i.e., picked the wrong villain;
> (b) co-signatories defaulted on their obligations: states, after all, cannot be expected always to honor their pledged word any more than individuals always can;
> (c) aggression might come through a "gap" in the Covenant.

Under the Charter, the potential victim might logically fear lest:

> (a) the Security Council misreads the situation;
> (b) he is subjected to the use of force before the Council can supervise effective action to aid him;
> (c) the Security Council becomes deadlocked by a veto by a permanent member;
> (d) a sufficient number of members default on their obligations, thereby making the United Nations action ineffective.

Concerned as we are with the institutional problem under the Charter we have to concentrate on (c); (b) we have already touched on previously.

The second institutional problem arises from the ever-present threat that a veto may be exercised—whether discreetly or indiscreetly—by a permanent member of the Security Council. By discreet exercise is meant the use by a Great Power of the veto when it is required to serve as a safety valve to prevent the Organization from being fragmentized as a result of its taking action against a member which is a Great Power. In Chapter I we saw how the Charter-in-theory placed the Great Powers outside, if not above, the law. The Charter-in-practice certainly takes them out of reach of the possibility of action being taken against them by the Security Council. This is how the veto was meant to operate. It was designed to be used in such a way that a permanent member should never be placed in a position where the combined forces of the rest of the membership were ranged against him.

Here lies the institutional fault line in an organization devoted primarily to the preservation of international peace and security. In the event of a member—which is not a Great Power—indulging in action likely, in the opinion of the Security Council, to lead to a breach of the peace, the member may find the combined might of the other members ordered against it by the Security Council. This, in the event of a showdown, is how the Organization is meant to function. But there is no guarantee that when the vital interests of a permanent member of the Security Council are likely to be affected adversely by a course of action proposed in the Security Council, that that member will not protect its interests by the use of the veto. This is also how the Organization is meant to function, i.e., not to function at all under such circumstances.

In addition to the function which was envisaged—to prevent action being taken which was inimical to the vital interests of a Great Power—it should be noted that there have been situations in which the veto has been applied where the vital interests of a permanent member were not necessarily involved. Extensive application of the veto, however, belongs rather to the days of post-war disunity. Under the circumstances then prevailing, the possibility of the Security Council taking action in a situation was extremely unlikely. For the Great Powers to agree to act in concert in the Security Council presupposes a convergence of interest, however fleeting, or, in the absence of this, at least a willingness to act due to the absence of any special interest which might prevent agreement.

Considerations of this kind might once have seemed unrealistic. However, in 1965 the Security Council acted to bring an end to the conflict between India and Pakistan. In late 1967, the treaty on outer space, signed and ratified by the U. S. S. R. and the United States, entered into force. In 1967 also, and again in 1968, resolutions were adopted unanimously regarding the conflict in the Middle East and its aftermath. In 1968 the treaty on the non-proliferation of nuclear weapons was presented to the General Assembly for adoption. Both in the Security Council and in other bodies of the United Nations, therefore, it has been possible to act on the basis of a convergence of interests of at least the majority of the Great Powers.

Important though these acts are in themselves, for the purposes of our study we should recognize that they are the product of a deliberate search for a common ground on the basis of which collective decisions can be taken. Seeking consensus has become an increasingly significant role for the United Nations. In the years immediately after World War II, however, the prospects for the emergence of such a practice did not seem likely in the face of international tensions that were then prevalent.

It became apparent in the early years of the United Nations that its functions in the realm of peace and security would disintegrate in the face of Great Power disunity unless an alternative security system within the Organization were found. Members, under United States leadership, turned to the General Assembly in an attempt to provide this.

"The Little Assembly." While the Security Council is given primary responsibility for the maintenance of peace and security, its functions are more or less confined to what are termed "critical situations." But although it has primary responsibility it does not exercise exclusive responsibility. To some extent, the General Assembly has a share in these matters.

The General Assembly is not designed to exercise power of direction over the members of the United Nations, as is the Security Council. It is essentially a chamber of public debate and reflection. As a deliberative body it is designed to define general lines of political orientation, leaving to the Security Council the taking of immediate action in dangerous or potentially dangerous situations.

In the years of Great Power disunity, the smaller powers, under United States leadership, moved within the General Assembly to establish an alternative mechanism to the Security Council. In 1947 the Interim Committee of the General Assembly was established to meet in permanent session. In this the U. S. S. R. never participated. It remains in existence but seldom meets. It has five main functions: It is designed to carry out preparatory work for the General Assembly between sessions; to consider ways and means of implementing Assembly resolutions; to assume a long-range study function; to exercise a constitutional function; and to handle certain specific assignments such as the Temporary Commission on Korea, the United Nations Special Committee on the Balkans, etc. In this way, a "Little Assembly," as it came to be called, could meet with sufficiently broad terms of reference at short notice to take up matters upon which the Security Council had failed to act satisfactorily.

The creation of the Interim Committee was an attempt by the General Assembly to place itself in a position to act, within its own institutional limitations, when the Security Council had failed to do so. Its functions have now possibly ended. The agenda and other arrangements for the General Assembly are ordered by the General Committee. Later, when situations arose in which the Interim Committee might have acted, the Secretary-General preferred to convene special *ad hoc* advisory groups drawn from carefully selected members to serve specific purposes. The Special Com-

mittee on the first Conference on the peaceful uses of atomic
energy, the Congo Committee and the advisory group on the
clearing of the Suez Canal serve as examples of Hammarskjöld's
special group procedure in such cases. Also, as we shall see at the
end of this chapter, the attempt by the General Assembly in 1950
to establish a much tighter security system overlaid its earlier
work in creating the "Little Assembly."

The experience of the General Assembly in these early years
showed that it could serve as a "chamber of second intention"
when the Security Council had failed. Also, because it is not endowed with specific powers, it can only exercise its right of direct
appeal to members and world opinion. This gives rise to a question
the answer to which might well determine the future of the Organization. Is not international peace and security more likely to be
fostered in a universal organ such as the General Assembly voicing,
in public debate, an appeal to public opinion all over the world
rather than in the deliberations of the Security Council where the
pursuit of Great Power unity is an illusion created by a war which
ended a generation ago? Perhaps not; but this provides us with a
question on which, at the end of our consideration of the institutional problems, we might wish to reflect.

Not victory, but peace. If war is to be abandoned as an
instrument of national policy then some machinery has to be
established and maintained to permit disputes, when they arise,
to be settled peacefully. The attempts to institute methods of
peaceful settlement in the early years of this century were embodied in the League of Nations. One of the weaknesses of the League
was that Article 19 of the Covenant remained a dead letter and the
League became not a facilitator but a "disallower" of peaceful
change.

Chapter VI (Articles 33–38) of the Charter describes the arrangements for the pacific settlement of disputes into which the
United Nations is drawn.

Disputes are indivisible. Basic concepts underlie the role of
the United Nations in fostering peaceful settlement.

War is firmly placed outside the law. Recourse to pacific settlement is not an alternative to the use of force but an obligation. A dispute cannot be considered as a private matter between the disputants, even if they wish to keep it that way, for an unsettled dispute, like a running sore, can spread and infect the whole system. As a corollary to that, wars cannot always be localized, therefore the recourse to pacific procedures established under the Charter is not only in the interests of the parties immediately concerned, but of all members of the international community. The well-being of the international community, consequently, calls for intervention not by third parties alone, but by everyone.

Procedures.   These general, underlying concepts are reflected in the procedures provided for in the Charter.

Members of the United Nations (and states not members, but which, in advance, accept the obligations of the Charter) must draw the attention of the Security Council to a dispute or a situation the prolongation of which might lead to a threat to the peace. The Security Council may invite the parties concerned to settle their differences by peaceful means.

The Security Council, nevertheless, may step into the situation at any point and call upon the parties to adopt procedures or methods to bring an end to the dispute. If the parties fail to reach agreement among themselves they are required to report back to the Council in which case it might recommend its own solution. The Charter also envisages a situation in which the parties actually ask the Security Council to make such a recommendation.

In its capacity as a chamber of second intention the General Assembly under Article 12 of the Charter may also discuss a dispute or situation and, in general terms, make recommendations to the parties. This intervention by the General Assembly is, of course, dependent on the matter not being before the Security Council.

Methods are varied.   The Charter, in matters relating to peaceful settlement, is extremely realistic. For the most part, it leaves, as it should, to the parties themselves the choice of means by which settlement is to be reached. The techniques of direct negotiation, of enquiry into the facts, mediation, conciliation or arbitration are all there to be drawn upon as needed. The Charter does not attempt to establish a monopoly role in supervising peaceful change. On the contrary, it recommends that parties attempt to seek agreement before recourse to the procedures provided by the United Nations.

It acknowledges the role of regional organizations and enjoins members to make every effort to settle their disputes peacefully through such regional arrangements or bodies. Chapter VIII (Articles 52–54) is devoted to such matters. Recourse to regional arrangements was required because by the time the Charter had entered into force such arrangements had already been made, for example, within the Pan-American system. Most regional defense pacts have built into them arrangements for the peaceful settlement of disputes which may arise amongst co-signatories.

Recourse to the International Court of Justice may also be recommended by the Security Council. Presumably it would do so when the nature of the dispute was primarily justiciable in character. As we shall see in Chapter VIII, the Charter is not based, as was the Covenant, upon the rule of law. Rather, emphasis is placed on the need to seek political compromise and mutual accommodation. Recourse to political settlement, therefore, is obligatory; recourse to legal procedures is not.

The fire brigade and the fire. The tendency in the United Nations to turn away from law in favor of mutual accommodation has been criticized. The Earl of Avon (formerly Sir Anthony Eden) has compared the United Nations practices in this respect unfavorably with those of the League. The League attempted to uphold through international law something called international order. The League Council, Lord Avon stated, was as serviceable a piece of diplomatic machinery as he had ever known. The United Nations, he implies, is less concerned with law and order and seeks constantly to reach through compromise and adjustment peaceful solutions, disregarding concepts of right and of lawful obligation. "There has been," he wrote, "too much accommodation between the fire brigade and the fire."

The comparison between the world of the Covenant and the world of the Charter is worth considering. The world we live in is one where disputes are seldom justiciable. They arise as the natural consequences of a world rapidly changing where relationships, obligations and responsibilities shift almost overnight. There is order, but order in a different sense from that of a static society held intact by the League and buttressed by generally accepted standards of right.

Be that as it may, within the flexible framework offered by the Charter for peaceful settlement, procedures and approaches can be varied. Basically, these are five and may be used in various combinations.

Characteristic of most situations is the public debate which, often spectacular, usually accompanies any consideration of a situation which is before the Security Council.

The public pleading of a cause, often useful in itself, also takes away much of the heat to which disputes naturally give rise. This enables patient negotiation to take place in quiet committees and small groups. Here the professional diplomat has his day. He requires, on such occasions, all the skills which Rosier writing in the fifteenth century considered so important. (See Chapter VII.)

Without information, it is difficult to negotiate. Expert missions to find out the facts usually visit the scene of looming conflict.

Of increasing significance has been the quiet and unobtrusive presence of the Secretary-General himself, playing as Hammarskjöld often put it, the role of "the honest broker." The phrase is historically inapt. The comparison of the role of Bismarck at Berlin in 1878 with that played by the Secretary-General in similar crises is not one that stands up to close examination. In contrast to Bismarck's performance, that of the Secretary-General is gentle and calm, giving disinterested service in the cause of peace. Individual, private conversations with the Secretary-General enable him to see what possibilities exist for finding common ground between the disputants and at what point other members may assist in moving toward a settlement.

Surrounding the debate, committee work, fact-finding missions and the quiet presence of the Secretary-General, are the corridors of diplomacy. Often discredited as being a glorified scuttlebutt, the

informal exchanges arising from the daily rubbing of shoulders with
diplomats and experts from other states in a multilateral setting
offer a continuing opportunity for discreet enquiry, exchanges of
views and, on occasion, negotiation.

Does it work? Here we would be well advised to hedge. Not
because the system does not work, for it does, but because we do
not know to what extent the United Nations can exclusively claim
the credit. Its role might be decisive, but marginal. However important the action of the United Nations may be, it will always be
only one factor in the situation.

Sometimes all that can be done is to assist, not so much in finding a satisfactory solution, as in assisting in the relaxation of tension,
thus permitting an atmosphere more conducive to negotiation and
settlement. Such a role can be played even in situations in which
the United Nations is not directly involved. This is one where
quiet diplomacy can take place and attempts to establish common
ground between the various parties be pursued. In others more can
be done. In the Dutch East Indies, for example, the patient participation of the Good Offices Commission and the vigilance of the
Security Council assisted in bringing about a peaceful withdrawal
of the Netherlands, and the achievement of independence by Indonesia in the presence of United Nations representation.

The revolt of the Arabs against Ottoman rule during World
War I resulted in disappointment for Arab nationalists. Instead of
achieving immediate independence, they found themselves placed
under British or French mandates. In 1917, partly in recognition of
the efforts being made by Jewish communities in the prosecution of
the war against Germany and her allies, the British Government
issued the Balfour Declaration which, in effect, committed the Government to the establishment, after the war, of a National Jewish
Home in Palestine.

That there might have been some inconsistency between the
purport of the Declaration and support for Arab irredentism was
not immediately apparent. Difficulties arose eventually with the increased influx of Jews into the Palestine Mandate as a result of
their persecution and massacre in Germany and other countries of

Central Europe immediately before and during World War II. After the War, Jewish refugees from the Continent of Europe moved to Palestine in increasing numbers and relations between Arabs, Jews and the Mandatory deteriorated into open conflict.

Early in 1947, the United Kingdom asked for a special session of the General Assembly to examine the question of Palestine. A Special Committee on Palestine established by the Assembly recommended in a majority report that there should be created an Arab State, a Jewish State, an international regime for Jerusalem and that all three should be joined in a customs union. These proposals were accepted by the Assembly which, at the same time, provided for the end of the Mandate and the withdrawal of British forces in Palestine by August 1948.

The Mandate actually expired in May of that year in a rapidly deteriorating situation. A Jewish State was proclaimed and Arab forces were engaged. A United Nations mediator, Count Folke Bernadotte, the President of the Swedish Red Cross, was appointed. Later in May, the Security Council called on governments and authorities to abstain from hostile military activities. In July, invoking Chapter VII of the Charter, the Security Council ordered military action to cease and for the authorities concerned to issue cease-fire orders. Thus the chain-of-events theory expounded by the makers of the Charter at San Francisco became a practice.

In September, Count Bernadotte was assassinated in the Israeli-held sector of Jerusalem. His functions were assumed by Ralph J. Bunche of the United Nations Secretariat. In November, fighting broke out in the Negev between Palestine Jews and Egyptians. In a series of resolutions, the Security Council called for a cease-fire. Early in 1949, on the island of Rhodes, armistice agreements negotiated by Bunche were concluded by Israel with Egypt, Jordan, Lebanon and Syria.

These agreements, together with the peacekeeping machinery of the United Nations Truce Supervision Organization and, from 1956 to 1967, of the United Nations Emergency Force, remained the sole barriers against the resumption of hostilities. The outbreak of fighting in the Middle East in June, 1967, represented a breach of these agreements. Their provisions, however, are regarded by the United Nations as still applicable. Three resolutions in that year were unanimously adopted by the Security Council. One called for a prompt ceasefire; another concerned the humanitarian aspects of the situation; the third included provisions for the appointment by the Secretary-General of a Special Representative. The impartial presence of the United Nations is an element of hope and opportunity in a situation characterized by animosity and suspicion.

The aftermath of World War II left many questions unresolved and due to the breakdown in allied unity it was difficult to reach agreement concerning them. The disposal of the Italian colonies, Libya, Eritrea and Somalia might be cited. Over a period of time, solutions were found within the United Nations. Somalia after a decade as a trust territory united with the Somaliland Protectorate to become the Republic of Somalia.

Although the Charter provides for action to be taken swiftly when dangerous situations arise, in practice success is more often achieved when action has been slow in coming. By a ceaseless vigilance to make sure that the situation does not get out of control, the slow withering away of the dispute is sometimes possible. The dispute over Trieste and the Anglo-Egyptian dispute of 1947 are examples of this practice by which the heat evaporates, the situation itself seems less pressing and solutions, when they are arrived at, pass almost unnoticed.

Violence creates habits of violence, and a climate can be created where violent habits become accepted not only in a city but also in the world. The climate which the United Nations attempts to create is one in which violence is normally eschewed. The habits of thought and behavior within the "House" are conducive to the creation of a setting which provides excellent opportunities for peaceful settlement or harmonious adjustment where conflict threatens. Peaceful behavior also can get to be a habit.

There are risks inherent in the system, however. The clamorous public debate appealing to public opinion in delicate situations can be found by those who use it to be a double-edged weapon. In diplomacy one should never say, "Never." Public intransigence makes adjustment difficult, particularly when public opinion itself becomes obdurate as a result, and makes the modification of one's position difficult by leaving little room to maneuver. Open agreements secretly arrived at is the post-Wilsonian practice. Just how to judge what the optimum dose of "public" as opposed to "private" diplomacy should be in any given situation is very difficult. It is perhaps for this reason that the quiet diplomacy of the Secretary-General is so often called upon to build the bridge between the two.

Collective resistance to aggression.   Since 1919, "collective security" has been the most majestic expression of the international ideal. Based perhaps mistakenly on Litvinoff's doctrine of the indivisibility of peace, such a concept is indispensable to an international organization devoted to the maintenance of peace and security.

In neither the Covenant nor the Charter is the term "collective security" used. The Covenant is more explicit than the Charter in that aggression is forbidden and condemned and an act of war against one was tantamount to an act of war against the rest of the membership. But in practice, the League almost always hesitated to give effect to the security provisions in the Covenant and thus became powerless as an effective instrument for maintaining peace and security.

The Charter, by contrast, is less eloquent in enunciating these principles but is much more precise and elaborate in stating what steps may be taken in the event of a threat to the peace, breaches of the peace and acts of aggression. "Collective security" as a concept enjoys an eminent position in the Charter, but it is not its essential feature. The role of collective resistance to aggression is to discourage or to punish illegal use of force; to use it in the construction of international order; to supervise the process of peaceful change; and to redress injustice.

The Charter delegates to the Security Council responsibility for taking collective action. The Security Council in exercising the powers given to it may decide on what forms that action will take. It may address itself to the parties, requesting or directing them to cease hostilities. It may order economic and diplomatic sanctions to be applied, or it may decide on military action.

As we saw earlier, the two structural weaknesses make action difficult. The forces to be placed at the disposal of the Security Council did not materialize in the way foreseen. Also, the veto can legally prevent action, which makes it difficult for members to accept absolute obligations in a system of collective security when there is no absolute guarantee that the international community will come to their aid if attacked. These institutional obstacles reflect the situation in the world outside. The world we live in, moreover, is a much more difficult one than the world of the interwar period in which to practice collective security. The configuration of forces then was much more favorable to a system of collective security when states were more approximately the same in size and weight. In the postwar period where power is concentrated in fewer hands, collective action is much more difficult.

Korea. Collective action worked in Korea, but the situation was a freakish one and is unlikely to occur again. On 25 June 1950, the forces of North Korea invaded South Korea. Witnessing the event was the United Nations Commission on Korea (UNCOK) which had been sent to effect the reunification of Korea and to watch for any untoward event. It reported the invasion to the Security Council, which, on the prompting of the United States, acted swiftly and called for collective measures to be taken to repel the invasion. Action by the Council was unimpeded by the veto (which doubtless would have been used had the U. S. S. R. been represented on that occasion), for, as a protest against the presence of the representative of China, the U. S. S. R. at that time was not participating in the deliberations of the Council.

The United Nations forces were made up of contingents from sixteen members. The main force and the logistical support aiding the army of the Republic of Korea came from the United States. In 1951 the Government of the People's Republic of China sent volunteers to aid the Northern forces. Thus the conflict, which had been prosecuted as a genuine act of collective resistance to aggression, began to escalate in the direction of a struggle between two major powers: Communist China and the United States. Three years later, with the battle lines rolling back to the former demarcation line between the two Koreas, an armistice was signed which to a large extent restored the *status quo ante*. Collective action had worked, but the conditions under which it came to work were not likely to be repeated.

An audacious innovation. The need for an alternative security system in the United Nations, foreseen by Secretary of State Marshall in 1947, found its expression in the establishment of the Interim Committee the same year. By 1950 the matter was of more than academic interest. How could the United Nations act if another "Korea" happened? The League had been almost finished as a security organization after it failed to act effectively when Japan invaded Manchuria in 1931, and completely finished when the sanctions applied against Italy in 1935 when it invaded Ethiopia were greeted with derision by Mussolini. The United Nations only accidentally escaped the same fate in Korea twenty years later.

In November 1950 the General Assembly adopted its Uniting for Peace Resolution. It empowered the General Assembly to consider any threat to the peace when the Security Council failed to deal with it. The General Assembly could be convened on twenty-four hours notice under such circumstances. Members were called upon to earmark contingents for service under the United Nations. The resolution established a Collective Measures Committee to consider ways of strengthening the peace. A Peace Observation Commission was established to be the eyes and ears of the Security Council, although this body did not succeed in operating as was originally envisaged.

This resolution based on the "Acheson Plan," named after the then United States Secretary of State, Dean Acheson, was followed by the Peace Through Deeds Resolution which called for prompt and united action against aggression, and condemned efforts to subvert legally constituted governments by interfering in their internal affairs. These resolutions were not designed to keep the peace but to *make* it and, if necessary, to use force to do so.

The Uniting for Peace Resolution is not a substitute for the security system established by the Charter. It does not transfer functions of the Security Council to the General Assembly. It is merely an alternative system which can be brought into play if the Security Council fails. It involves neither firm commitment nor firm guarantee of intervention in support of victims of aggression, for the General Assembly, unlike the Security Council, can only recommend what action should be taken. When the Security Council acts, the United Nations is an "it." When the General Assembly calls for action, it is to "them" (the members) that the appeal is addressed.

This does not mean that the alternative arrangements are negligible. History shows that, when governments fall down on their obligations, they can be brought to comply with them under pressure from public opinion. Nor does the slowness of the procedure under the alternative system block action. The General Assembly was remarkably effective in the 1956 Suez crisis, bringing about a prompt liquidation of the military phase, rapidly reopening the Suez Canal and creating a situation conducive to early agreement. In the accompanying crisis over the Hungarian uprising, the General Assembly had less room in which to act. However, in bringing timely aid not only to the Hungarian refugees but also to Hungarians in Hungary, steps were taken by the Secretary-General at the behest of the General Assembly to reduce some of the worst features inherent in the situation.

The action taken in the Congo was followed through by the General Assembly when the Security Council faltered. The new system, an audacious innovation, which is tantamount to a *de facto* revision of the Charter, enhances the role of the smaller powers when the Great Powers cannot agree. Its presence acts as a standing inducement for the Great Powers to reexamine their responsibilities.

The return of Great Power unanimity to the Security Council in the Indo-Pakistan Conflict of 1965 enabled the Security Council to call for a cease-fire with a clear indication that if it were not complied with by the two parties collective measures would be considered. Possibly the permanent members were more ready to act when their interests converged than they might otherwise have been if there had not been an alternative procedure available.

Accepting the concept. But it is not all as easy as it seems. The United Nations is not so structured that in a critical situation, collective action may be taken on the basis of well-established procedures. Nor, if a veto establishes a road block, do the diversion signs necessarily lead to the General Assembly.

Often writers studying the performance of the United Nations take as a guide the Charter and the official records of the Organization's deliberations. To do so gives us the same arid picture of the United Nations as we would obtain if we limited our study of the United States government to a reading of the Constitution and the *Congressional Record*. Moreover, the point is often missed.

The point is that the acceptance of the concept of collective resistance to aggression is more important than the reality. There was not this acceptance in the interwar period as we can recall from the anguished witness of pacifists, on the one hand, who wanted to resist the dictators but not fight them, and the hard-headed self-styled realists, on the other hand, who asked who was going to die for Danzig? In diplomacy, it is not the wielding of power that matters as much as the prestige which is the halo around power. Power is seldom in question; prestige is put to the test all the time. The general acceptance by international society that collective resistance to aggression is always present as an important feature is more important than what constitutional or military arrangements exist to underpin it. By its acceptance, we help to create the international order and habits of mind and behavior that underpin it. Thus, paradoxically, by creating an order based upon collective responsibility we make recourse to collective action less and less necessary.

Chapter V

PEACEKEEPING

The international institution, as opposed to the individual members who comprise it, is concerned primarily with international security. The pursuit of this aim is generally considered to depend to a large extent upon broad measures of worldwide disarmament or at least a degree of arms control and, at the same time, the establishment under international authority of an international peacekeeping force, or of national contingents available at short notice to serve under an international general staff. At different times these two aims are pursued independently; at others they are closely linked. In the present chapter we will trace these two developments and conclude with a few suggestions on the direction which discussion and negotiation might take in the future.

Aristotle and Kant. The first duty of a state, as Aristotle reminds us, is to exist. The task of preserving the state calls for its defense. Not to take reasonable measures to do so exposes the state to the predatory appetites of others. It is prudent to assume that states are by nature enemies although as we know, by simply looking around us, that in practice they seldom are. Each state, therefore, should be expected to maintain itself in such a way as to deter a potential aggressor. If a state does not do so, it risks disappearance or a radical change in the way of life of its citizenry.

It was Kant who drew attention to the dangers of maintaining a high level of armaments, and the desirability of states taking steps to bring about a degree of disarmament. Otherwise, the escalation of armed preparedness would continue into conflict, and even if it did not, the economic burden would reduce to poverty the states so profligate as to waste their substance in such a way.

The hope that disarmament might be possible has always accompanied attempts to develop a system of international cooperation. If arms could not be eliminated, at least they might be brought under some measure of control. The first Hague peace conference was convened in 1899 by Tsar Nicholas II, with the adoption of such measures vaguely in mind. It was the first conference of its kind, and as with some others that were to follow, it presaged not a period of disarmament but of rearmament.

A more sober mood prevailed among the drafters of the League Covenant. Article 8.1 reads as follows: "The members of the League recognize that the maintenance of peace requires the reduction of national armaments to the lowest point consistent with national safety and the enforcement by common action of international obligations." Implicit in this article was the recognition that national safety called for a measure of armed preparedness but that integration of an international society could never be advanced while nations maintained a heavy burden of armaments, thus constituting a standing threat to one another.

Die Reigen. The interwar period excelled in muddled thinking and humbug. This was particularly true over disarmament issues, and in the post-World War II period we still continue to be muddled, if humbug itself has ceased to be quite so fashionable. The arguments in favor of armaments have been used with the same force by those in favor of disarmament and vice versa at different periods. We should examine some of these as, over forty years, they have gone up and down round the carousel of international debate.

In the pre-Keynesian days of President Hoover, opinion in the United States favored disarmament because the diversion of a nation's resources to an unproductive activity was believed to cause economic slumps. The harnessing of these resources to productive activity would bring about an upswing in the economy. Armaments races brought on depression, so the argument ran.

Much contemporary discussion, however, has centered upon the prospects of the economic setbacks that may result not from rearmament but from a tapering off of arms production. The end of the Korean War boom and the economic setbacks that occurred after the hostilities had ended had a marked effect on the world economy. Worldwide disarmament, if it ever succeeds beyond being a pipe dream, will certainly call for major economic adjustment throughout more than one sector of the economy. For countries such as the United States, where whole new areas have been settled and their local economies structured entirely upon industry geared almost exclusively to armament production and related activity, a special problem is posed.

To counter this argument many point out that, in this post-Keynesian world, we know much more about how to manipulate an economy and we are capable of cushioning it from the adverse effects of major structural change which comprehensive disarmament would certainly bring in its train. But do we? We may know what to do, but there are many signs that we may not yet know how to do it.

There is no doubt, however, that there are channels into which such economic activity resulting from disarmament can be constructively diverted. As we shall see in Chapters X and XII the claims on the economically developed countries to help the poorer members of the international community to build up their economies are voiced continually. The argument runs among the developing nations not that disarmament would lead to an increase of resources available to them, but that in the light of their pressing economic needs, the developed countries have a moral obligation to disarm in order to create the productive elbow room which may be needed to transfer resources to a mass attack on the economic stagnation in most underdeveloped countries of the world.

Ceaseless innovation. A similar discussion centers upon the effect of disarmament on technology. Urgent and high priority problems await the attention of the scientist and technologist. Hiving off the best talent to perfect deadly instruments, or defensive weapons with which to fend them off, means that working on health, increasing the productivity of the earth, initiating breakthroughs to make life more comfortable and meaningful have to take a lower priority.

To a large extent this is undoubtedly true. If we could concentrate, for example, the talents, capital and organizing skill presently devoted to perfecting germ warfare instead to smashing the epizootics of East Africa, one of the world's greatest cattle industries could develop in a matter of years on those great tick and disease infested plains. But there is much to be said for the obverse. The ceaseless technological innovation and the relentless pressure to keep up or to keep ahead in weaponry has resulted in tremendous fringe benefits of a peaceful nature which have in twenty-five years changed much of our society. The interest aroused by C. P. Snow's lectures on the desperate but successful struggle by Sir Henry Tizard in the late nineteen thirties to provide for the defense of England against air attack has revealed to us something of the effort which went into the invention of radar. The navigational and other aids which have since been developed for civilian use, from what was essentially a military invention, have revolutionized transport and communications. Without the spur of danger of defeat it is unlikely that the pressure to innovate would have been so great.

These are, however, marginal arguments which, while they affect attitudes towards armaments control discussions, are not in any way decisive. Of greater significance is the discussion of the relationship between arms and conflict. Do armaments races cause war or does the fear of war cause an armaments race? History does not serve as a certain guide in these matters.

Writers before World War I and in the interwar period pointed to the increasingly heavy burden of armaments carried by the Great Powers and the high cost involved for the continental powers in maintaining great standing armies with long periods of conscription. The increasing burdens were felt by all and eventually a crisis occurred in 1914. The Anglo–German naval rivalry and the crushing financial burdens carried by such countries as Russia and Austria–Hungary in the building up of their armies had reached a breaking point, and when war seemed likely, there was less inclination to prevent a drift toward it as there would have been if the financial squeeze had not been felt so acutely. Or so we thought.

In World War II, allied airmen in moments of fantasy invented a mythological aircraft known as the woozle bird. Its principal characteristics were that it ascended in ever-decreasing spirals until it shot itself down. In the interwar period thinking about armaments was based on a similar mythology. Nations before 1914 had glared at one another's armaments, and then rushed to accumulate more until the process acquired a momentum of its own and finally ignited itself, bringing about a general conflagration. Now, if anything, the reverse is considered plausible. As nations acquire the instruments of mass destruction, they acquire with them an incitement to prudence. A balance of terror, in effect, is being struck with no nation prepared to let loose its arsenal, knowing that there is no guarantee that the instruments of retaliation will not inflict the same damage in return. This attitude, however, assumes that men of good sense behave, in moments of crisis, sensibly. As Captain Bluntschli found in Shaw's *Arms and the Man,* this is not a safe assumption.

If armaments do not necessarily lead to war, does disarmament lead to peace? The end of British–United States naval rivalry in 1923 helped to abolish any thinking that might have been present that these two countries could ever go to war against one another. But the low level of armed preparedness of the democracies did nothing to discourage the dictators from preparing for war in the nineteen thirties. The unwillingness of the democracies to recognize the dictators' intentions only encouraged the latter to be more belligerent. Moreover, sporadic attempts at arms control in this period caused dismay and loss of confidence in nations not directly parties to such agreements. The Anglo–German naval agreement of 1935 caused consternation in France and lent weight to the view that the British were indeed perfidious and could not be relied upon in the event of a confrontation with the dictators. Both unilateral and bilateral arms control measures have their hazards.

The chicken and the egg. There are many more arguments which form part of the warp and woof of the debate on armaments and arms control. But we have seen enough now to have some idea of its complexity and to draw two general conclusions. It is generally recognized that no effective international society can develop without disarmament or a measure of arms control. The constant threat of the unleashing of terror is not one which contributes to mutual confidence and willingness to work together in the interests of the world community. But disarmament cannot be treated in isolation from other and more deep-seated problems. Not taking them into account would be like the physician restricting himself to treating only the spots of a patient with measles. Disarmament considerations have to be examined almost exclusively in the light of what nations consider are their minimum demands for security. Without security there can be little hope for disarmament, and vice versa. Which comes first then—security or disarmament?

In the League, the French never had any doubt about it. When we can be assured of international security, the French stated, we can think about disarmament and not before. Other members of the League took the position that the search for security was a will-o'-the-wisp, and the sooner nations could be induced to disarm the sooner the craving for absolute security guarantees would go. In reality, neither security nor general disarmament was achieved. Disarmament can only be conducted in an atmosphere of confidence and that, in turn, can only be engendered by an assurance of security. The creation of conditions of security is assisted, if not predicated upon, measures of disarmament or arms control.

International security, however, is not achieved by arms control alone. Insecurity can still prevail even if nations have no arms. Arms comprise only one strand in the tangle of international relationships. The existence of a relatively stable balance of power is the most important element, and armed strength is only a part of that. The substitution of national defense systems and alliances by an international security machinery may also play a part.

Perhaps because of a lack of understanding of the relationship of disarmament to other factors and the excessive significance attached to the dangers of armaments, the League experience was not a happy one. Apart from the peremptory reference to disarmament in Article 8, the authors of the Covenant stigmatized, in Article 8.5, the private manufacture and sale of armaments. The

"merchants of death" were condemned but the League debates
contributed little. Most discussion, in fact, was outside the League;
for example the Washington Conference in 1922 and the Disarmament Conference in London in 1932.

The debates and conferences, however, made a contribution in
that they showed clearly three basic obstacles which confronted
those who sought agreement. They pointed up the psychological
difficulties preventing adherence to a general instrument of disarmament and prolonging a state of equilibrium in armed forces. Technological innovation brought about shifts in the balance of power;
nations realigned themselves in an endless quadrille. International
life is not static any more than national or individual life. Ceaseless
change does not admit of this kind of international arms freeze.

The second difficulty was the sheer technical impossibility of
applying common measures to different instruments of war. How
many bombers equal one submarine? Is a well-equipped tank brigade equal to an infantry division? No table of comparative values
is possible.

Governments also could not surmount the third obstacle—the
supreme difficulty in agreeing to a system of comparison among
countries of diverse strength. A long frontier might call for more
troops than a country with a short frontier or none at all. But
strength is not just a matter of troops easily mobilized. Victories
are not always to the swift but sometimes to those with massive
industrial and financial strength who slowly gird themselves for a
war of attrition. Economic strength and the availability of allies to
bear the brunt of attack might count for more than the superior
fleets, armies and airplanes of the enemy.

With the best will in the world meaningful agreement was not
possible. And the will was not of the best. Naval powers such as
Great Britain sought to reduce the size of land armies. States with
large standing armies such as France wished to reach agreement
on naval forces. Countries militarily weak all around and with long
frontiers to defend such as the U. S. S. R. called, as Litvinoff did in
1927 before the League Disarmament Conference, for complete
and comprehensive disarmament. Finally, the demands of a re-

surgent Germany for parity in armaments ushered in a period not of disarmament but rearmament.

Before considering the experience of the United Nations we should sum up five general conclusions: (a) A degree of arms limitation and control is called for in our attempt to integrate and further the well-being of the international community; (b) without an atmosphere of mutual confidence, steps toward arms control must falter; (c) control and confidence building measures have an interaction in that each advances the other; (d) even with a will to negotiate, the technical, strategic and political difficulties are almost insurmountable; (e) arms control questions cannot be treated in isolation from other factors entering into international life such as the quest for a stable balance of power and the elaboration of an adequate machinery of international security.

A new sense of urgency. The United Nations Charter gives to the General Assembly the tasks of defining the general lines to be followed in disarmament matters. Article 11.1 states that the General Assembly "may consider . . . the principles governing disarmament and the regulation of armaments, and making recommendations with regard to such principles to the Members or to the Security council or to both." Under Article 26 the Security Council is given the responsibility of elaborating precise plans.

The destruction in Hiroshima and Nagasaki by atomic bombs at the concluding phase of World War II lent a new sense of urgency to the task of formulating plans for the regulation of armaments. Efforts were immediately directed towards the control of the atom. By its first resolution at the first session of the General Assembly in January 1946, the Atomic Energy Commission was established. It was instructed to make proposals which would restrict atomic development to peaceful purposes only, eliminate atomic weapons and establish safeguards for inspection.

The Baruch Plan. The political setting was one of deepening suspicion between the Western powers and the Communist countries. The wartime alliance was beginning to crumble as the dangers that had called it into being were removed. Strategically, the situation was one in which the United States had a monopoly of atomic weapons, and the U. S. S. R. had a massive preponderance of land forces in Europe.

The United States, recognizing that its monopoly was of a temporary nature, saw the need for early control of atomic weapons. At the same time it was clear that scientific and technological progress could not be halted, nor would it be possible to distinguish between atomic development for peaceful and for warlike use. Control of atomic power, therefore, was necessary at the source.

It was with these considerations in mind that the United States presented the "Acheson-Lilienthal" or the "Baruch" Plan. The essence of the plan was that there should be established an international monopoly of atomic materials covering all aspects: ownership, exploitation, research and development. To ensure this establishment, an international atomic agency would be set up to exercise the monopoly. Thus, all countries would be guaranteed against atomic attack, and at the same time work could proceed on the elaboration and application of the atom for peaceful purposes. Following the adoption of these measures, there would be a destruction of existing atomic weapons and the making of further bombs would be prohibited.

The U. S. S. R. rejected the concept of placing the atom under an international monopoly and proposed instead that priority should be given to prohibition of all atomic arms, placing little stress on the need to have foolproof systems of international inspection in order to insure compliance with the atom ban.

The discussion continued with variants on these rival proposals until a sudden shift in the balance of power occurred. In July 1949, the Commission suspended its work, following the withdrawal from participation by the U. S. S. R., heralding by one month the explosion by the U. S. S. R. of its first atomic device. The General Assembly dissolved the Commission in 1952. Some months later in 1953 the United States exploded its first hydrogen device to be followed by the U. S. S. R. a year later.

The conventional approach. Heretofore, the consideration of the reduction in conventional (i.e., non-atomic) arms had been pursued by the General Assembly through its Commission for Conventional Arms set up in 1947 with the same membership as the Security Council. Apart from fruitless attempts to reach agreement on a census of arms as a prerequisite to the discussion of their control and institution, little headway was made by 1950 when the U. S. S. R. withdrew as it had done from the Atomic Commission, ostensibly over Chinese representation, and the arms commission also was subsequently dissolved in 1952.

The second attempt after this double failure was to link the discussion of atomic arms with conventional weapons and tackle both simultaneously. There was much to be said for this, as the abolition of one without the other foretold security for no one. The General Assembly thus created a Disarmament Commission in 1952. It never got off the ground and the procedural hindrances were overcome in 1953 when the General Assembly created a subcommittee of the Commission providing in this way a more flexible framework for the discussions.

In the years that immediately followed proposals were presented thick and fast. So much so, in fact, that each side in the discussion presented all the possibilities in the form of their own proposals only to reject them when presented by the other side. It should be recognized that, during this period particularly, members were prone to propose plans which, by their nature and timing, they knew must have been unacceptable to others. Knowing that they would not be accepted and losing no advantage by proposing them, as much propaganda mileage was obtained from them as possible before they were overtaken by another crop of proposals.

To a large extent due to the persistence of Jules Moch of France, the following three general points of agreement were arrived at in these years:

(a) atomic arms should be banned;
(b) conventional arms should be reduced to a point of equilibrium between the powers;
(c) an effective system of inspection and control should be instituted to supervise these arrangements.

The snag was, which should receive priority? To give priority to either of the three involved a risk which none was prepared to take. To abolish one's atomic arms, subject to control arrangements designed to make sure the other fellow did likewise, was dangerous. To do so with conventional arms was, if anything, more hazardous. And to submit to inspection by the other side was to expose one's strength and military capability.

It should be added that the proposal to reduce conventional arms was never studied in the strategic and tactical detail as was done in the League. Perhaps such details had come to be looked upon as more political than technical.

The piecemeal approach. The third phase started in 1955, in the new climate of confidence which developed after the death of Stalin. The comprehensive approach was not abandoned. The U. S. S. R. pursued its policy, originally expounded in 1927 by Litvinoff, for complete all-round disarmament. The United States and the Western countries continued to place special emphasis on inspection and control. The underdeveloped countries increasingly began to make their presence felt in public debate on the need to devote the resources from worldwide supervised disarmament to the establishment within the United Nations of a fund for their economic development.

Attention, however, began to concentrate on specific matters in an attempt to reach agreement on aspects of the general question which could be settled without comprehensive agreement. It was felt that the demonstration of some progress, however marginal, would help to build up the climate of confidence without which political agreement would be difficult, but not impossible as we shall see later. Besides, new problems were beginning to present themselves.

With the perfection of the hydrogen bomb great strides had also been made in delivery systems. First came the intermediate range ballistic missile (IRBM) and then the intercontinental one (ICBM). These advances in rocketry made the possibility of detecting a surprise attack too late for interception a frightening prospect. Proposals for the abolition of nuclear warheads and the dis-

cussion of measures to prevent surprise attack were linked, by the
U. S. S. R., with the elimination by the United States of its foreign
bases. The "open skies" plan of the United States was an attempt
to institute a partial or complete aerial photographic inspection
system.

Discussion also centered upon the abandonment of nuclear testing due to the threat of nuclear fallout. During this period the discussion continued outside the United Nations in a four-power conference comprising France, the U. S. S. R., the United Kingdom
and the United States.

In 1955 the first Conference on the Peaceful Uses of Atomic
Energy was held in Geneva, with full participation by the atomic
powers under the chairmanship of the head of the Indian Atomic
Energy Commission. It was a remarkably successful conference,
brilliantly prepared and directed by a special team comprising the
best talents available to and within the United Nations Secretariat.
At that time too, on the initiative of President Eisenhower, the International Atomic Energy Agency was established to further international cooperation in the peaceful application of atomic power
and to act as an international "bank" for fissionable materials.

Sputnik I. The launching of Sputnik I by the U. S. S. R. in 1959
(following which Khrushchev, at the General Assembly that year,
presented to the United Nations a model of the space craft now
hanging high above the public lobby), resulted in a sharp shift in
the balance of power. Along with United Kingdom disarmament
proposals, the U. S. S. R. presented to the General Assembly a
Declaration of the Soviet Government on General and Complete
Disarmament. These events led to the fourth stage in the work on
arms control. The essence of the U. S. S. R. proposals took the form
of a stage-by-stage progression to complete disarmament over a
period of four years with a control organ to supervise the steps
taken.

The old subcommittee on disarmament, in which the U. S. S. R.
had declined to participate in 1958, was wound up and a new Ten-
Nation Disarmament Committee began its meetings in 1960. At
those meetings, the United States made its own proposals which,

in effect, placed special emphasis on the arrangement to oversee and verify the steps taken at each stage before proceeding to the next and to give greater priority to the prohibition of orbiting vehicles.

Proposals and counterproposals were again presented with a broad measure of agreement again being reached on abolition of nuclear arms, the lowering of conventional arms levels and the introduction of inspection systems. The problems were not only of a technical nature but also of time. Technological innovation constantly bypassed agreement. The "open skies" inspection proposal was overtaken by technological improvements in the techniques of avoiding detection. Also, what constituted peaceful as opposed to warlike use was almost impossible to determine in the same way; as in the interwar period, it had been found a fruitless exercise to attempt to distinguish between defensive and offensive weapons.

A not-so-exclusive club. The fifth stage focused attention on the dangers inherent in nuclear proliferation. In 1945 the United States had exploded its first nuclear device; in 1949, the U. S. S. R.; in 1952, the United Kingdom. France joined the club in 1960, and Mainland China in 1964. Although two of these may not have delivery systems of any magnitude there is no technological reason why they should not very soon have them and indeed be joined by a dozen other states.

Breakthrough. Throughout the League and United Nations experience with the many committees and proposals which have come to little or nothing, and now with a beginning of modest achievement, we have learned many lessons. Basically as we saw earlier the pursuit of disarmament, as of security, is a will-o'-the-wisp. In the absence of a foolproof international security system, international security will depend upon the degree of stability being maintained in the balance of power. Armed strength and preparedness are important factors in this, and no nation can be—or indeed should be—expected to forego the protection that armed preparedness affords it. Where nations can see their way to lowering their guard, without losing their present balance of advantage, then agreement is possible.

These steps can be furthered by confidence-building measures toward which the Test-Ban Treaty of 1964 made a notable contribution. As Bismarck was fond of remarking (in a different context): "One hand must wash the other." Arms control measures can contribute to a "relaxation of tension," as the newspapers would have it. An increase in confidence can lead to the adoption of further measures in the direction of controlled complete disarmament as long as —and here's the rub—they do not tamper with the balance.

The modest achievements resulting so far may represent the end of the beginning in reaching settlements. A limited start was made in 1959 with agreement on the demilitarization of the Antarctic. This was, in itself, an insignificant step. In diplomacy, agreement on peripheral matters should be reached first if only as confidence-building measures. In this way, at least it is possible to demonstrate that agreement can indeed be reached and so improve the climate for negotiation when the time comes to discuss more serious matters.

In the meantime, nuclear proliferation and the explosion of other greater bombs caused a heavy groundswell in opinion in many parts of the world to stop testing and to stop the proliferation of the bomb. The General Assembly has called repeatedly for a halt in these matters and in 1961 requested the U. S. S. R. not to explode a 500-megaton device in the atmosphere. Except for the French tests in the Sahara, the moratorium on testing was effective from 1958 until late in 1961 when testing was started again by the U. S. S. R.

In 1963, two further steps were taken. The first was to establish a direct telephone link between Moscow and Washington— the so-called "hot line." The second was the renunciation by the U. S. S. R. and the United States of placing nuclear weapons in orbiting devices. In the following year, agreement was also reached on the reduction of the production of fissionable materials.

A diplomatic consensus on the part of the non-nuclear countries on the desirability of stopping further test series and the vigorous efforts made in the United Nations to bring about a cessation of such tests at last bore fruit in the Test-Ban Treaty of 1964. More than one hundred states have ratified the treaty, which became effective in 1964. It does not forbid testing below the ground, nor does it prevent the building of further bombs. Parties to the treaty, however, have ended the exploding of such devices above the ground. Neither Mainland China nor France is a party to the treaty. France, in 1966, resumed testing in the Pacific, and Mainland China exploded a large hydrogen bomb in 1967.

Obviously, a breakthrough is not the same thing as a breakout. The Disarmament Committee, increased in membership in 1961 from ten to eighteen (although as late as 1967 France was not participating) continues its work. Agreement on a non-proliferation ban on the manufacture of nuclear devices by non-nuclear countries or on the sale to them of such devices, or the materials with which to make such bombs, has now been reached.

Mastering the unthinkable. All that has been achieved so far has been a series of impressive confidence-building measures. In thinking about the way ahead on controlling and reducing conventional and atomic arms, we should jot down a few additional items on our agenda.

Even if non-proliferation of arms removes the danger of the "nth" country acquiring atomic weapons, there remains the awful danger from those which already have them in their arsenal and are constantly refining them. The reduction of stockpiles might not be easy but it is comparatively simple compared with coping with the continuous innovation which makes present weapons, together with their counter-weapons, obsolete as well as the international agreements concerning them.

Also, the question of surprise attack remains. The prophylactic war, threatened by Bismarck against France in 1875, has become a reality in more than one area in recent years. The search for a foolproof mechanism that will prevent surprise attack should not apply solely to the missile-happy country, which seeks to destroy an enemy at a moment when it considers it has the strategic edge in hardware, but to countries anywhere with a sizeable military establishment.

One area in which some early progress might be made is in the introduction of international measures to control the private sale of armaments. Immediately before and for some time after World War I, much attention was paid to the private international traffic in arms. It would seem that this commerce is again increasing, and the adoption of limitation measures cannot but serve the interests of the international community.

Finally, there is CBR: chemical, bacteriological and radiological warfare. Research in the use of tactical weapons, including nerve gases and incapacitating agents, biological weapons using living organisms or their toxic products and radiological devices such as encasing bombs with cobalt to heighten destruction from fall-out, has made tremendous strides in recent years. Apart from fallout, these tactical weapons are old. The difference now is that they have been perfected and have a tactical attraction (for some) in that they destroy only people and do not devastate land or crops. Some do not even do that. Some nerve gases, as they only incapacitate, have the added attraction that they seem to "take death out of war."

Although such discussions have and will be "taken out of" the United Nations when it seems appropriate, the Organization stands as the most suitable place in which opinion may find its voice in these matters. There new compromises may be formulated and given an airing. There, also, where simultaneous progress can be made on a number of other fronts in the creation of a more integrated international society, a setting is provided and a climate created where further control measures can find their way to adoption and implementation.

An international gendarmerie. As was stated at the beginning of the present chapter, the steps to be taken to limit national armed forces have often been linked to the creation of an international security force which would reduce, if not remove entirely, the need for nations to maintain a heavy burden of armaments and armed forces. In the balance of this chapter we will examine past and present experience against which we can consider the possible ways in which such an international force might be organized and made available in the service of the international community.

The early writers on international cooperation saw the need to replace national forces by a European international force either to fight the Turk or to keep the peace nearer home. Both Sully and Penn were aware of some of the problems of mustering and maintaining such a force. Neither proposed an international standing army but, more realistically, envisaged national contingents being made available to serve under a European commander-in-chief. Their proposals were based on the successful experience of the Greek city-state leagues where each state supplied its quota of men, money or ships as the need arose. Other writers foresaw the need to take drastic steps to exact from the participating states the payment of dues. In those days, soldiers had to be resigned to serving for long periods without pay, and it was recognized that an international paymaster would entertain even more difficulties in paying his troops than would his national counterpart.

It was not until the last stages of World War I that troops of many nations found themselves under an allied General-in-Chief, Marshal Foch of France. But this was a desperate war remedy made possible by Prime Minister Lloyd George's healthy mistrust of his own British generals. The experience seems to have had little bearing on institutionalized cooperation in establishing an international field force.

The Bourgeois plan for the League, which embodied the French proposals for a League of Nations, provided for a strong international force to be placed at the disposal of the League to ensure the security of its members. This proposal was one which did not find acceptance in the Covenant, but provision was made in it for a permanent commission to advise the Council on military questions. French policy in the interwar period was dominated by a preoccupation to insure France's security from a renascent Germany. In disarmament discussions in 1927 and in 1932, France proposed the creation of an international police force as part of any disarmament measures. The other major powers were not prepared to see such a force created. To have done so would have drastically altered the League and the nature of the obligations of its members. Also, the thought could not be dismissed from the minds of many that the French proposal, impossible of acceptance, was one way of justifying publicly the maintenance in that country in peacetime of large land forces.

The actual experience of the League in the field was modest. In 1934, after the end of a series of incidents between Peru and Colombia over an area of the Upper Amazon known as the "Leticia Trapeze," a League commission administered the area for a year with a small force of Colombian troops under League command. After a happy issue to the quarrel, the League withdrew.

As part of the reparations awarded France under the Treaty of Versailles, the rich coal basin of the Saar was placed under French administration for fifteen years, after which its future status would be determined by plebiscite. In 1935, an international force of 3,300 men commanded by a British officer was present while the Saarlanders, in a plebiscite supervised by the League Council, voted peacefully and overwhelmingly to return to Germany.

An international force under the League was planned in considerable detail by Marshal Foch and General Weygand to occupy the no-man's-land between the Polish and Lithuanian troops around Vilna in the bitter struggle for that town and its environs in the nineteen twenties. The proposed nine-nation force was not used.

More General than Secretary. The Bourgeois proposals, defeated in 1919, had to await the establishment of the United Nations before being accepted. The structure of the United Nations, described in Chapter II, made provision for a Military Staff Committee to advise and assist the Security Council. To a large extent, these provisions were based on the highly successful allied experience during the latter stages of World War II, when a unified command of allied forces was achieved in the western European theater of operations. The Charter arrangements presupposed a continuation of the wartime alliance into peacetime. That such an assumption has no historical foundation we have already recorded. With the breakdown of the alliance, the Military Staff Committee has not been able to function substantively.

Since the specific provisions of the Charter in these matters have not been applied, the calls upon the United Nations to provide peacekeeping forces has been on an *ad hoc* basis, and the mobilization of the resources of the Secretariat and of the forces involved has been for the most part improvised and provided on an emergency basis. Basically there have been three kinds of peacekeeping operations: the United Nations "presence," observer groups, and peacekeeping forces. The first does not call for the provision of armed forces. The second may, and the third normally would.

The concept of the United Nations "presence" was devised by the late Secretary-General Hammarskjöld. In periods of rapid transition to independence under what might have appeared as economically and possibly politically precarious circumstances, where a small state was feeling the effects of exposure to political turbulence in which it had no direct part to play, the Secretary-General might send a representative.

The dispatch of such observers has usually been taken at the initiative of the Secretary-General himself although Thailand, in 1954, requested the presence of an observer at a time it felt the activity of the Viet-Minh on its borders constituted a danger. The request was subsequently withdrawn. The concept of the United Nations presence was something typically characteristic of Hammarskjöld's personal diplomacy which he exercised with consummate skill and discretion. The posting of the Secretary-General's representatives in 1966 to Thailand and Laos, were in many ways a revival of the late Secretary-General's practice.

Some constitutional niceties. A list of peacekeeping operations involving military personnel in chronological order can be found in Table 1 on pages 106–107.

In spite of the many situations in which peacekeeping forces have been engaged there is no consensus among the members on what actually constitutes a peacekeeping operation. The Charter is silent on the subject. Many members see such operations as falling outside the category of enforcement action under Chapter VII of the Charter. Peacekeeping operations, therefore, are not mandatory or of a coercive nature and are undertaken only with the consent of at least one party involved in the situation which calls for United Nations intervention.

Other members take a stronger view, considering that such

action is executive in nature interposing the United Nations in a situation likely to lead to a breach of the peace. Some members see the need to consolidate the peacekeeping role of the United Nations by including a new chapter in the Charter should an opportunity be found to amend it. Others are almost entirely reserved about the further use of peacekeeping forces and consider that armed strength should be used only under Chapter VII of the Charter and its deployment be determined exclusively by the Security Council.

The Blue Berets. To obtain a clearer idea of the problems and possibilities of peacekeeping operations, we should examine briefly past and present experience. The size and scope of the operations have varied greatly. Apart from the Secretary-General's presence, they can, as was stated earlier, be divided into two categories: observer operations and peacekeeping forces. In the first category are UNTSO, UNMOGIP, UNOGIL, UNIPOM and UNYOM; in the second, UNEF, ONUC, UNTEA and UNFICYP (see Table 1).

The initiative for peacekeeping operations originated in every case in the Security Council, with the exception of UNEF and West Irian; for these the General Assembly took the required action. The situations with which the peacekeeping forces were concerned varied greatly. In Kashmir, Palestine, Lebanon and Cyprus, fighting had actually broken out when the United Nations acted. The possibility of further violence is always present in the case of the Truce Supervisory Organization in Palestine and Kashmir. In the Congo, Lebanon and Cyprus civil strife was accompanied by the added danger of involvement in the situation by other countries.

The composition of the United Nations force in each situation has been different. In West Irian the troops serving in UNTEA came from one country only. Thirty-six countries sent national contingents to the Congo. Great care was exercised by the Secretariat in drawing on the armed forces of members most acceptable to the countries within whose territories the forces were to operate.

The mandates under which the forces operate have varied in content and detail. In West Irian the task was limited in scope and

Table 1

CHRONOLOGY OF UNITED NATIONS
PEACEKEEPING OPERATIONS

1. *Greece*

Committee of Investigation concerning Greek frontier incidents, 1947.

Special Committee on the Greek Question, 1947.

Special Committee on the Balkans, 1948–1952.

United Nations Military Observers in Greece, 1952–1954.

2. *Palestine*

Special Committee on Palestine, 1947.

Mediator, 1948.

Supervision of Ceasefire by Military Observers, 1948.

Armistice Agreements and United Nations Supervision Organization (UNTSO), 1949–

Conciliation Commission, 1951–

3. *India-Pakistan*

United Nations Commission for India and Pakistan, 1947–

United Nations Military Observer Group in India and Pakistan (UNMOGIP), 1948–

United Nations Mediator, 1958–

United Nations India and Pakistan Observation Mission (UNIPOM), 1965–1966.

4. *Suez Crisis and Cessation of Military Action in Egypt*

United Nations Emergency Force (UNEF), 1956–1967.

5. *Lebanon and Jordan*

United Nations Observer Group in Lebanon (UNOGIL), 1958.

Special Representative of the Secretary-General in Amman, 1959–

6. *Congo (Kinshasa)*

United Nations Operations in the Congo (ONUC), 1960–1964.

Conciliation Commission, 1960–1961.

Table 1 (*continued*)

7. *West Irian*	United Nations Temporary Executive Authority (UNTEA), 1962–1963.
8. *Yemen*	United Nations Yemen Observer Mission (UNYOM), 1963–1964.
9. *Cyprus*	United Nations Force in Cyprus (UNFICYP), 1964–
10. *Dominican Republic*	1965–1966.

time, covering as it did a period of transition during which the territory passed from the Netherlands to Indonesia. The force in Cyprus has, through its mandate, been drawn deeply into the complexities of the relationships between the Greek Cypriot and Turkish Cypriot communities. UNEF patrolled the armistice line in Gaza and on the international frontier covering some 280 miles. The early experience of this operation was later drawn on in the emergency provision of a peacekeeping force for the Congo.

The frailties of the existing machinery. What general conclusions can be drawn from the Congo and other experiences in peacekeeping? The "smart" answer might be "none." Circumstances and situations have been so varied, the types of peacekeeping force, the directives and the tasks so many, as to make generalizations difficult and possibly imprudent. But in seeking a guide to the development of international institutions we should strive to make good the ground as we go along and in so doing develop a body of collective experience on which we can draw when considering the future of international organizations in field operations such as these.

Peacekeeping forces can be used usefully in six different types of situations. Groups can be used to assist a country in maintaining order where requested by that country and in conditions where peace and security might otherwise be disturbed. Where a truce has been agreed to by contending parties, peacekeeping forces can observe or supervise the cease fire lines. Forces can also be used to support investigative or fact-finding operations, when there has been

alleged interference from outside. Missions of mediation and conciliation may, in certain circumstances, call for armed forces. Finally,
a force can observe conditions on one or both sides of a frontier
where trouble may be brewing.

Whatever the task, peacekeeping should not be undertaken
without the consent of at least one of the parties involved, and the
retention of the force after the consent has been withdrawn would
be difficult although there may be circumstances where the Security Council or the General Assembly may not wish to authorize
withdrawal.

The deployment of a force may be of an emergency nature
leaving many questions unanswered regarding the legal basis on
which the troops are supplied, maintained and stationed. It may
also be difficult to determine the exact scope of the operation in
every case. Information on the ground may be incomplete or faulty.
The United Nations has no intelligence system. Furthermore, the
local political or strategic situation can change rapidly making the
original mandate of the force less meaningful. The peacekeeping
force, therefore, calls for tremendous diplomacy, tact and political
awareness as well as the more easily recognizable military virtues.

Peacekeeping by itself is little more than a palliative unless it is
accompanied by the necessary measures to resolve the problems
which called the force into being in the first place. The United
Nations has a variety of such techniques at its disposal. If we look
again at Table 1 we shall see how conciliation missions, arbitrators
and various other means of providing good offices are built into
peacekeeping operations. The work of these individuals and groups
is of course underpinned by diplomatic initiatives and other approaches of which the provision of large-scale economic support
for the rehabilitation and economic development of the areas in
question is becoming an increasingly significant element, as for
example in the Congo.

The financing of these operations has been varied. UNTSO,
UNMOGIP, UNOGIL, the mediator in Cyprus and the Secretary-
General's representative in the Dominican Republic have all been
financed from the regular budget of the United Nations. UNTEA

and UNYOM were financed on the basis of the governments principally concerned sharing the costs between them. UNFICYP is financed by voluntary contributions.

UNEF and ONUC financing was complicated and remains partially unresolved. A special account meets the arising costs. It is replenished by a combination of assessed and voluntary contributions. The difficulties which have arisen in these matters have been referred to in a preceding chapter and will again be touched on in Chapter VIII. The Special Committee on Peacekeeping Operations established by the General Assembly has been considering the financing of such operations as well as many other matters referred to in this chapter.

The late Ambassador Adlai Stevenson when referring to the peacekeeping operation in Cyprus stated that it had "vividly exposed the frailties of the existing machinery." He suggested that the position of the United Nations should be strengthened by the creation of a standby force available at short notice. This really brings us back to the relationship of such forces to broader measures of arms control and of international security.

Creating as we destroy. An awareness of this possible relationship may have been in the mind of the late President Kennedy when he stated that "To destroy arms . . . is not enough. We must create as we destroy—creating worldwide law and law enforcement even as we outlaw worldwide war and weapons."

There are many proposals for a standing international peace force. In the United Nations itself proposals for a United Nations Guard Force of one thousand to five thousand men were put forward by Secretary-General Lie in 1948. Again, within the framework of the Uniting for Peace Resolutions, Lie put forward proposals to the Collective Measures Committee for a United Nations Legion, later to be called a United Nations Volunteer Reserve. Those who were not hostile to the proposals were lukewarm either on financial or political grounds, or because of the many problems to which the control, enlistment, training, stationing and deployment of such a force would give rise.

The creation of such a standing force and its relationship to disarmament is a subject which had been dropped for fifteen years but is now again being discussed. But the emphasis is not so much on a standing international force as on a standby force composed of national units earmarked for international peacekeeping operations and trained for such purposes. Arrangements of this kind would be of little or no cost to the United Nations. It would be possible to mobilize and move troops at even shorter notice than before, given a favorable political climate.

It is difficult to see how an arrangement of this kind can have a major effect on international security and contribute to the confidence building measures called for in arms control discussions. But the accumulation of experience and the development of a modest body of competence in the marshalling and deployment of such forces enables the Organization, even if its role may be marginal in the quest for international security, to be decisive in local situations. In any case the tangible achievement of peacekeeping forces is a vast improvement on the pipe dreams of the past.

Going non-nuclear. Earlier in the present chapter, we considered how the creation of a climate of confidence was necessary before significant steps could be taken on arms control measures. At the same time, until some tangible agreements had been reached, and it had been demonstrated that the balance of power would not be disturbed by their implementation, it could hardly be expected that the climate would appreciably improve. Confidence-building measures, and the creation of an atmosphere more conducive to agreement, therefore, needed to be pursued simultaneously. We also saw how, starting on the periphery of the problem, with agreement on such matters as keeping Antarctica demilitarized, it was possible to move closer to agreement on more substantial matters such as the treaty banning nuclear weapon tests in the atmosphere, and the Treaty on Outer Space, which provided that weapons of mass destruction will not be placed in orbit, and that the moon and other celestial bodies should remain demilitarized.

In the more favorable climate thus created, the negotiation of further instruments, more far reaching in their implications, gathered momentum. These include the adoption, in 1967, of the Treaty for the Prohibition of Nuclear Weapons in Latin America, and, in 1968, the Treaty on Non-proliferation of Nuclear Weapons.

An event of historical significance. Ever since Podiebrad, a fifteenth-century king of Bohemia, sought to create a community of states in Europe ostensibly to unite Christendom to fight the Turk, but really to secure the safety of small states against their more powerful neighbors, the interest of smaller powers has been in strengthening international arrangements that might contribute to their security. So extensive would be the devastation, and so incalculable the effects of nuclear bombardment, that the hazards of conflict involving weapons of mass destruction would probably not be localized to the antagonists using them. In the many resolutions of the General Assembly on disarmament, often sponsored by smaller powers, there has been an almost universally expressed sense of urgency on the need to reduce the danger of nuclear conflict.

Of more immediate significance, however, is the possibility of nuclear proliferation. As we saw earlier, the powers with nuclear weapons numbered five in 1967. The likelihood of several more acquiring or manufacturing them has become increasingly probable.

As an inducement to the nuclear powers to move more vigorously in limiting the spread of nuclear weapons, and in order to keep their own continent nuclear free, the countries of Latin America gave expression to their own strong sense of community in deciding to ban nuclear weapons from their continent. Encouraged by the General Assembly, the Latin American governments established their own Preparatory Commission for the Denuclearization of Latin America. It held four sessions in the presence of observers from many other states, culminating in the adoption of the Final Act in January 1967 in Mexico City. On that occasion the Preparatory Commission adopted and opened for signature the Treaty for the Prohibition of Nuclear Weapons in Latin America. This treaty, which was warmly welcomed by the General Assembly as "an event of historic significance," by mid-June 1968 had been signed by eighteen states.

The treaty (and its two protocols) totally prohibits the use and manufacture of nuclear weapons, and weapons of mass destruction of every type, in Latin America. The treaty recognizes, however, that states should not be hindered from using nuclear power for peaceful purposes.

As part of the treaty, the Agency for the Prohibition of Nuclear Weapons in Latin America is created with its headquarters in Mexico City. Following the pattern of the Specialized Agencies, which is discussed in Chapter XI, the Agency is provided with a conference, a council and secretariat. The treaty has a built-in control system designed to verify that the treaty provisions are observed and to ensure that nuclear activity in Latin America is devoted exclusively to peaceful pursuits. Special inspection powers are granted to the Council when one party suspects another of activity prohibited by the treaty or, when a party suspected of such activity, requests a special inspection. The parties are required to conclude agreements with the International Atomic Energy Agency (IAEA), which is also granted special inspection rights regarding the application of its safeguards to nuclear activities. The Agency for the Prohibition of Nuclear Weapons in Latin America is to report to the General Assembly and the Security Council. In the event of an unsettled question or dispute concerning the treaty, there is recourse to the International Court of Justice.

Non-proliferation.   The Eighteen-Nation Committee on Disarmament was created by the General Assembly in 1961. Following the successful conclusion of the Test-Ban Treaty in 1964, the committee concentrated for four years on the preparation of a draft treaty on the non-proliferation of nuclear weapons. That body's co-chairmen were the United Kingdom, the U. S. S. R. and the United States. Together they presented a draft treaty and, in June 1968, it was adopted and opened for signature. Within a month almost sixty states had signed the treaty.

It had become widely recognized, as the Secretary-General stated in 1967, that the successful conclusion of such a treaty was an indispensable first step toward disarmament. For the spread of nuclear weapons clearly would make the eventual task of moving from arms control to disarmament much more laborious. Moreover, a further increase in the number of countries with such weapons at their disposal would increase international instability and uncertainty, as well as divert resources from development.

Urged by the General Assembly to give priority to non-proliferation, and finally pressed to submit its report to that body by mid-March 1968, the committee eventually met continuously to complete its work. Common ground had first to be found between at least a majority of nuclear powers themselves. Then the positions of the non-nuclear members, who participated fully in the work of the committee, had to be accommodated.

In establishing common ground, the nuclear powers had to reach an understanding on the question of non-nuclear states in alliance with nuclear states. If the aim of the treaty was to prevent non-nuclear states acquiring nuclear arms, how could this be reconciled with defense pacts where nuclear allies might share their weapons with non-nuclear parties? The treaty as finally adopted is clear in this respect. Article I forbids each nuclear-weapon party to transfer nuclear weapons or other nuclear explosive devices, or control over them, directly or indirectly, to any recipient whatsoever, whether that recipient be a party to the treaty or not. Each party also undertakes not to assist, encourage, or induce any non-nuclear-weapon state to manufacture or otherwise acquire or obtain control over such weapons or devices. On the other side of the medal, Article II forbids a non-nuclear-weapon party to receive or transfer such weapons, or devices. It undertakes not to manufacture or otherwise acquire them, and not to seek or receive assistance in their manufacture.

The treaty in these respects follows the Latin American treaty, and so did the concerns expressed in its adoption. Many members wished to make sure that the non-proliferation treaty would not be an obstacle to the development of nuclear power for peaceful purposes. For many of the economically developing countries facing severe economic and resource problems, the prospect of being able to take a "technological leap" over them with the help of nuclear power or technology was increasingly attractive. Any agreement that would deprive them of ready access to the economic benefits and technological spin-offs of the nuclear age would be unfair. The treaty contains assurances on this. The problem was rather how to ensure that benign development was not accompanied by any malignant side effects. (Nuclear power stations as a by-product can produce plutonium which is used in the manufacture of bombs.) Safeguards had to be found. These, it was intended, should be verified by inspection, the responsibility for which would lie principally with IAEA.

Under Article III of the treaty, each party undertakes to accept safeguards to be set forth in an agreement to be concluded with IAEA in accordance with the Statute of that agency and its safeguards system. These safeguards are elaborate and include detailed provision for inspection by the agency. It would seem that the concept of inspection previously found unacceptable by many states, while still exceptional, has been accepted in some important treaties, including those on the demilitarization of Antarctica, and of Outer Space, as well as the present treaty.

Of greater moment to some non-nuclear members was the question of their own security. If threatened by a nuclear power, are they to be deprived of access to nuclear weapons, or prevented from making them, in order to defend themselves or, at least by demonstrating parity, to stave off the threat? Apparently so, for it was not found possible to include in the treaty guarantees of nuclear protection for non-nuclear parties. But, in presenting the draft treaty in the General Assembly, the co-chairman of the disarmament committee submitted to the Security Council a resolution, that was subsequently adopted, and accompanying declarations on security assurances to non-nuclear countries. The declarations by the U. S. S. R., United Kingdom and the United States stated that they would regard any act of aggression with nuclear weapons, or the threat of aggression to any non-nuclear state party to the treaty as "creating qualitatively a new situation" which required their immediate action and response. They agree to meet actively and collectively through the Council to take the necessary measures to counter a threat or an act of aggression under such circumstances.

Finally, there might have been additional hesitation over the treaty, as it would perpetuate the nuclear supremacy of the Great Powers. Unless there were guarantees that they would regard the treaty as a step towards the eventual abolition of nuclear weapons, it might appear to set a seal of international endorsement to their special status. The treaty holds the promise that this is not so and foresees further steps being taken in the direction of disarmament. This was confirmed by the co-chairmen in the General Assembly.

The way ahead. While some important countries still need to be brought into the framework of these new international agreements to make them fool-proof, new initiatives may now be considered, possibly applying, in a broader context, the experience accumulated in negotiating the Non-proliferation Treaty. Priority may be given to scaling down missile delivery systems or to reducing nuclear stockpiles. In any case, the high hopes expressed in the Charter on disarmament and the creation of a less insecure world appear now more like realistic possibilities than the foolish expectations they might once have seemed.

Chapter VI

THE ROAD TO EMANCIPATION

In no other field of human endeavor has the United Nations been more successful than in assisting dependent peoples on their way to self-government and independence. In the present chapter we shall examine what we mean by "the road to emancipation." For many it has been a long one, but for most it has not been as long as we sometimes are inclined to suppose. To understand what has been achieved, we need first to understand something of the nature and characteristics of colonialism and imperialism in their heyday, then to see how the anti-colonial movement developed, gathered strength and finally triumphed. We can thus place the work and achievements of the United Nations in some perspective and, finally, see what residual tasks remain and what new responsibilities this remarkable success story brings in its wake for the United Nations.

There is nothing odd about some people ruling others. Romans ruled from the Euphrates to the Clyde and Norsemen from Sicily to Greenland. In history we accept this as one of the facts of life. The colonies settled by the Romans or the Norsemen were not weak because they were colonies; they were colonies because they were weak. We are, however, concerned more immediately with the contemporary world where such observations are less palatable.

The golden road. In the sixteenth, seventeenth and eighteenth centuries Portuguese and Spanish adventurers, following in the wake of Columbus, conquered and then colonized Central and South America. Great Britain sent its peoples to colonize North America, and later New Zealand and Australia. To a lesser extent the Dutch settled the Cape of Good Hope and, moving northwards across the veldt, met the Bantu moving south.

Strategic considerations. From 1815 to 1870 imperialism assumed a strategic aspect. Imperialist countries seemed less interested in extending their empires than in consolidating their gains by making secure the sea routes to them. Footholds were established along the coasts, and in islands considered strategic, to guard the highroads of empire. Where strategic considerations were not present, often little interest was shown. In 1815 at Vienna, Britain, for example, returned to France the possessions captured from her during the Napoleonic Wars with the exception of a few islands in the West Indies thought then to have strategic importance. Not everyone welcomed the obligations inherited by the metropolitan power from the ebullience of previous generations. Even Disraeli, later an imperialist of a highly romantic kind, grumbled, "These colonies will be a millstone round our neck."

Fits of absence of mind. With the exception of the latter-day imperialism of Italy and Japan in the nineteen thirties, modern imperialism was restricted almost completely to the period between 1870 and 1914. The heyday of the heyday was in the twenty years between 1880 and 1900. During that period the whole of Africa, with the exception of Ethiopia and Liberia, was carved up between the imperialist powers. Anglo-Indian power had extended into Burma, and France had become dominant in Annam, Laos and Cambodia. The United States took over the remnants of the Spanish Empire. Led by Great Britain, who by then had kicked open the door into China, the United States and other imperialist powers moved into the Middle Kingdom. In all likelihood, if World War I had not interrupted that process in 1914, China would have been as divided as Africa already was.

In the nineteenth century the two great forces of change were the British industrial revolution and the national, constitutional and liberal movements that sprang from the American and French revolutions. Imperialism was a by-product of the first, and the eventual dismantling of empire was the inevitable consequence of the second.

The mercantilist stage of imperialism was soon overtaken as the economic drive for raw materials and easy markets was stimulated by industrial growth, first in Great Britain and subsequently throughout Europe and North America. When "Galloping Jack" Seeley suggested in the House of Commons that the British had "acquired an empire in a fit of absence of mind," he was not being wholly facetious. Imperialism (and colonialism too, for that matter) was not always the product of a conscious policy of government, although subsequent endorsement was nearly always granted to the man on the spot. General Kaufmann in Central Asia, Karl Peters, Cecil Rhodes, Richard Francis Burton, John Speke and Jean Baptiste Marchand in Africa were often on their own, even if Henry Stanley, Horatio Kitchener and Louis Lyautey were not. Empire was acquired not so much by the tramp of marching boots, as by traders, adventurers, explorers, missionaries and anti-slavers penetrating where no white man had been in modern times. Territories thus opened up were often annexed unwillingly at first. But governments were inexorably drawn in for reasons of prestige, or to keep the other man out, or finally because appetites became whetted, and the practice of satisfying appetites eventually became a habit. Nor did the process stop there. Imperialism had its own built-in local patriotism which in Australia, South Africa, India and Canada took command over events in a way that distant Whitehall could not.

The scramble for empire.   Great soldiers and administrators followed the Russian traders across Asia through territories far removed from other influences, only to be checked at Penjdeh Afghanistan. The Portuguese resisted British attempts to oust them in India and Africa and took over Angola and Mozambique. The British said little but did a great deal of penetrating to the north from the Cape Colony. Belgium entered Africa relatively late but under King Leopold took over the Congo as a giant trading company. Italy also came late, taking over the desert lands of Libya from the Ottomans and the Horn of Africa from Somali nomads. The French came under the guiding genius of Jules Ferry to move into North Africa with the Spaniards and to take over west and central equatorial Africa, in an attempt to make up for her weakness in Europe after defeat at the hands of Prussia in 1870.

Bismarck was a continental politician. After he had unified Germany, he was not anxious to enter into colonial adventures. Rather he preferred to deflect French attention from the defeat he had inflicted on them by encouraging them to seek compensation in the development of an overseas colonial empire. He used the exposed position of Britain in Egypt as a whip to beat the British, and French ambitions as a wedge to drive between France and Great Britain so that they would not join together against the growing might of Germany. But Bismarck had to bow to popular pressure at home and enter the game. Germany, although she took over South-West Africa, Tanganyika, Zanzibar and portions of West Africa, never attached much importance to them. By 1914, there were fewer than 24,000 Germans in their overseas dependencies.

Meanwhile the rivalry between France and Great Britain increased the sense of urgency for British influence to be extended, and dangerous clashes between French and British interests and between those of other powers became imminent. The scramble was becoming dangerous. In spite of increasing preoccupation with their stake in Africa, the powers always kept their eyes on Europe, for there was the flashpoint, not in Africa. Generals taught their staffs to think in terms of the Rhine, the Danube and the Vistula—never the Nile, the Congo or the Zambesi. In 1885, very sensibly, the Great Powers called for a breather and met in Berlin for the Conference on Tropical Africa.

This conference was one of the most successful in history. And, as after most successful conferences, the negotiators returned home to mixed receptions. It is easy to charge "sell out" when concessions have to be made to gain something. For once a conference was well organized and governments sent teams of experts of the highest order to work out the ground rules for the division of Africa. It was agreed that there would be free trade in Central Africa, spheres of influence were defined and the Concert of Europe laid down that territorial claims had to be justified by effective occupation by the government voicing the claim. From then on, apart from the failure of Italy at Adowa to conquer Ethiopia, and the struggle of Great Britain to dominate the Boers in the south and to reach the headwaters of the Nile in the north before the French, the imperialist take-over in Africa was complete south of the Sahara.

Satiated powers. By 1914, Africa was roughly parcelled out, with the exceptions of Ethiopia and Liberia, among the imperialist powers. In terms of land area taken, they were, in a descending order of magnitude: Great Britain, France, Germany, Belgium, Portugal, Italy and Spain.

Roughly too, subjugation of one sort or another took place from the Cape to Cairo. In some areas, native authority was overthrown. In others, an understanding of its nature and effectiveness only later came to be understood and indirect rule through native rulers and chiefs was developed. In some areas, as with the French association with Beylical authority in Morocco, existing power was not displaced but extended beyond its traditional limits. It should be remembered, however, that Africa, south of the Sahara, when the imperialist arrived was not unlike North America when the colonists pushed westward.

China remained closed to external influence until 1800, with the exception of the Portuguese settlement in Macao and some trading by the British East India Company through Canton. In 1833 the monopoly of the East India Company was broken, and other traders forced their way into China, introducing an ugly period in which the Chinese were pressed to take opium in barter for the goods bought from them. These practices resulted in the Opium War with Great Britain culminating, in 1842, in the Treaty of Nanking. This treaty opened the door to British penetration and behind Britain came traders of other nations as well, principally those of the United States.

By 1860, the Russian traders had come down the Amur River from the north. Britain and the United States were joined by other powers in the race to obtain concessions from the Chinese. Japan, which had been opened to Western influence by the United States and developed by the British, rapidly acquired Western habits and with them Western ambitions. Japan consequently joined the Western powers in forcing their presence on the Chinese. United States missionaries and traders penetrated far north into Korea until that country was taken over by Japan in 1895.

Chinese civilization was and is deep and solid and in many ways remained remarkably unaffected by imperialist incursions. But the Chinese government was a government in name only. Its authority was a cobweb that was blown away by the foreign interloper. In the 1890's when the race for concessions, treaty ports and other extraterritorial rights was at its height, the Dowager Empress, bent on her own pleasures, was only dimly aware of what was happening to her great country. However, toward the end of the century, the scramble for railway concessions by Russia and the Western powers revealed the danger not only for China herself but also for the rivals jostling one another for concessions.

Possibly because imperialist rivalry did not reach a pitch where conflict was a likelihood between the powers in China until the eighteen nineties—later than in Africa—and because the imperialists were no longer exclusively European, there seems to have been no attempt on the part of the Concert of Europe to intervene.

In the face of imperialist incursions, chaos in China deepened, punctuated by periodic outbursts against the foreigner, of which the Boxer Rebellion in 1900 was the most violent. Attempts in the 1860's and in the 1890's were made, however, to reform the Chinese administration. These were localized and were not successful. Toward the end of the century dedicated and farsighted foreigners, such as Sir Robert Hart, attempted with some initial success to assist the government in introducing much needed reforms. But as with similar attempts during that period by foreigners to introduce reforms in the Ottoman empire, the efforts of the few in China failed.

During this period nationalist, constitutionalist and socialist movements began to appear first among the students and eventually among their elders. Sun Yat-Sen emerged as the leader of not only the anti-barbarian movement but also of the anti-Manchu movement. In 1911, Sun Yat-Sen and his followers overthrew the Manchu dynasty in Peking (at the same time as the Young Turk movement overthrew the Sultan at the Sublime Porte) and declared China a republic.

From then on it was a race between nascent nationalism on the one hand, and imperialist penetration on the other, to determine whether China would hold together or be divided. The war clouds of August 1914, however, drifted over Asia, and China with Japan joined the war on the side of the Entente. Thus China was saved in the nick of time from suffering what seemed likely to be the same fate as Africa.

Rough riding. During this period the Monroe Doctrine went through many stages of transition and application. What began as an American concern to keep the Old World from meddling in the New had been transformed into a policy which regarded South America as something of a *chasse gardée* of United States interest. In the Spanish-American War of 1898–99, fought ostensibly to relieve Cuba from Spanish oppression, the United States divested Spain of her remaining colonies in the New World and, in the Pacific and Caribbean, took over a colonial empire of some 120,000 square miles and 8,500,000 people.

Oddly enough, this acquisition of empire has been regarded much less unfavorably than the more peaceful attempts at penetration south of the border. President Theodore Roosevelt's policies in the opening years of this century of "dollar diplomacy" in the Caribbean and of the "big stick" in South America brought the United States much disfavor. But distasteful though such aggressive policies may have been to the Latin American republics, they represented policies, even when they were streaked with violence, of a markedly diluted kind compared with contemporary behavior in other continents.

"Bliss was it in that dawn . . ." It was stated earlier that of the two dominant forces at work in the nineteenth century, one created imperialism and the other destroyed it. The shot that was fired at Concord in 1775 was indeed heard round the world. It is true that the French Declaration of the Rights of Man, hung above the judges in the Conciergerie, may not have impressed those who were hastily condemned in its name and promptly led off in the tumbrel to the Place de la Concorde. We have also less excuse than Wordsworth to romanticize over the revolution. But there is no doubt that its effects gave inspiration to millions and, as we shall see in Chapter IX, continue to play a distinct role in the work of the United Nations in many directions.

These two events, the American and French revolutions, changed the world. Nationalism triumphed in Europe, culminating in the Treaty of Versailles, a triumph for the Wilsonian principles of national self-determination. It was only a matter of time before the influence of the revolutions made itself felt among the dependent millions of Asia, Africa and South America.

The imperialist not only brought order and law of his own kind; he also brought with them the fundamental concepts of common law and standards of right upon which they were based. When missionaries set up schools, colleges and eventually universities, no one could insist upon the student restricting his learning to that which was politically innocuous. And as the arts of administration came to be practiced—at the lower levels—by the local peoples, new habits of authority were acquired. Exposure to the effects of the industrial revolution was thus accompanied by conversion to the principles of the political revolution.

Not that dependent peoples needed imported ideas to make them aware of what others assumed was their birthright. Resentment of the interloper was always present, particularly where a difference in skin color emphasized the division between the ruler and the ruled. The foreigner was not always hated as he was in China. In parts of Southeast Asia he was not disliked at all. But resentment was ever present.

Also, as we will have reason to remark later, revolution does not necessarily occur when oppression and suffering make man's condition intolerable. Normally such events take place when he who revolts has never had it so good. In 1789 the French peasant lived better than ever before; he was buying up land at an increasing rate and he was relatively well off. A mood of rising expectations came with this new prosperity, and he found residual feudal rights, such as the *taille* and the few remaining inherited monopolies and privileges of the aristocracy, suddenly intolerable. The French experience came to be repeated all over the world. Later, as anti-imperialist movements of the twentieth century gathered force, the slogans on the banners were the same rallying cries of the irredentist and independence movements of the nineteenth century in Europe and Latin America, joint legacies of the two revolutions of the eighteenth century.

Port Arthur.   Where and when did the anti-colonialist and anti-imperialist movement start? In a certain sense it was always there. Imperialist domination was not won without resistance. Whether it was Aguinaldo, Toussaint l'Ouverture, Abd-el-Krim, El Mahdi, or Lobengula, resistance leadership was seldom lacking. But the defense of one's way of life is one thing; a worldwide movement is something quite different.

The starting point of the anti-colonial movement was the Russo-Japanese War of 1904–05. The fall of Port Arthur to the Japanese and the defeat of the Russian fleet at Tsushima was greeted with joy throughout Asia by peoples who had little if any knowledge of the protagonists or where the fighting took place. All they knew was that the hitherto invincible white man had been beaten at his own game. Peasants in the fields of Annam planted corn flowers in commemoration of the victory of the Japanese. Throughout Asia there was rejoicing.

The successful Chinese revolution led by Sun Yat-Sen in 1911 was the first tangible witness of the movement. War gave it new impetus. Indian troops fought gallantly in the mud of Flanders, the beaches of Gallipoli and throughout Mesopotamia. The Chinese ousted the Germans, and Africans saw battle in their own continent and in Europe. India had a seat at the conference table at Paris in 1919, was a signatory of the Treaty of Versailles, and as such entered the League of Nations.

At Versailles the anti-colonial mood began to make itself felt, particularly in the case of the former German and Ottoman colonies.

The Mandates System.   It was Jan Smuts who, in 1918, first raised publicly the question of what steps should be taken at the

Paris Peace Conference to fill the void left by the crumbling empires experiencing revolution. He proposed that the former enemy colonies in Africa, the Middle East and Asia should not fall as spoils to the victors but should be held in trust by them on behalf of the international community. The powers concerned would, within the framework of the League of Nations, assume responsibility for the administration of these territories under mandate from the League. He had in mind not only former imperialist possessions but was also concerned with the fate of such peoples as the Armenians.

To many these proposals may have appeared as a thin veneer designed to disguise what was tantamount to annexation of the territories concerned. Whatever the motivation, the League in assuming its responsibilities in the name of the international community did not permit this to happen. The wording of the Covenant in Article 22.1 makes the responsibility of the League clear:

> To those colonies and territories which as a consequence of the late war have ceased to be under the Sovereignty of the States which formerly governed them and which are inhabited by peoples not yet able to stand by themselves under the strenuous conditions of the modern world, there should be applied the principle that the well-being and development of such peoples form a sacred trust of civilization and that securities for the performance of this trust should be embodied in this Covenant.

The Article went on to state that the best method of giving practical effect to this principle was for certain powers to administer the territories concerned under the supervision of the League. It stated that some territories were at a stage of development where their independence could now be foreseen; in others it was more distant, and in some cases their location or the sparseness of their population suggested that they be administered as integral parts of the mandatory power. Direct rule by the international community through the League was not proposed, possibly because of the difficulties that had occurred when the Concert of Europe in the nineteenth century, had been embroiled in assuming collective responsibility for the Congo Free State.

Consequently, it was decided that there would be three categories of mandate. Those in Category A were the countries of the Middle East which were becoming independent from the Ottoman empire and where the mandatory power did not need to administer so much as to carry out a handholding operation with the local authorities. Category B mandates were those which were to be administered as separate territories under the arrangements established for the mandate. Category C mandates were those which, subject to certain safeguards, would be administered as part of the mandatory power's own territory. The territories included in the mandates system and the administering power in each case are listed in Table 2.

An accountable trust. The Supreme Council of the Allies allocated the territories to be mandated among the allies. In so doing it prepared drafts of the agreements to be concluded by the League and each mandatory power concerning its responsibility for the territory involved. The C mandates agreements were adopted by the League Council in 1920 and the B and A agreements in 1922 and 1923 respectively with the governments which had assumed the responsibility for administering them.

In 1921, to assist the League Council in carrying out its responsibilities under the Covenant in these matters, a Permanent Mandates Commission was established. It met biannually to receive and examine annual reports on the mandates, following which the Commission would report to the Council on the compliance of the mandatory powers with the agreements. The members of the Commission were not government delegates but were appointed by the Council in their personal capacity. They numbered less than a dozen and were assisted in their work by an assessor from the International Labor Office who was principally concerned with labor conditions in the territories concerned. The Commission held its sessions in private but published full reports on the proceedings following each meeting.

The mandatory authorities probably viewed somewhat askance the new mandates idea, and its Commission with some suspicion. Sceptics who had regarded the mandates system as a cloak to place

Table 2

LEAGUE OF NATIONS MANDATE TERRITORIES AND MANDATORY POWERS

The A Mandates in the Middle East

Lebanon ⎱ Syria ⎰ Iraq	France
Palestine ⎱ Transjordan ⎰	Great Britain

The B Mandates in Africa

Ruanda-Urundi	Belgium
Cameroun ⎱ Togoland ⎰	France
The Cameroons ⎱ Tanganyika ⎰ Togoland	Great Britain

The C Mandates in the Pacific

New Guinea, New Ireland ⎱ New Britain and the ⎰ Solomon Islands	Australia
Nauru	under the mandate of the British Empire exercised through Australia
Western Samoa	New Zealand
The Marianas, Caroline and Marshall Islands	Japan

The C Mandate in Africa

South-West Africa	Union of South Africa

a spurious moral gloss on what were outright acts of seizure by the mandatory powers soon came to realize that this was not, as it worked out, the case. The Commission carried out its functions scrupulously, and in time its work came to be viewed as less of an irritant than a stimulant to the mandatory powers, who came to respect its role and eventually to share with the Commission some of the headaches of administration of dependent peoples.

Of the A mandates, scheduled for early complete independence, Iraq was the only one to acquire complete sovereignty during the interwar period. Admitted to the League as a member in 1932, it was required to enter into a minorities treaty with the League for reasons outlined in Chapter IX. The British mandate at that time was withdrawn. Thus the ambition of King Faisal was realized before he died in the following year. One of the main leaders in the Arab revolt against the Ottoman empire in World War I, Faisal's vision which he and T. E. Lawrence had shared in the desert revolt was shattered when they found that what had become his country had been placed under British tutelage. By adroit political handling of the disgruntled factions at home and adept diplomatic dealing with the mandatory power, Faisal kept domestic peace and won eventual complete independence for his country.

The massacre of the Assyrian minority shortly afterwards, however, created a new situation in the League. The protracted but unsuccessful negotiations by the League regarding the resettlement of the remaining Assyrians, and the devotion of the League officials appointed to work with them served to bring home to the League the obligations that went with the responsibilities it had assumed in the name of the international community, and the difficulties to be encountered when it came to giving effect to them.

The mandates system was not concerned with imperialism or colonialism. The League did not question the right of peoples to rule others except when Japan invaded Manchuria, and Italy attacked Ethiopia. The League's specific responsibilities related to the mandated territories only, and only in the case of A mandates was full sovereignty foreseen. That such responsibilities were vested in the League and that it was able to exercise them arose primarily from the changing climate of opinion. Ever since the second Boer War at the turn of the century, when British forces eventually subdued the Afrikaner, in the face of the strongest criticism in Europe and the United States, the extension of imperialist power was discouraged. The mood had indeed changed although, strangely enough, the Permanent Mandates Commission was not one which vigorously pressed for the independence of any of the territories under mandate. In fact, it viewed with increasing reserve, after the experience of the Assyrians, any indication by a mandatory power of its intention to withdraw from its responsibilities.

Such was the case, as the British in Palestine encountered increasing difficulty in carrying out their responsibilities following the Arab revolt in 1936, and in the face of increasing numbers of Jews emigrating to Palestine as persecution of them mounted in Germany and other countries in Eastern Europe. The Commission reacted similarly at the prospect of the withdrawal of the French mandate in Lebanon or Syria, preoccupied as it was with the need to construct adequate safeguards for the many religious and ethnic minorities living in these countries.

The mandates system worked. It reflected in a deep and lasting sense the principles expounded by Edmund Burke in the debate on Fox's East India Bill in the House of Commons in 1783. He said, ". . . all political power which is set over men . . . ought to be in some way exercised for their benefit . . . such rights or privileges, or whatever else you chuse to call them, are all, in the strictest sense, a trust; and it is of the very essence of every trust to be rendered accountable."

It is unlikely that the mandates system would have ever been established had it not been for the First World War. It is unlikely, too, that the anti-imperialist, anti-colonial movement would have gathered so much momentum so quickly had it not been for the Second World War. Once again troops from dependent territories fought all over the world; Indians in Italy, Nigerians in Burma, Palestinians in the desert, Africans in France, and Nepalese in Malaya. The overcoming of much of the Pacific and Southeast Asia by the Japanese armies focussed world attention on such countries as the Philippines and Burma. Native administrators assumed new responsibilities in this radically changed situation and resistance groups fought bravely against the enemy.

Few were in the mood, having fought the occupier, to accept

without comment the return of the imperialist power in the wake of the victory they themselves had helped to secure. Nor was the mood of the imperialist powers unchanged. The United States had declared its intention to grant independence to the Philippines, and the election of the Labor Government in the United Kingdom in 1945 reflected to a considerable extent the desire of many in Great Britain to grant independence to the Indian subcontinent and to reestablish the independence of Burma after its long night under Japanese occupation.

In the Netherlands East Indies resistance greeted the return of Dutch authority. In the Middle East, with the withdrawal of French power during the war, Lebanon and Syria became independent, formally, in 1945 and 1946 respectively. Jordan also became independent in 1946. Thus, with the exception of Palestine, the former A category mandates had all become independent, although even before, they had enjoyed and exercised a wide measure of self-government. It might be more accurate to refer, not to their achieving independence, but to their assuming full sovereignty on the withdrawal of the mandatory power.

The pace quickens.   In Chapter I we saw how the allies slowly shaped the United Nations in the war years. At Dumbarton Oaks, the drafters were silent on the mandates system of the League and on the future institutional setting within which such responsibilities should be pursued. At San Francisco in the wider spectrum of international representation, the establishment of an international trusteeship system had been placed on the agenda. Previously agreement had been reached at Yalta that there should be a trusteeship system established within the United Nations but only the machinery and the principles of trusteeship should be formulated by the San Francisco conference. Exactly what territories should be included would be decided not by the conference but by subsequent agreement.

Based on a United States draft proposal submitted to the conference, the international trusteeship system was adopted to include the three categories of territory listed in the Yalta statement: territories which were under the League mandates system but which were not independent; territories detached from enemy states; and territories voluntarily placed under the system.

The keystone of the trusteeship structure is Article 76(b) of the Charter which states the responsibility of the United Nations for the promotion of the political, economic, social and educational advancement of the inhabitants, and their progressive development toward self-government or independence. Trust territories, whatever their condition, might therefore look forward to achieving self-government or to attaining independence. The body for seeing that these obligations were met was not a commission composed of specialists meeting privately as in the League, but the General Assembly itself and, under its authority, the Trusteeship Council. The Council was a public, governmental body which, in addition to receiving reports from the Administering Authorities and petitions from inhabitants of the Trust Territories as under the League, could also send out visiting missions on periodic inspections of the Trust Territories themselves.

The anti-colonial mood of many delegations at San Francisco was not prepared to let matters rest there. The Charter does not remain silent on imperialist possessions as did the Covenant. Fresh ground was broken at San Francisco by the inclusion in the Charter, after considerable debate, of the *Declaration Regarding Non-Self-Governing Territories.*

How the anti-colonial movement gathered strength and finally triumphed can now be examined. To do so it would be best to consider first how the trusteeship provisions were implemented, then how the non-self-governing territories moved up to the center of the stage, and finally how the domestic jurisdiction provisions of the Charter were moderated by the General Assembly and other bodies concerned.

"Tutelle" rather than trusteeship. Agreements were subsequently drawn up, and signed by each Administering Authority for each Trust Territory under its stewardship. The highwater mark was reached by the end of 1949 when ten such agreements had been approved by the General Assembly and the eleventh, the Trust Territory of the Pacific Islands under United States

administration, by the Security Council. In Table 3, the Trust
Territories, the Administering Authority and the year the agreement was approved are given.

Table 3

TRUST TERRITORIES, BY THE END OF 1949

Pacific

Nauru	Australia (on behalf of Australia, New Zealand and the United Kingdom)	1946
New Guinea	Australia	1946
Western Samoa	New Zealand	1947
The Marianas (with the exception of Guam), Caroline and Marshall Islands	United States	1947

Africa

Ruanda-Urundi	Belgium	1947
Cameroun Togoland	France	1946 1946
Somalia	Italy	1949
The Cameroons Tanganyika Togoland	United Kingdom	1946 1946 1946

It will be seen that countries of the Middle East no longer
appear as Trust Territories, but that the table otherwise is not unlike that of the mandates system on page 127. The United States
took over from the Japanese in the southern Pacific more or less
what Japan took over from Germany after World War I. Australia
and New Zealand remained responsible for territories in the southern Pacific. France, Belgium and the United Kingdom retained
responsibility for six territories.

Stalin at Potsdam mentioned that the U. S. S. R. might like to have responsibility for one former enemy territory. The suggestion was not pursued. Possibly Stalin, true to Russian traditional interest in the Mediterranean, had in mind Libya, then recently liberated from Italian rule.

The disposal of the former Italian colonies, Libya, Eritrea and Somaliland, presented a thorny problem to the Great Powers immediately after the war. Libya became independent in 1951, after close association with the United Nations with which it has always had a special relationship. Eritrea became federated to Ethiopia in 1952. Italian Somaliland, in 1950, was returned to Italian administration as a Trust Territory for a period of ten years, after which it was joined with the neighboring protectorate of British Somaliland to form the Republic of Somalia.

Former German South-West Africa, a C mandate under the then Union of South Africa, was administered as an integral part of the Union. As a member of the United Nations, South Africa was expected to enter into an agreement to place South-West Africa under trusteeship. The provision of the Charter in these matters is not mandatory. Article 77.2 states, in part:

> It will be a matter for subsequent agreement as to which territories . . . will be brought under the trusteeship system and upon what terms.

South-West Africa was not a matter for subsequent agreement.

The trusteeship system was brought into existence by the conclusion of an agreement between the United Nations and each Administering Authority for each territory to be placed under trusteeship. By March 1947, eight agreements between the United Nations and each Administering Authority had been concluded; thus, the initial membership of the Trusteeship Council was decided—Administering Authorities, permanent members of the Security Council not Administering Authorities, and other members of the United Nations to effect a balance between the former.

In setting up the system, the governments responsible for the

Trust Territories took on specific tasks which were not assumed by the powers concerned but which were given them by the United Nations on behalf of the international community. In so doing the United Nations gave to the peoples of the Trust Territories precise guarantees which placed them under international protection and gave assurances regarding their future.

The Trusteeship Council settled down promptly to its business. New techniques were introduced by the Council in carrying out its responsibilities. In addition to an annual report on each territory by the government exercising the trusteeship, a questionnaire was devised by the Council and addressed to the Administering Authorities which was designed to probe more deeply into the political, economic and social condition of each territory. Petitions were received from the individual inhabitants and social groups. They ran sometimes to 10,000 pages a year and a subcommittee had to be established to examine them. Petitioners themselves appeared before the Council to present their grievances orally.

Of perhaps greatest importance was the visiting mission which, every three years, was appointed to inspect each territory. Such visits, on occasion, were supplemented by special missions. One of the first of these was dispatched to Tanganyika in 1948. It was typical of many which followed. The visiting mission made some sharp observations on such questions as land policy and migrant labor. It also suggested that a target date be fixed for independence. Criticisms were levelled against the mission that its members were inexperienced, lacked familiarity with local conditions and stayed too short a time. Particular criticism was voiced on a proposal to set a target date for independence.

The question of the adoption of target dates on which Trust Territories would become independent became an issue over which increasing appeals were made by the anti-colonialist groups in the General Assembly. In 1936 the United States had promised independence to the Philippines, setting a date ten years later. On a tighter timetable could not the same practice be followed for the Trust Territories? After all, the British not only had set a date for the independence of the peoples of the Indian subcontinent, but also then advanced that date by one year. With some vigorous prodding by the General Assembly, independence dates became the order of the day.

At this stage we should examine the work of the Trusteeship Council as it affected the territories themselves.

Togo. Togo was the first area to emerge from trusteeship. Yet it presented problems of such complexity for the United Nations, the governments and the peoples involved that, in many ways, the future of the Togolese peoples was one of the most difficult to determine.

This narrow corridor running into the interior from the Gulf of Guinea is occupied by a mosaic of different tribes, the principal ones being the Ewe who settled in the area in the twelfth to fourteenth centuries; with the Adja-Outchi they form the main tribes in the south. In the north live the Kabrai-Losso. Colonial boundaries set up towards the end of the nineteenth century were not concerned with the niceties of maintaining tribal homogeneity or identification. Consequently, the Ewe could be found not only in Togoland but in Dahomey and on the Gold Coast as well. In Togo itself, the Ewe live among many other tribes often of a different ethnic origin.

In 1914, British and French forces ousted the Germans. Under the League mandates system and later under the United Nations trusteeship system, the British administered the western area, and the French the eastern.

In 1947, the Ewe tribes appealed to the United Nations for unification. Later appeals were for the unification of Togo and its many peoples. The problem of the future of the area arose not only from a reluctance on the part of the Administering Authorities to change the status of the territories but also from the sharp divisions between the tribes themselves.

In British Togoland, in 1956, a United Nations supervised plebiscite was held in which the inhabitants were asked to declare whether they favored (a) union with the Gold Coast (then about to become independent), or (b) continuation under trusteeship pending an ultimate settlement of their future. A majority favored union with the Gold Coast. The General Assembly accepted this indication of the inhabitants' wishes, and accordingly the territory was united with the Gold Coast, which became the independent State of Ghana and a member of the United Nations soon afterwards.

This was the first plebiscite supervised by the United Nations. A plebiscite is a clumsy instrument at the best of times. It will be noted that the peoples were not offered the possibility of independence, except as part of another country.

In 1956 also, a referendum was held in French Togoland and a majority favored to end trusteeship and enjoy autonomy in close association with France. This was, in effect, the first step in what amounted to a unilateral withdrawal of the trusteeship without consulting the United Nations. In 1958, following the recommendations of a mission despatched by the General Assembly, new elections were held under United Nations supervision. A gifted leader, Sylvanus Olympio, led his party to victory and became Prime Minister. Two years later the country became independent and was admitted into membership in the United Nations.

The world is short on leadership. In Olympio, who became President on independence, the Togolese found a wise leader and the world a constructive statesman. He was assassinated in 1963.

The Cameroons. The Germans established a protectorate in the Cameroons at about the same time they established themselves in Togo. Here again they found an ethnic and cultural complex. After World War I, during which French and British troops drove out the German forces, the British assumed the mandate over the area bordering on Nigeria, and the French the remaining four-fifths of the country. These too, in turn, became Trust Territories.

In 1958, in the French Cameroons, the new legislative assembly, created the previous year, voted for independence. France and the United Nations General Assembly agreed. In so doing, the latter expressed the hope that new elections would be held. These took place in 1960. A new constitution was drawn up and later in the year the Republic of Cameroun became independent and subsequently a member of the United Nations.

Neighboring Nigeria was scheduled for independence in 1960. In anticipation, the General Assembly, in 1959, recommended that a plebiscite be held in British Cameroons to determine whether the peoples wished to join Nigeria or remain under trusteeship pending a settlement of their future at a later date. The plebiscite when held in the northern region favored the latter.

In the south, the situation was more complicated by an absence of agreement on what questions should be asked. After a series of consultations it was recommended by the General Assembly that a plebiscite should be held in both regions, inviting the populations to state whether they wished to join Nigeria or the new Republic of Cameroun. The north then voted for union with Nigeria, and the south to join Cameroun. British trusteeship was withdrawn and the wishes of the inhabitants respected. Thus they became not independent but self-governing in a wider setting.

Tanganyika. General von Lettow-Vorbeck held the British and South African forces at bay in Tanganyika for four years in World War I. The territory subsequently became a British mandate and then a Trust Territory. It was the largest and most heavily populated territory in the international trusteeship system. Problems arose during trusteeship because the United Nations considered that political union with the other British-administered lands of Kenya and Uganda was not appropriate under the trusteeship agreement. Elections were held in 1958 and 1959. These were conducted, however, in such a way as to maintain balanced representation between the African, Asian and European communities. The General Assembly viewed these measures as transitional and, in 1960, electoral reforms were introduced. After the General Assembly had been informed in 1961 that self-government had been completed the previous year, the trusteeship was withdrawn and Tanganyika became a member of the United Nations.

Ruanda-Urundi. As late as 1962, few thought the Belgian-administered territories of Ruanda-Urundi ripe for independence. These mountainous little countries in Central Africa had not developed any of the institutions of modern government, nor had the inhabitants been trained to assume the responsibilities that go with independence. In 1962 the Belgian trusteeship was withdrawn, and the two million inhabitants were divided into two states, Rwanda —the most densely populated state in Africa—and Burundi. Presumably in recognition of this lack of preparedness, the General Assembly called upon the United Nations and the Specialized Agencies to bring all aid possible to these countries.

Unhappily, Rwanda continued to be the scene of intertribal conflict leading to a massacre by the Bantu people (the Bahutu) of their tall, tribal Nilotic overlords, the Tutsi. The swift provision of support through international programs of assistance has, nevertheless, eased the passage of these two states through the initial period of their independence.

Western Samoa.   A land in the South Pacific which recalls the Vailima letters of Robert Louis Stevenson (who spent his last years there), Western Samoa presented the United Nations with an independence petition as early as 1947. Under New Zealand trusteeship, Western Samoa developed democratic institutions, and in a plebiscite held in 1961 the inhabitants overwhelmingly declared in favor of independence. The trusteeship ended and Western Samoa became independent, and her government did not apply for membership in the United Nations, but joined some of the Specialized Agencies.

A thousand islands.   The areas remaining under trusteeship are Nauru, New Guinea and Micronesia, all in the Pacific. Nauru, a small island with a population of five thousand, faces an uncertain future. The phosphate deposits on which the island depends for its livelihood will be worked out in less than forty years. The island became independent in 1968.

New Guinea is administered, together with Papua, by Australia. In the wake of the 1962 visiting mission's recommendation, representative institutions have been further developed. An International Bank Mission in 1963 has also proposed a number of measures designed to stimulate the growth of the economy of the area.

In Micronesia the United States administers some 2,141 islands set in more than three million square miles of the Pacific Ocean. The hundred thousand inhabitants now have representative local government and the Council of Micronesia was set up in 1961 to represent the whole area. Four-fifths of the area's budget continues to be met by funds from the United States.

Article 73e. At San Francisco, the drafters of the Charter settled for a *Declaration Regarding Non-Self-Governing Territories.* Under Article 73e, members of the United Nations with colonies are invited to transmit for information purposes to the Secretary-General, subject to certain limitations, statistical and other technical information relating to the economic, social and educational conditions in the territories for which they are responsible.

The wording of the Charter is, by comparison with the trusteeship provisions, positively diffident. After all, these territories under the Charter were to be groomed not for independence but self-government.

Independence presupposes sovereignty, self-government does not. The anti-colonial members in the General Assembly rapidly moved to bring the same principles to bear regarding colonies as had been established for Trust Territories. As far as possible the milk and water provisions of Article 73e were replaced by the firmer procedures of the trusteeship system.

In 1949, the General Assembly established its Committee on Information from Non-Self-Governing Territories to examine the information which was to be transmitted to the Secretary-General under Article 73e. Membership provided parity between colonial and non-colonial members. Taking upon itself what might normally have been considered a responsibility of the Secretary-General, the Committee drafted its own questionnaire addressed to the colonial members, asking for reports on conditions in the colonies. There ensued a cycle of reports on economic, social and educational conditions in the various dependencies.

With these reports before them, the Committee dug deep into colonial conditions and did not hesitate to stretch its terms of reference to discuss political developments—or the lack of them—and the need to advance the colonial areas not so much toward self-government as toward independence. The Declaration, included in the Charter as a shield to bring a measure of protection for colonial peoples, in the hands of the Committee and with it the urgings of the General Assembly, was forged into an instrument to provide for their self-government and independence.

Forcing the pace. The General Assembly, particularly as new members joined the anti-colonial groupings led initially by India, began to develop to the fullest possible extent the provisions of the Charter. It adopted calenders for independence. It called for political information, and in 1961 the "73e Committee" had its terms of reference enlarged so that it could discuss such information. It laid claim to the right itself to decide when a country was ripe for independence; these were matters which could not, the General Assembly considered, be left entirely to the members responsible for the territories concerned. In the wider frame of activity of the United Nations, the anti-colonial representation made itself felt. Its effect can be found in the Universal Declaration of Human Rights. When the Declaration came to be converted into draft international covenants, the right of self-determination was inserted into the preamble of each of the two drafts, as will be seen in Chapter IX (p. 210). In practically every forum of the United Nations the anti-colonial movement made itself felt whether it dealt with measures for keeping the peace, the financing of economic development or discussions on international commodity trade.

In the years 1959–61 the most striking changes took place as a result of the election of General de Gaulle as President of the French Republic. With the exception of Algeria (which had to wait until 1962 to become independent), each French colony was given freedom to determine its future through the means of a referendum. Guinea became independent in 1959. In the following year eleven African territories chose independence within the framework of the French Community.

The General Assembly of 1960, at which most of these new states were admitted to membership, was an historic occasion for other reasons. Heads and Chiefs of State from many countries including some of the Great Powers attended, and in their presence historic debates took place. One such debate in plenary session led to the adoption of the Declaration on the Granting of Independence

to Colonial Countries and Peoples. The Declaration was blu
to the point. It stated that while many colonies had become
pendent, many had yet to be emancipated. All peoples had a right
to self-determination, and for those that had not yet attained independence immediate steps should be taken to transfer all powers
to the peoples without any distinction.

A year later, in 1961, the General Assembly established the
Special Committee of Seventeen to examine the application of the
Declaration and to make recommendations on the progress and
extent of its application. The old Committee on Information was
wound up, and its responsibilities vested in this new Committee.
Two other General Assembly committees, the Special Committee
on Portuguese Territories and the Special Committee on South-
West Africa, both established in 1961 (the latter succeeding an
earlier committee), had their functions similarly merged in the
Special Committee by the General Assembly in 1962. Thus the Special Committee which, in 1963, had its membership enlarged to
twenty-four, became the only United Nations committee, with the
exception of the Trusteeship Council, with direct responsibility for
giving effect to the Declaration.

The winds of change. The Committee first drew up a preliminary list of sixty-four territories not yet independent. It then
began, through discussion, consultation with the colonial powers,
receiving and hearing petitions, to direct attention to the different
territories in turn.

Several countries have become independent in the period following the adoption of the Declaration. Of those of concern to the
Committee, Kenya became independent in 1963; so did Zanzibar,
to unite, in 1964, with Tanganyika to form Tanzania. The settler-
dominated Central African Federation, created by the United
Kingdom in 1953, was dismantled in 1964 with Northern Rhodesia
becoming the independent state of Zambia; Nyasaland became
Malawi. Malta became independent in that year. The winds of
change had indeed begun to blow since Prime Minister Churchill,
when questioned in the House of Commons about constitutional
advance in Malta, retorted, "Can you have a constitution for a

battleship?" Gambia, whose future possibly lies in closer relationship with neighboring Senegal, became independent in 1965. All of the above became members of the United Nations almost immediately following independence. In 1966 British Guiana, under its new name Guyana, became independent and a member of the United Nations.

The protectorates in Southern Africa, Basutoland, Bechuanaland and Swaziland had been of concern to the Committee. Geographically they are for the most part large, impoverished, drought ridden enclaves within the Republic of South Africa, and many inhabitants of the protectorates migrate seasonally to work in the Republic. In 1966, Basutoland became independent under its new name Lesotho, and Bechuanaland as Botswana. Both were admitted to membership in the United Nations and like all former British dependencies, with the exception of Burma, elected on independence to become members of the Commonwealth. With the "Little Eight" Leeward Islands in the Caribbean, which missed self-government when the British-sponsored Federation of the West Indies disintegrated in 1962, for the most part becoming independent with Barbados in 1966, of the former British Protectorates and dependencies only some islands in the Pacific and South Atlantic, the Rock of Gibraltar and sheikdoms in the Persian Gulf remain as residual responsibilities. Their constitutional future, for reasons of their size, local interests, or strategic significance, remains in doubt. Special reference here may be made to the creation, in 1963, by the United Kingdom of the Federation of South Arabia comprising the Aden Colony and Protectorate and eleven small Arab states. Such constitutional changes, brought about as a result of the new Federation, were not acceptable to some of the groups concerned. Following consultations and the hearing of petitioners, the Committee called for new elections under United Nations supervision. The United Kingdom Government, while taking steps to consult over constitutional changes, considered that a transitional period was required during which an attempt should be made to make the Federation work. At the end of 1967, the Federation achieved independence as Southern Yemen.

A ride on the tiger. From 1923 to 1965, Rhodesia was a self-governing colony with the United Kingdom retaining certain constitutional powers. In 1953, the Central African Federation was formed out of Northern Rhodesia, Southern Rhodesia and Nyasaland. Ten years later this federation, too, was dismantled and Northern Rhodesia and Nyasaland became independent under their new names of Zambia and Malawi. Southern Rhodesia did not receive independence, because the British were not prepared to grant independence to a country which was being governed by a minority of its peoples. On 11 November 1965, Ian Smith, the Rhodesian Prime Minister, made a unilateral and illegal declaration of independence.

In consultation with the Commonwealth, the United Kingdom immediately imposed political, financial and economic sanctions. Within a matter of days, the Security Council, at the request of the United Kingdom, called upon all members to sever economic relations and to impose an oil embargo. In April 1966, because of blockade runners delivering oil to Mozambique through the nearby port of Beira, the United Kingdom received authority from the Security Council to prevent by force the arrival at Beira of any vessels reasonably believed to be carrying oil destined for Rhodesia.

In December 1966, after exploratory discussions with the Rhodesian Government and in consultation with the Commonwealth, the British Prime Minister Harold Wilson met with Ian Smith on board HMS Tiger off Gibraltar. They produced a working document which provided for the end of the rebellion and progress toward unimpeded majority rule with built-in constitutional safeguards. Smith's colleagues found part of the document unacceptable.

The United Kingdom promptly returned to the Security Council and called for economic sanctions as provided for in Chapter VII of the Charter. George Brown, the British Foreign Secretary, requested and obtained a Security Council resolution calling for "effective and selective" mandatory sanctions against Rhodesia. Mandatory sanctions on selected Rhodesian export commodities were imposed as well as on the sale of arms to Rhodesia. The Security Council also called on all members to prohibit the sale of oil to Rhodesia.

For the first time in the history of the United Nations, the Security Council had applied economic sanctions. These required all members to take and enforce powers to prevent their nationals from buying or shipping prohibited Rhodesian exports or sending banned commodities to Rhodesia.

Sanctions, however, can prove to be a two-edged weapon. They can, if applied indiscriminately, result in relatively greater economic damage to those countries applying them than to those against whom they are applied. The selected list agreed to by the Security Council had been drawn up with three considerations in mind. It was composed of those items the ban on which can effectively be applied. They include those most likely to inflict the maximum economic damage on Rhodesia. At the same time, the list was so prepared as not to endanger through any side-effect the economics of Rhodesia's neighbors, particularly of Zambia.

Most impervious.   Most impervious to the winds of change are the oldest colonial powers: Spain and Portugal. Spain has recently become more responsive to representations regarding its old pockets in West Africa, Fernando Po, Ifni, Río Muni and Spanish Sahara. Portugal, a member of the United Nations since 1955, does not consider it appropriate to transmit information on its territories to the United Nations. These total about 900,000 square miles and include 12 million inhabitants. The main areas are Angola and Mozambique in Africa and Timor at the end of the island chain, the bulk of which is now Indonesia.

The position of Portugal is that, as these areas are constitutionally overseas provinces of metropolitan Portugal, they do not come within the purview of the Charter. (France and the Netherlands had taken similar positions regarding certain of their overseas areas.) Only South Africa has occasioned more ire among the anti-colonial members of the United Nations. Attention has repeatedly been drawn to the alleged ill treatment of prisoners, harsh repression and the absence of constitutional reforms other than paper ones. A series of committees has devoted special attention to the Portuguese territories and the Special Committee has drawn the attention of the Security Council to what it considers to be a deteriorating situation in these territories. The United Nations High Commissioner for Refugees has been invited to act on behalf of the refugees from those African territories where rebellion is a continuing feature.

The cobweb of domestic jurisdiction. Toward the end of Chapter I we examined constitutional features of the Charter, in the light of its purposes and principles. One of these related to the provision contained in Article 2.7 of the Charter which, except in matters relating to enforcement measures, placed outside the Organization questions which were within the domestic jurisdiction of a state.

On many occasions, in different Organs of the United Nations, this clause has been invoked in an attempt to prevent discussion of conditions in an area which the member claimed to be essentially within its domestic jurisdiction and therefore outside the scope of the Charter. While such claims have succeeded in preventing an item relating to the matter from being inscribed on the agenda of, say, the General Assembly, this protective clause has seldom, if ever, prevented the matter from being discussed.

In most cases, the protection claimed arose when anti-colonial members wished to give a public airing to conditions prevailing in what was considered by them to be a dependent territory. As has been seen previously, the refusal of Portugal to submit information to the Secretary-General as required by Article 73e is based on the position that Angola and Mozambique are components of a constitutional whole of which Portugal itself is only a part. This has not prevented full discussion of conditions in these and other areas by a succession of committees and by the General Assembly itself.

France made similar claims in respect to Algeria before that country became independent and like South Africa, on occasion, had declined to participate in debates on matters considered to be domestic. But to no avail; such has been the force of the anti-colonial movement that the protection of domestic jurisdiction has been blown away like a cobweb, and has not prevented international debate.

This is a major constitutional departure, as far as the Charter is concerned. At least here it has, in practice, admitted flexibility. For those who have expressed grave reservations regarding this fundamental change, it might be relevant to recall the signing of Magna Carta six hundred years ago. The only reason why the Magna Carta remains significant on this planet, when half a dozen similar charters of the thirteenth century have passed almost unnoticed into the limbo of history, is that the fundamental concepts of individual freedom and the rule of law enshrined in that document were developed beyond all recognition and came to be applied to millions who were never given a passing thought by its drafters.

South Africa. The rock against which the wave of anti-colonialism has so far broken in vain is the Republic of South Africa. The practice of *apartheid*, or racial separation, by which the minority of Afrikaners predominate over the overwhelming majority of Bantu and "Cape Coloured" (those of mixed descent) has caused more emotion and less analysis than any other issue before the United Nations. To the great majority of governments the continued pursuit of racial separation by the government in Pretoria or Capetown is now morally repugnant, politically imprudent and an invitation to violence. The harsh legal measures taken to enforce *apartheid* have given rise to continued protest and demands for action to bring the Republic to change its policies. The General Assembly, in 1962, took the unique step in calling for an embargo on trade with South Africa.

If this were not enough, the treatment of peoples of Indian origin in South Africa has been a matter of constant concern and enquiry by the United Nations. Also, the refusal of South Africa to conclude a Trusteeship Agreement for South-West Africa remains a running sore, so much so, in fact, that the Governments of Ethiopia and Liberia, the two other African members of the League, filed applications before the International Court so that the Court could order South Africa to cease and desist from the practice of *apartheid* and other policies of racial discrimination in that territory. (See Chapter VIII.)

It is for the South African government to attempt to justify what its policies are and the underlying reasons for them. The government has not found it easy to do so. While pressures mount, experiments in the first steps towards separate government by the Bantu in the Transkei, buttressed by programs of economic development, go forward. Whether these moves towards political and economic betterment have been accelerated by debate in the United Nations, or have been retarded as a result of the obdurate mood that outside criticism has generated, is something we do not yet know.

Harambee. In East Africa, the chant of the laborers as they haul together is "Harambee!" The old cry of "pull together" is today the motto of an independent Kenya. In a way, it symbolizes the strength and triumph of the anti-colonial movement. In this chapter we have examined the twin forces of the nineteenth century which gave rise both to colonialism and—at the turn of the century—to the anti-colonial movement. We have seen how this force gathered strength and, in the United Nations, found expression, and eventually a machinery was fashioned to bring about, in almost every case peacefully, independence and membership in the Organization.

Lord Caradon, himself a former colonial governor, has described this success story as "one of the most spectacular developments of our generation and this century." It is unlikely that such development could have taken place, as it did, without the United Nations and the pulling together of the anti-colonial members themselves.

At first the Trusteeship Council moved leisurely. A forced draft from the General Assembly made it move more rapidly to complete its task of bringing independence to most of the peoples of the Trust Territories. Only certain islands of the Pacific remain, and there significant constitutional advances towards self-government have been made. Fortunately, with the possible exception of Tanganyika, racial issues did not present themselves, thus making the task of the Council much less complicated than moves toward independence elsewhere.

The first state in what used to be called Black Africa to become independent in the post-war period was the Gold Coast. When, in 1956, Ghana reappeared as an African state, the pace of the independence movement quickened.

Some are large countries such as the Federation of Nigeria with a population totalling more than 60 million. Others are small such as Gambia, looking on the map almost like a towpath on the lower reaches of the Senegal River. Some are wealthy such as copper-rich Zambia. Others are poor, as is Somalia in the dry Horn of Africa. Nearly all are having to make great domestic adjustments upon becoming independent. But almost everywhere, compared with European liberation movements in the 19th Century, independence has been acquired peacefully if not quietly. To a large extent this has been due to the quiet, effective and moderating influence and control of the United Nations. It did not attempt to create a dam against the rising waters of change, but to create a sluice gate to control them.

Good government is no substitute.   Although the anti-colonial debates in the United Nations have been often acrimonious and members have been sharply divided, since 1956 practically all the colonial powers have disagreed not so much on whether a dependency should become independent but when and under what circumstances. Should not a country be first economically viable and have order, law and good government before it assumes autonomy? For ten years, at least, such questions met with the same answer: good government is no substitute for self-government. When self-government has been achieved in our own way, then we shall set about good government—in our own way. Whether we have been disillusioned with the outcome depends on the extent of our initial illusions.

Decolonization was considered by many to be a prelude to a blood bath, and indeed internal strife has followed independence in some countries. But the whole anti-colonial movement, with the

United Nations channelling constructively the forces at work, has triumphed peacefully compared with the similar nation-making process of nineteenth century Europe or America. There has been no Solferino or Gettysburg.

In many of the new states the constitution adopted on independence has been overturned with the replacement of political groupings by a monolithic nationalist party. We forget, perhaps, that the two party system is peculiar to the English-speaking world and is as much a product of the plasticity of the language itself as it is of centuries of organic growth.

Apprehension was felt at the spectacle of peoples often ninety per cent illiterate ruling themselves. But for the most part the electorates of new nations are extremely articulate and have a healthy lack of reverence for authority. Here, too, we may have forgotten that the franchise gives rise to a demand for education and not the reverse.

Many of the new states are, in a certain sense, synthetic creations. Their boundaries are derived from the lines arbitrarily drawn during the colonial carve-up of the nineteenth century. What was there to hold the plural society together in the face of divisive tribal and social differences once disinterested authority was withdrawn? In the West Indies, East Africa and elsewhere attempts to group weaker countries into stronger federations collapsed because nationalism, once thought to be a nineteenth century anachronism, emerged again as the strongest form of political reality in the most unlikely situations. Also, federation is seldom a popular movement, but a political solution enforced from the top as the United States itself experienced.

The golden bowl.   What residual tasks and what new problems now face the international institutions, and particularly the United Nations, which have done so much to pave the way to emancipation?

The residual tasks relate mainly to those dependent areas where constitutional measures are directed towards independence. In Chapter III and earlier in the present chapter, we saw how the largest dependencies have become independent, and joined in the world community through membership of the United Nations and the Specialized Agencies. Now, as we have seen, mini-states have been created. These are now likely to be followed by micro-states such as Fiji and Pitcairn Island with populations not much larger than a good-sized housing complex. In 1967 U Thant drew the attention of the General Assembly to the economic and political difficulties which would accompany the assumption of membership in the United Nations of such new states, which could be many. He has suggested that some form of association would benefit both the United Nations and such small entities.

The almost intractable problems, however, are economic. They confront most of the new states both big and small. Few are fortunate to have rich mineral resources such as Ghana and Jamaica, which if carefully exploited could create moderately prosperous urbanized industrial countries. Few have the startling entrepreneurship of Singapore. For the most part the new countries are agricultural, practicing the shifting of cultivation when growing food crops, and heavily overgrazing denuded pastures where there is animal husbandry. Export earnings are dependent on primary products, the prices of which are notoriously unstable in the world market and the secular trend in overseas demand not very favorable. Here the United Nations family can move decisively to mobilize on a massive scale world food surpluses for transfer to poorer areas. This can become part of the accepted pattern of international behavior. The United Nations Development Program, particularly if it is given a new sense of purpose and direction through being able to provide capital funds for development, can join with the older financing institutions in training the labor force and opening up the natural resources of the new countries to make the most of their economic opportunities. The United Nations can also encourage regional economic and trading groupings so that the emergent nations can negotiate with their stronger trading partners on less unequal terms.

The American literary scene is familiar with the social and personal problems defined by Henry James as a "search for identity in a world of circumstance." Depending on our environment and background the very process of living is to a large extent for each one of us the search for identity in shifting surroundings. This is true for nations whether they are older ones such as the United States, or newly arrived on the world's scene. These states present the United Nations with new tasks of considerable complexity. The problem lies in assisting them to find political and economic identity in a world of circumstance. It is fitting that this should be so, for the new states are to a large extent a product of the United Nations, having joined the Organization to find their place in the world community, then in turn taking their share in shaping its destiny.

Chapter VII

THE INTERNATIONAL
PUBLIC SERVANT

Today's diplomat has his origins in the Italian Renaissance, when the techniques of diplomatic intercourse were developed to a fine art. An ambassador came to be looked upon not as one who was concerned with peace and the furtherance of the public good, but rather as one who represented the interests of his country. An ambassador who interpreted his instructions in the interests of humanity as he conceived them instead of in the best interests of his government might find himself looking for a job. A seventeenth century ambassador, Sir Henry Wotton, once wrote in a visitor's book "an ambassador is an honest man who is sent abroad to lie for the good of his country." His employer, King James I, was deeply shocked at this frivolity and never used him as an envoy again in spite of Sir Henry's protestations that he was only trying to be funny.

In medieval times, however, this concept of the ambassador's duties might have occasioned some surprise. Diplomats often saw themselves as public officials. By that they did not mean, as nowadays, officials employed in the public service, but officials who, while employed by their governments, served the wider interests of Christendom and the cause of peace. The writings of Rosier and Bartolus, both practicing diplomats, suggest that the life and duties of the pre-Renaissance ambassador were not too far removed from the international official serving the interests of the world community rather than those of his own country.

It was William Penn who first proposed that there should be and could be an international public service. In his writings published in 1693, Penn saw the need for a disinterested and dedicated group of officials who could serve the European diet. He modelled his official after the clerks of the House of Commons who, throughout those turbulent times, continued to record the debates and decisions in Parliament with the strictest impartiality. If such officials could do their duty in such times, then similar officials could also serve an international parliament objectively and with integrity. But Penn's suggestions remained of academic interest only, until Smuts in 1918, when making his proposals for a League of Nations, stated that the League should have an international secretariat.

The drafters of the Covenant, in much the same way as the makers of the Charter a generation later, at one point toyed with the idea of the Secretariat of the League being headed by someone with exceptional powers and responsibilities. In 1919, Lord Robert Cecil had in mind an executive head who would be given the title of "Chancellor." The British made the mistake of tailoring the job to suit a particular man they had in mind. He was Eleutherios Venizelos of Greece, an experienced, brilliant statesman with a worldwide reputation.

When it became known that Venizelos did not wish to leave the service of his country, the drafters of the Covenant lowered their sights and thought more in terms of an administrative head. This they found in Sir Eric Drummond who was appointed by the Peace Conference as Secretary-General. He was so designated in an Annex to the Covenant.

The Covenant was almost laconic as far as its provisions related to the Secretary-General and his staff. Article 6 (1) states:

> The permanent Secretariat shall be established at the Seat of the League. The Secretariat shall comprise a Secretary-General and such secretaries and staff as may be required.

Apart from the first Secretary-General, his successors were to be appointed by the League Council with the approval of the majority of the Assembly. The staff was to be appointed by the Secretary-General with the approval of the Council, and all positions were to be open equally to men and women. The Secretary-General was to "act in that capacity at all meetings of the Assembly and of the Council."

These were the main references to the Secretary-General and his staff. It was left to Sir Eric Drummond to fashion the Secretariat as he considered most appropriate and to build through his example an enduring tradition for the international civil servant.

Sir Eric by experience and personality represented the highest traditions of the British civil service. As we would say nowadays, he was a member of the Establishment. He belonged to a world where discretion, absolute probity, integrity and complete devotion to duty were the distinguishing characteristics of the senior public servant. He was also personally self-effacing, shy and most reluctant to move upstage. Under his leadership a secretariat in Geneva was recruited and trained, and came to adopt his standards and to follow his precepts. Although he brought his traditions and practices with him and could never be considered anything but an Englishman, from the day he took up his duties until his retirement in 1933, he devoted himself entirely to the interests of the League.

He never addressed the Assembly or the Council. In committee he spoke always as if he were the committee's secretary rather than as a factor in events. Behind the scenes he was always available to play a creative and constructive role, to give impartial counsel or to exercise a moderating influence in moments of crisis.

The first Secretary-General established during his tenure two major principles of his position. The first was that it should have international responsibilities, and secondly that the secretariat should be international in composition. These concepts were subsequently reflected in the Staff Regulations of the Secretariat of the League of Nations by which members of the Secretariat were enjoined to regulate their conduct with the interests of the League alone in view, and which prohibited them from seeking or receiving instructions from anyone outside the Secretariat.

This, today, may seem self-evident. If so, it tends to confirm how well Drummond shaped the Secretariat. In 1920, however, such concepts were not so obvious. If anyone had thought about the question at all, as like as not he would have considered that the Secretariat would be intergovernmental in character with the staff seconded from the various member governments; in effect, an intergovernmental staff to service an intergovernmental body. Such, in fact, were the views of Italy and Germany when, in 1930, the German and Italian representatives on a committee to advise on the staff arrangements of the League, submitted a minority report at variance with the majority of the committee which advocated that the international character and responsibilities of the Secretariat be maintained.

Under Drummond, the Secretariat was recruited on an international basis. Budget stringency and the overwhelming European membership of the League resulted in the staff being mainly drawn from Europe. Coming from a country which, in the previous century, had replaced patronage by merit and haphazard selection of the civil service by open competitive examination, the Secretary-General recruited the staff as far as possible on the grounds of merit and competence. He was not wholly successful, but some of those he brought into the service as young men still occupy posts in the United Nations Secretariat, and they remain a source of inspiration to the newcomer.

The criticism of Drummond lay in his apparent passivity and lack of any sense of the dynamic role the Secretariat could play, and eventually came to play in the next generation. His performance, according to his critics, made a poor showing in contrast to the verve and dash of his more extroverted colleague, Albert Thomas of France, the first Director of the International Labor Organization. By comparison, the Secretary-General seemed somewhat anemic.

Confident of strong trade union backing in an organization with a tripartite structure composed not only of government representatives but also representatives of management and trades unions, Thomas played a dominating and formative role in the development of ILO. He was vigorous, controversial, forceful and not averse to indulging in a little swashbuckling in order to further the interests of his organization. Thomas, his subordinates and his successors, in the interwar period, were responsible for improving the condition of the worker throughout almost all the world. But their field of activity was a different one from that of the League, and the political climate in which they operated was much less uncertain. Nevertheless, it is interesting to speculate on what might have happened if each man had occupied the other's position.

Joseph Avenol of France, who succeeded Drummond in 1933, took over the Secretary-Generalship when the League, following its inability to act decisively in the Manchurian crisis in 1931, was already beginning to decline. He canvassed for the readmission of Italy to the League after the conquest by Italy of Abyssinia. He may also have contributed to the inactivity of the League when in 1936, Italy intervened in the Spanish Civil War. In 1940 Avenol resigned and returned to France where he placed his services at the disposal of the Vichy authorities.

Breaking new ground. The Great Powers foresaw at Dumbarton Oaks the need for a chief officer of the United Nations who would have effective administrative and executive functions. The proposals adopted there followed the suggestions put forward by the United States. In 1919, as we have seen, some of those engaged in preparing drafts for the Covenant had in mind creating a chief officership with great prestige and authority. Similarly, the United States when preparing for the Dumbarton Oaks conference toyed for a time with the idea of having a President of the United Nations as well as a Secretary-General. The former would have had political and executive functions, and the latter would have carried the administrative responsibilities. In a somewhat diluted form, these functions were subsequently invested in the Secretary-General.

At San Francisco, the Dumbarton Oaks proposals were built into the Charter. Basically, they provided for an enhanced administrative role for the Secretary-General, specific international political responsibilities and a constitutional independence.

The chief administrative officer. Thus Article 97 of the

Charter designates the Secretary-General. As such he appoints the staff, not subject to the approval of the Council as in the case of the Secretariat of the League, but under staff rules as adopted by the General Assembly. As Secretary-General he acts in that capacity in all meetings of the Principal Organs. As the chief administrative officer of the organization, the Secretary-General's responsibilities range far beyond hiring and firing the staff and seeing that conferences and other meetings are run on time. They place firmly on his shoulders the many executive decisions necessary to give effect to the requests and recommendations made by the various organs. In other words, while it is basically the responsibility of members to decide *what* should be done, it is the job of the Secretary-General to decide *how*. As the prestige of his office and, with it, that of the Secretariat has been enhanced over the years, the Principal Organs have become increasingly prepared to observe this functional dividing line.

Article 98 calls upon the Secretary-General not only to act as administrative officer in the meetings of the Principal Organs, but it also requires that he "shall perform such other functions as are entrusted to him by these organs." The Covenant made no such provision for the Secretary-General of the League. It is implicit that, in the exercise of these responsibilities, the Secretary-General may be required to take political and other action which could place him in situations of conflict between members. His position, therefore, is one which by its nature exposes him to the sharpest political winds that blow. He cannot always remain above the storm and, on occasion, however careful his navigation might be, he may well find himself in the eye of it.

Under Article 98, the Secretary-General is not called upon to take political initiatives, but to carry out such tasks as may be entrusted to him. The onus is on the Principal Organ—such as the Security Council or the General Assembly—to request him to act. Article 99, however, gives the Secretary-General a major political role. As Dag Hammarskjöld stated in his speech at Oxford in 1961 on "The International Civil Servant in Law and in Fact", "It is Article 99 more than any other which was considered by the drafters of the Charter to have transformed the Secretary-General of the United Nations from a purely administrative official to one with an explicit political responsibility."

This Article does indeed give the Secretary-General broad powers of political initiative. Under the Covenant, the Secretary-General of the League could convene a meeting of the Council only in the event of an outbreak of war. As was found to the world's cost, for the Secretary-General to take action when hostilities had actually broken out was too late in the game. The makers of the Charter clearly wished the Secretary-General of the United Nations to have wide powers of discretion to act when danger, in his opinion, threatened. Obviously, hazards may await a Secretary-General who sets the machinery of the Charter in action under this Article. The powers conferred are great and are to be used with discretion and great care.

It is perhaps for this reason that Secretaries-General have preferred methods of action other than those specifically provided for under Article 99. Although Trygve Lie claimed that his intervention in the Security Council when hostilities broke out in Korea had been based on Article 99, the statement almost had the air of an afterthought. During the Suez crisis in 1956, Hammarskjöld informed the Security Council that he would have acted under Article 99 had not the United States already called for a meeting of that body. When the government of Laos called for assistance in 1959, Hammarskjöld, in asking the Security Council to meet, went out of his way to point out that he was not acting under the powers conferred upon him under this Article, as he did not have sufficient facts on which to act. Only when he moved during the Congo crisis in 1960, did he specifically act under Article 99.

It is not so much the *explicit* powers that are conferred upon him that make his position so significant, as the *implicit* powers which may be inferred from the Secretary-General's responsibilities. In order to meet his obligations under this Article he needs to have, as Hammarskjöld put it in his Oxford address, "a broad discretion to conduct enquiries and to engage in informal diplomatic activity in regard to matters which 'may threaten the maintenance of international peace and security.'" These responsibilities require ceaseless vigilance, knowledge, wisdom and tact. Above all, the Secretary-General has to try to act in a way that does not compromise him with any of the parties engaged, for as soon as the mutual confidence between him and the individual parties is lost, his usefulness may be at an end.

Two sides of the coin. It will be seen from the foregoing that when Trygve Lie referred to his post as being "the most impossible job in the world," he was not overstating the case. The burdens placed on the Secretary-General and his staff are far greater than those carried by national civil servants. Until traditions have developed and with them the *esprit de corps* that is the hallmark of the great public services, however, some uncertainty is bound to prevail regarding the inviolability of the international civil servant.

A measure of protection, nevertheless, is provided by the Charter in Article 100. While, under the Covenant, the Secretariat of the League was established on the concept of *administrative* independence, the Charter grants to the Secretary-General and his staff a *constitutional* independence. This Article, in part, builds into the Charter the language of the staff regulations of the League referred to on p. 154. Article 100 assures the independence of the Secretary-General and his staff from governments or any other authority outside the United Nations. On the other side of the coin, members of the United Nations undertake to respect the international character of the responsibilities of the Secretary-General and his staff, and in so doing undertake not to seek to influence them in their work.

The Article taken as a whole gives to the Secretariat a constitutional independence. To underpin the Secretariat's position, Article 105 provides that the Secretariat should enjoy such privileges and immunities as are necessary for the independent exercise of its functions.

Composition. The Secretariat of the United Nations includes the Secretary-General and the staff. Before proceeding we should establish some idea of the size and composition of the Secretariat. Although numbers are subject to immediate change, a few figures are helpful.

In 1968, the professional and senior staff numbered some 2,795 including under-secretaries-general. The remainder were professional officers, directors, and principal officers. The balance of the established staff was made up of 3,830 general service, field service and manual workers.

Article 101.3 of the Charter states that "The paramount consideration in the employment of the staff . . . shall be the necessity of securing the highest standards of efficiency, competence and integrity." It also goes on to state that "Due regard shall be paid to the importance of recruiting staff on as wide a geographical basis as possible."

Line and staff.   In the Office of the Secretary-General are three staff units: the Offices of the Controller, of Legal Affairs and of Personnel. In addition, there are the Executive Office (under which the Division of Human Rights and the Division of Narcotic Drugs presently operate), the Offices of the Under-Secretaries-General for Special Political Affairs and other units and posts.

The main, line departments are those for Political and Security Council Affairs, Trusteeship and Non-Self-Governing Territories and Economic and Social Affairs as provided for in Article 101 of the Charter. The largest, the Department of Economic and Social Affairs, includes regional secretariats in Europe (Geneva), Latin America (Santiago, Chile), Asia (Bangkok), and Africa (Addis Ababa) to service their respective regional economic commissions. Some of these have sub-offices. There is also a United Nations Office in Geneva located in the *Palais des Nations,* originally built to house the League of Nations.

These line departments are serviced by staff offices. They include offices for general services, conference services and public information. The latter maintains some 43 information centers and offices throughout the world.

In addition to the Secretariat proper are the United Nations agencies or bodies which in different ways enjoy within the United

Nations a degree of substantive and administrative autonomy. The agencies and programs are the United Nations Children's Fund (UNICEF) based at United Nations Headquarters, New York; the United Nations Relief and Works Agency for Palestine Refugees in the Near East (UNRWA) based in Beirut; the United Nations High Commissioner for Refugees and the United Nations Conference on Trade and Development (UNCTAD) both located in Geneva; the United Nations Development Program (UNDP) at United Nations Headquarters in New York and the United Nations Industrial Development Organization (UNIDO) in Vienna. UNICEF and the UNDP maintain field offices in practically all economically developing countries in which they have assistance or development programs.

Compared with the size of bureaucracies engaged in the administration of great cities, the United Nations Secretariat must seem pitifully small if we consider that the world is its parish.

The international civil servant. In many large American corporations the most aggressive and successful of the younger executives with an eye on the loftier reaches of management are often selected for special training in order to groom them for senior appointments. An interesting exercise often conducted at an early stage in such courses is for the whole group to list what, in its opinion, are the qualities required to be president of the corporation. Subsequently, they are called upon to list the qualifications needed for the post each at that moment occupies and, finally, to state what, as interviewers, they look for in applicants seeking jobs under their supervision. It often comes as an eye-opener when the eager aspirants for high office find that the qualities called for are the same at all levels and divisions.

The qualities required by an international official, whether he is a Filipino lawyer, an Indian general, a French hydrologist, an Iraqi economist, a Russian interpreter or a Panamanian conference officer, are identical to those required in the Secretary-General, although the technical training called for may be different.

Much has been written about the qualifications needed by an international official. Sydney Bailey's little book, *The Secretariat of the United Nations,* is perhaps the most useful. In Alexander Loveday's *Reflections on International Administration,* a former high official of the League writes with some reserve of the United Nations Secretariat. Both refer to the qualities needed for a staff member. Bailey: integrity, independence, impartiality and loyalty to the Organization; Loveday: understanding and consequential loyalty, diplomatic capacity, constructive imagination, capacity for leadership, administrative ability, nervous energy, determination, specialized knowledge and what he terms *convivencia*—a sense of "live and let live."

There is, however, a critical element in the makeup of the international public servant which is constantly reiterated in Hammarskjöld's writings and statements on the subject. It might almost be considered the main thread running through his speeches, collected by Wilder Foote in *The Servant of Peace.* It is simply that the international public servant, under the Charter, serves the international community as a whole and until he accepts this, and the concept becomes part of his life and work, he is not a fully integrated international official. In different ways both Bailey and Loveday make this point. But it is the pivot on which the whole structure of the Secretariat is poised.

In the seventeenth century, the Abbé Fénelon suffered at the hands of the great Bossuet for the perhaps incautious expounding of religious attitudes which he had developed from his earlier exposure to the ideas of his friend Madame Guyon. Fénelon suggested that man's relationship with God was made possible by the soul's receptivity and readiness to accept His gift of love, and to become spiritually at home with Him.

In order that this spiritual conditioning could take place, man should cast off his preoccupation with personal interests, hates and desires so that his spiritual awareness could be increased and deepened, a *désoccupation de soi.* This did not mean a retreat into an ivory tower for, as a result of this spiritual conditioning, it was possible to reengage in the day-to-day business of living, with new attitudes made possible by the release of oneself from previously held prejudices and concerns. Fénelon called this quality *souplesse*

—an adaptability and flexibility which developed when the great adjustment or commitment of *désoccupation* had been made.

This disinterring of one of the eighteenth century's many religious disputes might seem to be a strange diversion from the matter in hand, if Fénelon's reflections did not help us to understand something of the adjustment and rededication demanded of the international civil servant.

When the new recruit to the United Nations is inducted, he states:

> I solemnly swear (undertake, affirm, promise) to exercise in all loyalty, discretion and conscience the functions entrusted to me as an international civil servant of the United Nations, to discharge these functions and regulate my conduct with the interests of the United Nations only in view, and not to seek or accept instructions in regard to the performance of my duties from any government or other authority external to the Organization.

This may not seem a solemn moment to him as he scrawls his signature on the printed form, together with a sheaf of others relating to his appointment. But even if he does not yet know it, this is the beginning of an act of dedication. He commits himself to serve the Organization and the international community as a whole. He can only do this by a withdrawal from involvement in many of the daily concerns of his national life which heretofore had been so important to him: a *désoccupation,* in fact. Having done this, he finds that he has acquired that degree of *souplesse* that gives him the freedom to think and act not in terms of a national of his country, but rather in terms of the long-run interests of the international community as a whole.

The change does not come in a blinding flash. For most, the period of withdrawal is the result of self-discipline, working with others in order to acquire the necessary attitudes and habits of mind, and so to become a part of the "house."

Does this mean that the international official becomes a polyglot, without roots, at home everywhere and at the same time calling nowhere home? Is he a man without a country as the French would say, *métèque?* Far from it. In the first place, it is best if he is a man of his own country. The most pervasive force in the world remains nationalism. The international civil servant must be aware of this, and how better than being an expression of it? For otherwise in setting about his job, he would be like an atheist discussing faith: he would have no experience of what he was talking about. Furthermore, having gone through the conditioning of the "house," he becomes a man who can bring to his work the wealth of tradition and accomplishment of which he is a part and a product.

Theory and practice.   Given, then, this concept of the nature of his office, how should the international civil servant comport himself? Much too has been written on this delicate matter, both by official bodies within the international family and observers without. In searching for a guide for conduct, we might do as well to look back to Bernard du Rosier who, in the fourteenth century as theorist and practitioner, laid down the precepts of behavior for the public servant. Rosier was Provost and later Archbishop of Toulouse. On Christmas Eve 1436, he finished at the Court of Castille his *Short Treatise About Ambassadors.* It was meant to serve as a handbook for diplomats. He was not only a theorist but he also had a firsthand knowledge of what he was writing about. He had been a plenipotentiary at the Congress of Arras, one of the world's first "summit" conferences.

What the diplomat should never attempt, warned Rosier, is to try to bluff, intrigue or indulge in deceit in his work, or in anyway try to bedazzle or befuddle those with whom he is negotiating. Such victories as might result are Pyrrhic, and occasion others to hold his integrity in question. Once confidence is lost, his role has ended. In his work, the public servant should always listen attentively, and however intractable the problem may seem, constantly seek for special points or areas of possible agreement. Always do the easy things first: settle the points on which agreement is readily reached; leave the harder nuts for cracking later. Always be prepared to make concessions, for without them few concessions will be made to him. But make sure that they are consistent with the dignity of his office and organization. Adapt the methods of negotiation to circumstances, but keep in mind the real issues at stake.

The public servant should press persistently but patiently toward agreement; he should never be disheartened. If possible he should reach agreement swiftly, for time is always a factor and protracted negotiations may bring with them the danger of a changing situation introducing new and disrupting elements.

Be always polite and considerate, never prod or irritate and do not make a fuss over trifles. Above all never be carried away by a vain desire to triumph, or score off those with whom negotiations take place. Seek only mutual understanding and accommodation, bearing in mind the interests of the Organization and the community of which it is an expression.

These canons of behavior (freely adapted from Rosier's advice) may well serve to illustrate the standards called for in the quiet diplomacy elaborated by Hammarskjöld and his successor.

From this international commitment, and working in the spirit of Rosier's public servant, everything else flows. In the world of man, the international civil servant needs to be a man of the world. He needs, consequently, to have a basic understanding of international society, as far as he can firsthand knowledge of the countries which are members of the Organization, and an awareness of the possibilities for institutionalized international cooperation. This calls for more than a fleeting acquaintance with governments, peoples and history, and a list of national or racial stereotypes. A deeper understanding and awareness are called for, and this can only be acquired over many years, although the process can be accelerated, as will be suggested later, by a degree of training (or would it be better to term it "conditioning"?).

The limit to a man's ability is seldom only intellectual. It is often simply a question of stamina. The man of the world has to be fit and have great stamina. He is called upon to travel huge distances at short notice in varying climates under often trying conditions. The terms of his employment often compare unfavorably with others in similar positions, and his conditions of work are often varied. Not only stamina, but as Loveday remarks, nervous energy is also required. The nature of the international official's work is such that he is often called upon to work with great concentration for sustained periods. The stresses are often considerable, and only those with this particular kind of physical and intellectual strength can emerge without strain. On occasion the work is extremely hazardous, as evidenced by the growing number of commemorative bronze plaques outside the Meditation Room at United Nations Headquarters.

It was once remarked by a distinguished United Nations director that the task of the international secretariat was to know how far to go too far. This was probably his way of defining the qualities listed by Loveday as constructive imagination and leadership. The international official who keeps in mind the provisions of the Charter has more than anyone else the responsibility of seeking ways in which the United Nations can be made a more effective tool of the international community, and of fashioning its development towards this end. For this an imaginative brilliance (not to be confused with a brilliant imagination) is called for, linked to an ability to provide discreetly and sensibly a high degree of leadership.

It is these qualities which, when properly harnessed, give to the Secretariat that dynamic spirit which has characterized so much of its work in recent years, particularly with the influx of new member nations for the most part appearing upon the international scene for the first time and finding, in this initial period, valuable assistance in an experienced and readily available international secretariat.

In theory, then, the foregoing describes some of the ideal characteristics of the international public servant. Although theory and reality rarely coincide, with some justification not only the United Nations Secretariat but also the staffs of all the agencies comprising the international family have come to be well thought of. There have been cyclical movements in this popularity, but the secular trend has been one of enhanced prestige and standing. Let us look, however, in the following order at some of the criticisms and the problems to which they are addressed: recruitment, training, supervision and conditions of service.

Recruitment. With the exception of tests for translators, there is no competitive entrance examination, such as those found in national and state civil services. To conduct such examinations would be extremely difficult to organize, and the results almost impossible to assess. Usually applications are made, the candidate interviewed and his references consulted. Critics have pointed out that these arrangements sometimes appear haphazard and result in a high turnover in staff, which is expensive in terms of investment in the recruit who does not turn out to be suitable.

A greater difficulty seems to be the need to adhere to the concept of equitable national distribution not only quantitatively but qualitatively; i.e., to maintain the concept in terms of numbers but also at the different levels of the Secretariat. This is not easy particularly when we consider the demand for indigenous skilled administrators in the public service of the new countries for whose candidates room has to be found in the Secretariat. In ensuring proper adherence to the provision of Article 101.3 in this respect, the career opportunities for advancement of the other staff members have to be borne in mind if morale is not to suffer.

By and large this issue which has occasioned perennial debate in the General Assembly has now been resolved. The complexion of the Secretariat, largely American, European and Commonwealth in the early years has now changed to a more even spread, particularly with the retirement of many of the League staff who continued with the United Nations.

Another issue, which also gives rise to an underlying question of principle, is how to maintain an international secretariat with career opportunities and have at different times the highly specialized personnel which are needed on occasion. Specialists the Secretariat must have, and these need to be brought in for short periods. To maintain them as career staff would involve the risk of building up excess capacity and with it the continued employment of experts after their specialty is no longer called for. How to maintain a balance between short-term and career staff is a delicate matter. If everyone were a short-term appointee, it would be impossible to maintain the international character and outlook of the Secretariat; to shun short-term appointments would be to introduce rigidities to staff administration which would make it difficult for the staff to bring to bear the necessary degree of competence, specialized knowledge and training in emergency or rapidly changing situations. As a rule of thumb, short-term staff should not rise above one-third of the total complement.

To be a good orator . . . What makes a civil servant loyal, efficient and hardworking? Does the secret lie in the raw material, catching the best of the crop when it is young? Or is it in the training the new entrant receives; making silk purses?

Traditionally in the best public services, the approach has been that of the Greeks. To be a good orator, you must first be a good man. By this the Greeks presumably meant that his sense of values, background, rearing, attitudes, behavior and bearing should be such as to produce a good man. Without being one, he could never carry the responsibilities or enjoy the privileges of the public orator. But this is all very well in a service where traditions are the product of generations of disinterested service, and the entrant is selected from potentially the same human material. The career service enfolds him, the landmarks are familiar, his cocoon of red tape will always protect him if, administratively speaking, he loses his trousers; the extent and nature of the tasks before him are clearly identified, and the opportunities to act and the limitations on his actions are clearly demarcated.

The international civil servant has few if any of these advantages. Would not careful induction and in-service training serve as a partial substitute? The International Labor Organization, the International Bank for Reconstruction and Development, and the World Health Organization for many years have run such training programs. The *esprit de corps* of these agencies has always been high. Whether this is due more to professional solidarity—particularly in the case of IBRD and WHO—or careful training would be difficult to determine.

By comparison, training programs in the United Nations Secretariat have in the past tended to be perfunctory. The establishment at Headquarters of a United Nations Institute for Training and Research (UNITAR) may provide the setting for the establishment of a staff college where recruits and mid-career officers may be offered intensive training and refresher courses.

Emerson on institutions. "An institution," as stated by Ralph Waldo Emerson, "is the lengthened shadow of one man." An organization is to a large extent the institutionalized personality of its head. This is true not only of the Secretary-General, the Managing Director, the Director-General or whatever he may be called, but also of all of those who have supervisory responsibilities under him.

It is not enough for a supervisor, as Churchill once referred to his own role, "to fight for his corner." In the international service, the officer with supervisory responsibilities has to care for his staff, help fashion them, foster their careers and do all he can to mold them as men better than he to be civil servants. For if the pupil is not better than his master, has not the master failed? Perhaps the critics here have been mindful of the problems that are present when a secretariat with widely diversified tasks is recruited from a world of diverse cultural backgrounds. The responsibilities of supervision, to the outsider, appear stupendous. He reckons, however, without taking into account the inherent strength of the "house."

Efficiency, competence and integrity. In twenty years the international civil service has taken great strides to meet the standards required of it by the Charter. The difficulties encountered have been partly in the nature of the task and partly man made.

The operational demands of an international organization call for a great deal of flexibility. The civil servant needs to be a Jack-of-all-trades and master of many. But in the early years the secretariats of the United Nations and many of the agencies were developed on the basis of narrow job specifications called "job descriptions," and men and women with some claim to specialized training were recruited to fill these positions. As a result a high degree of rigidity developed in the Secretariat at the expense of flexibility.

The early practice followed rather old-fashioned American concepts of public administration, and criticisms were soon levelled against these procedures.

While these practices persist here and there in the secretariats, under Hammarskjöld a determined effort was made to streamline the Secretariat and its work, and to introduce the concept of flexibility so that staff members not only could move relatively freely from one department to another, but would accept this as part of the job. The process was accelerated by events forcing the Secretariat to make such adjustments overnight. Suez, Hungary, Lebanon and the Congo found staff members at all levels working and excelling in areas of activity which, until pitchforked into them, they might reasonably have considered as falling outside their job classification.

This introduction to assuming administrative responsibilites in widely differing situations is rather more in keeping with British traditions in this respect, and oddly enough did not cause an increase in the feeling of insecurity that at times has assailed the Secretariat. On the contrary, in forcing members to make rapid psychological adjustments in a dynamic situation, it did much to weld the Secretariat into a body with a high morale and a hitherto unsuspected high degree of resilience. A staff, after all, is like an economy. When it is static or contracting, modifications are difficult; in an expanding and growing economy, there is elbow room for adjustment.

So much for some of the critics and a selection of what they consider are shortcomings in the international civil service. That there is much to study and ponder on concerning the improvement of the service few doubt. The Consultative Committee on the European Civil Service has begun an interesting study on the workings of the bureaus of the various Western European organizations that have come into existence since 1948. The heightened role of the International Civil Service Advisory Board, set up by the General Assembly to study such matters in the international family, is a sign of the importance attached to a closer examination of general working conditions, salaries and pensions.

The points touched on here, however, are pinpricks compared with the two great criticisms of the Secretariat which strike at the whole concept of the internationality of the Secretariat and its international responsibilities. The criticisms came first from the United States and subsequently from the U. S. S. R.

Commenting on the events of 1952 and 1953, Hammarskjöld stated in his Oxford address:

> Various authorities of the United States Government, host to the United Nations Headquarters, conducted a series of highly publicized investigations of the loyalty of its nationals in the Secretariat. Changes were made which, although relating to a small number of individuals largely founded upon inference rather than on direct evidence or admissions, led to proposals which implicitly challenged the international character of the responsibilities of the Secretary-General and his staff.

It was an unhappy period, and it coincided with a strong emotional reaction against the United Nations at the close of Korean hostilities. It is not the emotion of those days that concern us here but a fundamental question of principle. Can the international character of the staff be preserved if the Secretary-General no longer can make an independent evaluation of those he is considering to select for recruitment, and if he can no longer have freedom to exercise his choice? After a period of some uncertainty the independence of the Secretariat was indeed preserved.

No Secretary-General would knowingly recruit to his staff anyone who had been disloyal to his country. The Secretary-General naturally would be prepared to receive information concerning the suitability of a candidate forwarded by the government of whose country he was a national. But, in keeping with Article 100 of the Charter, the choice was that of the Secretary-General and no one else.

In 1914 Walter Hines Page, the United States Ambassador to the Court of St. James, wrote home to Washington at the outbreak of World War I that while countries could be neutral, a man could not. Walter Lippmann, when interviewing Khrushchev in 1961, reported him as saying that "while there are neutral countries, there are no neutral men." These statements place in question the premise upon which this chapter and the whole concept of the international public service is based. In giving disinterested service on behalf of the international community the international civil servant had to be impartial. This did not mean he had to be neutral. Or as Hammarskjöld humorously remarked, ". . . the civil service had to be 'politically celibate' (though not perhaps politically virgin)." In other words, one could certainly hold political opinions, but not express them publicly. As Hammarskjöld remarked in his Oxford address:

> It can fairly be said that the United Nations has increasingly succeeded in affirming the original idea of a dedicated professional service responsible only to the Organization in the performance of its duties and protected so far as possible from the inevitable pressures of national governments, and this has been done in spite of strong pressures which are easily expanded in terms of historic tradition and national interests. Obviously, however, the problem is ultimately one of the spirit of service shown by the international civil servant and respected by Member Governments. The International Secretariat is not what it is meant to be until the day when it can be recruited on a wide geographical basis without the risk that then some will be under—or consider themselves to be under—two masters in respect of their official functions.

Geographical representation. The Charter requires, in Article 101, that the paramount consideration in the employment of the staff and in determining the conditions of service should be the necessity of securing the highest standards of efficiency, competence and integrity. The Article concludes: "Due regard shall be paid to recruiting the staff on as wide a geographical basis as possible." As Hammarskjöld stated, it is ultimately the spirit of the house which will determine the standing of the Secretariat and this in turn partly depends on the extent to which the staff is recruited on a geographical basis. On the whole, appreciable attention is devoted to ensuring this, not only quantitatively but also qualitatively.

Perspective.   The experience of the Greek City States lies far back in history, yet it may be possible to see in it the origins of to-day's international public servant. The concept of an official appointed by the States to serve the interests not of one of them but of all of them was well known in the sixth century B.C. Such officials, notable among them the guardians of Delphi, were granted certain immunities in recognition of their functions. At Delphi, the meeting place of the Amphictyonic Council and the seat of the Pythian Games, the guardians of the oracle provided a source of information, a continuing presence and a unifying influence in a society whose ancient malady Herodian called "a love of discord."

Although the international civil servant is only a recent creation, his functions are similar to those of the ancient guardians. But in this century the quality, integrity and disinterested service of the international official may have a determining influence on the role of the organization he serves in furthering the integration and, perhaps, even the preservation of the international community.

Chapter VIII

THE ROLE OF LAW

Legal doctrine and jurisprudence have played a significant if not a decisive role in major issues before the United Nations. The Charter makes but fleeting reference to international law. Article 1.1 calls for conformity with the principles of international law. Article 13 refers to its progressive development and codification. In settling disputes, Article 33 includes arbitration and judicial settlement among the methods to be applied. Article 33.3 is more precise in referring to the role of the International Court, the Statute of which forms part of the Charter. But there is no overriding language in the Charter that states that the Organization, its organs or its members must be subject to the rule of law.

This is in sharp contrast to the wording of the Covenant of the League of Nations which is imbued with the idea that international order was to be upheld by law and the sanctity of treaties. Law, it might well have been thought, did not create order, but upheld it. The Charter in contrast to the Covenant, as we have observed already, is somewhat coarser in its concepts, although, perhaps because of that, more serviceable in a turbulent world.

The world of the Charter is not one of international order, as such, but rather one of international change. Karl Marx mistakenly saw national law, as being essentially an instrument of oppression and exploitation of the masses—mistakenly because he conceived law as something imposed on society by the class that held the keys to power. Marx's over-simplification, however, helps us to understand something of how international law has been regarded by many. The majority of the members of the United Nations are bent not on upholding an order of things in which many were subject peoples, but on change, rapid and fundamental. In this sense the United Nations may be seen as a body fashioned to channel peacefully and constructively the forces of revolution—for that is what rapid and fundamental change means. There is no need to shy away from this. The law was not on the side of the farmers at Bunker Hill any more than it has been on the side of their revolutionary heirs. Then, as now, law too often seemed an obstacle to change and an upholder of an outmoded order. For most sovereign states, the rules of international law were formulated before they, as states, existed. They naturally are prone to view such law as reflecting and protecting the older and more economically developed members of the international community. Recent experience by African members in attempting to use the International Court as a means of political change in South-West Africa, and in the General Assembly to prevent the World Bank from extending loans to Portuguese African territories, for example, may tend to confirm this view.

Both in theory and in practice, therefore, it would be difficult to establish that there is an acceptance of the continuing validity and binding effect of international law in the United Nations system. This does not mean, however, that the United Nations is a tool for the internationally lawless. If law does not rule, it has a role, nevertheless. The Charter itself is a multilateral treaty binding on its members, and to which the rules of treaty interpretation apply. There is a substratum of law upon which most of the work of the United Nations system is based. It lies below the surface, but an awareness of its presence permeates the United Nations in its legislative techniques, the daily use of legal instruments, of diplomatic practice and the approach of the Secretariat to its responsibilities.

In this setting we should now examine the role of the International Court of Justice, the work of the International Law Commission, the Legal Committee of the General Assembly and *ad hoc* conferences. We can then conclude by discussing the emergence of new international law as a result of the work of legal, political and economic organs of the United Nations.

Arbitration.   The horse and buggy era of the use of law in the settlement of international disputes produced the techniques of arbitration. By arbitration we mean the settlement of a dispute between states by arbitrators of their choice, who give effect to existing law and whose decision is binding on the parties to the dispute. The immediate origin of the practice can be found in Jay's Treaty concluded in 1794 between the United States and Britain, which stipulated that disputes between the two countries should be settled by arbitration. In the nineteenth century a slender structure for peaceful settlement, based on the earlier experience, began to appear.

A landmark in arbitration occurred in 1872 when the arbitration provisions of Jay's Treaty were applied to the *Alabama* claims. A commerce raider, fitted out in Liverpool for the Confederacy during the Civil War, the *Alabama* did great damage to Northern shipping before it was finally driven aground and destroyed on the coast of France. The United States rightfully claimed compensation from Great Britain for damages suffered. An award was handed down in favor of the United States, although the amount to be paid was scaled down considerably from that originally demanded.

The techniques of arbitration were further elaborated and more widely adopted as a result of the two peace conferences convened by the Tsar Nicholas II at The Hague in 1899 and 1907. While these conferences failed in their principal purpose, which was to obtain agreement on disarmament, the 1899 conference resulted in the first Hague convention for the pacific settlement of international disputes. It was widely ratified and all the Great Powers became parties to it. To date, some sixty-one states have ratified the convention. The second Hague convention of 1907, which was meant to supersede the earlier instrument, was not so widely ratified. The Permanent Court of Arbitration established by the 1899 convention provides a speedy, cheap and, if necessary, private setting in which states may voluntarily submit their differences to arbitral settlement. In association with these arbitral procedures there also developed related techniques of impartial commissions of enquiry, good offices and other methods of international conciliation.

The Court's effectiveness was soon demonstrated when Russia

and Great Britain submitted the *North Sea* or *Dogger Bank* case to arbitration. In 1904, during the Russo-Japanese war, the Tsar's Baltic fleet, sailing round the world only to be sunk on arrival by the Japanese navy at Tsushima, ran into some Hull trawlers fishing in a heavy fog on the Dogger Bank in the North Sea. Possibly thinking that the trawlers might be Japanese torpedo boats, the Russian ships shelled the fishermen and wrought considerable damage. Fortunately, there were cool heads at the helm of each government, if not on the bridge of the Russian ironclads. The incident, which inflamed opinion in both countries, was submitted satisfactorily to arbitration in 1905.

As we shall see later in this chapter, arbitration facilities are becoming increasingly available in settling international commercial and investment disputes. Also, as recently as 1962, the Permanent Court (using a commission of inquiry to assist it) took up the *Red Crusader* fishing dispute submitted to arbitration by Denmark and the United Kingdom. One of the attractions of the Permanent Court of Arbitration is that recourse to the court is voluntary. The unhappy reception accorded by the General Assembly to the International Law Commission's attempt to bring up to date the outmoded Hague conventions, by drafting its own convention on arbitral procedure, was to some extent based on the provisions to make recourse to arbitration mandatory. There is no doubt that the U. S. S. R. and the socialist states of Eastern Europe, which are parties to the 1899 convention, find the voluntary nature of that convention's stipulations more acceptable.

It has to be recognized, however, that much of the procedure of the Court is outmoded. As early as the original Hague Conference, it was pointed out by a United States representative that the court was neither permanent nor a court, as it was not composed of judges in permanent session. Also, it has never been integrated into the United Nations system, although its work is closely linked with the activities of the United Nations. But the Court's functions were, to a large extent, taken over by the Permanent Court of International Justice in 1920.

The International Court of Justice. Established at the same time as the League of Nations, the Permanent Court of International Justice with its seat at The Hague functioned throughout the interwar period until the German occupation of the Netherlands in 1940.

At Dumbarton Oaks, the Great Powers recommended that the new international organization to be established should have an international court associated with it. At San Francisco, where some of the judges of the Permanent Court participated in an advisory capacity, the old Statute of the Permanent Court was revamped slightly to form part of the Charter of the United Nations. The word "Permanent" was deleted from its title. Provision was made for the court to sit elsewhere than at The Hague, although it has never done so. (It has on one occasion—the *Corfu Channel* case— sent a committee of enquiry.) The Optional Clause, Article 36, was redrafted and shortened, although it is not quite clear why this was done.

With these small modifications, the present Court, in 1946 rose from the ashes of the Permanent Court to become the principal judicial organ of the United Nations. This continuum is important, for the Court today follows the procedures of its predecessor and its jurisprudence forms a significant part of the growing body of public international law. Members of the United Nations become automatically parties to the Statute of the Court and, following prewar practice, non-members of the Organization can become parties on conditions determined by the General Assembly on the recommendation of the Security Council. Non-members are also encouraged to use the Court whether or not they are parties to the Statute.

The extent of the rule of law is measurable against the extent of the judicial function. In spite of the General Assembly periodically enjoining members to use the Court, there seems to be a remarkable reluctance to do so. In the first ten years after World War II, fewer cases were heard than in the first year of the old Permanent Court after World War I. Between 1946 and 1967, the present Court has decided thirty-four cases and has given thirteen advisory opinions.

Litigation, internationally as wel
business and there is a natural tende
we have become increasingly aware
dispute which are, by nature, non-j
gredient in almost all disputes but, in
states prefer to seek political compr
tion rather than submit their dispu
on their possibly limited legal merits.

The judicial function. The sc
national Court were described in C
touch on them again. The Court, with its fifteen judges, nine or
whom make up a quorum, sits in permanent session except for the
somewhat generous legal holidays. Decisions are taken by a majority vote of those judges present and voting. For reasons of sickness, death or for reasons which are not readily apparent, the bench
is not always full. The President, in the event of a tie, as in the
South-West Africa case in 1966, has a casting vote. He not only
presides over the Court, but he is the chief administrative officer as
well.

Judges serve a nine-year term and represent the world's principal
legal systems. No two judges can be nationals of the same state.
They are elected by the General Assembly and the Security Council,
voting separately. This is a somewhat bizarre arrangement and
should be changed. In contentious cases, the Court itself may also
appoint *ad hoc* judges, one from the country of each litigant if
they are not already represented on the bench. In the United States
there remains a link with the Permanent Court of Arbitration in that
the individuals comprising the American group on the Court's
panel of arbitrators are those who nominate candidates for election
to the International Court.

The staff of the Court is called the Registry and this comprises
the Registrar, Deputy Registrar and other officials. The Registrar
negotiates a good many procedural matters with the parties in contentious cases. He sits robed on the bench with the judges and
occupies, together with his deputy, positions of importance and
considerable prestige.

as two functions. It decides on cases brought before
dvisory opinions. States may seek the judgment of the
interpretation of a treaty; any question of international
existence of a fact which, if established, would constitute
ach of international obligation; and the nature and extent of
reparation to be made for a breach of an international obligation.

The General Assembly, or the Security Council, may request
an advisory opinion on any legal question. Other organs of the
United Nations and the Specialized Agencies (with the exception of
the Universal Postal Union which has its own arrangements for
arbitrating its disputes) may request advisory opinions within the
scope of their activities when authorized to do so by the General
Assembly.

In cases brought before it, the Court's decisions are binding.
With the exception of the *Corfu Channel* case, when Albania refused to pay the damages awarded to the United Kingdom by the
Court, all other judgments have been respected, and generally upheld by international lawyers. Advisory opinions are not legally
binding on states and are often the subject of controversy as in the
Certain Expenses of the United Nations case. But within the United
Nations system advisory opinions, particularly on constitutional
matters, have been of major significance.

The reluctance of states to accept without reservation the compulsory jurisdiction of the Court was recognized when the original
Statute of the Permanent Court was drawn up. For that reason
Article 36 was inserted and except for some minor editing was
retained in the Statute of the present Court. By virtue of this article,
parties may accept the jurisdiction of the Court with, or without,
reservation.

Article 36 reads as follows:

> 1. The jurisdiction of the Court comprises all cases which
> the parties refer to it and all matters specially provided for in
> the Charter of the United Nations or in treaties and conventions
> in force.
> 2. The states parties to the present Statute may at any time
> declare that they recognize as compulsory *ipso facto* and with-

out special agreement, in relation to any other state accepting the same obligation, the jurisdiction of the Court in all legal disputes concerning:

    a. the interpretation of a treaty;

    b. any question of international law;

    c. the existence of any fact which, if established, would constitute a breach of an international obligation;

    d. the nature or extent of the reparation to be made for the breach of an international obligation.

    3. The declarations referred to above may be made unconditionally or on condition of reciprocity on the part of several or certain states, or for a certain time.

    4. Such declarations shall be deposited with the Secretary-General of the United Nations, who shall transmit copies thereof to the parties to the Statute and to the Registrar of the Court.

    5. Declarations made under Article 36 of the Statute of the Permanent Court of International Justice and which are still in force shall be deemed, as between the parties to the present Statute, to be acceptances of the compulsory jurisdiction of the International Court of Justice for the period which they still have to run and in accordance with their terms.

    6. In the event of a dispute as to whether the Court has jurisdiction, the matter shall be settled by the decision of the Court.

The Connally Amendment, inserted by the Senate into the declaration by which the United States accepted the compulsory jurisdiction of the Court, excludes "disputes with regard to matters which are essentially within the jurisdiction of the United States of America as determined by the United States of America." Whether subjective reservations of this kind are consistent with other provisions of the Statute of the Court, notably Article 36.6, is open to question and the executive branch of the United States Government has frequently criticized the action of the Senate. Other states have now followed the example of the United States. Such reservations do indeed heavily erode the authority of the Court and would reduce its role to a relatively minor one. As a result, certain judges of the Court, notably in the *Norwegian Loans* case, have challenged the validity of such reservations.

Between the wars, vigorous campaigns were launched to encourage governments to accept compulsory jurisdiction without reservation. A greater understanding of the judicial function has led many interested in the development of international society to be less insistent on this point. Not all reservations nullify, or even substantially reduce, the competence of the Court. Moreover, international law is still, in many areas, of a fragmentary nature and, not being subject to a superior body as courts are under most national constitutions, there is no control over the degree to which the Court can exercise its discretion. Many states, therefore, are not prepared to enter lightly into an arrangement by which they accept the Court's compulsory jurisdiction without reservation.

"The aristocracy of the robe." Alexis de Tocqueville, writing of America in the early nineteenth century, spoke of the respect for lawyers and the law. This was not only because of the traditional attachment of Americans to keeping their actions lawful, but also because the Supreme Court is the supreme interpreter of the law of the land, and the practice of judicial review is a central feature of the Constitution. In the United Nations, none of the Principal Organs is supreme. It was suggested by the Australian delegation at San Francisco that the Court be given compulsory and final authority to interpret the Charter. The U. S. S. R. position was that the Court should not have jurisdiction in this matter. The Australian motion was defeated and it was agreed that each Principal Organ should interpret the Charter for itself. The interpretation of one organ should not be binding on another.

Problems of conflicting decisions of different organs and each body interpreting the Charter in its own way do not in fact present a major problem. This is mainly due to the fact that the Secretariat of the United Nations acts as the guardian of the Charter. Imbued with the concepts of the Charter and serving as the repository of legal wisdom relating to its interpretation, the Secretariat can, for the most part, make shift for itself without recourse to the Court. Much of this work falls on the distinguished Office of Legal Affairs which, in addition to transacting a vast amount of legal business, is responsible for the registration of treaties.

In recent years, however, beginning in 1960 with the *Constitu-*

tion of the Maritime Safety Committee of the Inter-Governmental Maritime Consultative Organization case, interest has been renewed in this "gap" in the Charter over the legal effects of possible illegal acts committed by international organizations. In the absence of compulsory recourse to a suitable machinery for determining whether such acts are illegal and of any clear rules to be followed in such situations, the legal validity of the actions of international organizations cannot always be challenged. As has been stated above, advisory opinions can be requested of the Court and, on occasion, the United Nations and, less frequently, the Specialized Agencies have used the Court to obtain such opinions. But recourse is not compulsory and the opinions are not legally binding. This arrangement may be compared with that contained in the three treaties establishing the European Community where judicial review is both compulsory and inescapable.

In spite of these institutional shortcomings, we should, because we are concerned with the development of the United Nations system, end our discussion of the International Court by reviewing two recent judgments of considerable constitutional significance to the United Nations: the *South-West Africa* cases and the *Certain Expenses of the United Nations* case.

A procedure in utter futility? On 4 November 1960, two applicants, Ethiopia and Liberia, filed proceedings and, in brief, accused the Government of South Africa of violating its duties as mandatory of South-West Africa by practicing *apartheid* and other policies of racial discrimination. The Applicants were in fact asking the Court to find that the League of Nations mandate was still in force; in the allotment of status and rights on the basis of race, color, national or racial origin, South Africa had violated the mandate; South Africa had also violated the mandate by militarizing the area; and that it was South Africa's duty to accept, as mandatory, the supervision of the United Nations.

South-West Africa, as we saw in Chapter VI, became a C mandate under the League with the then Union of South Africa becoming the mandatory, with authority to administer South-West Africa as an integral part of the Union under its own laws. It will be recalled that Article 77.2 of the Charter provided that it would be a matter of subsequent agreement as to which mandates would be brought under the United Nations trusteeship system and upon what terms. No such agreement was reached by South Africa and the United Nations.

There was, therefore, a certain ambiguity concerning the relationship of the territory to the United Nations. The General Assembly decided to obtain from the Court clarification on this matter. In the original *South-West Africa* case, the Court, in its advisory opinion of 11 July 1950, stated that the League of Nations mandate remained in force and the obligations assumed by the Union of South Africa still applied. Here the Court gave an opinion which, in the view of Lord McNair then President of the Court, amounted to a piece of "judicial legislation" for the Court had stated that although the League of Nations no longer existed, the obligations assumed by South Africa under the mandate survived. While South Africa was under a duty to comply with the mandate, the Court found that South Africa was not under legal obligation to place the territory under trusteeship. Two further advisory opinions were sought by the General Assembly on this matter in 1955 and 1956.

The mandate agreement entered into by the League with South Africa required the Union, in article 2, paragraph 2, "to promote to the utmost the material and moral well-being and the social progress of the inhabitants of the Territory. . . ." Under article 7 of the mandate, it stated that the Union agreed to submit to the Permanent Court of International Justice any dispute with "another member of the League of Nations relating to the interpretation or application of the provisions of the mandate. . . ."

In 1960, at the second conference of the independent African states held in Addis Ababa, the institution of proceedings was recommended. Subsequently, the United Nations Committee on South-West Africa lent support to the proposal. As Ethiopia and Liberia had been members of the League, the Applications were filed by them.

The filing of the Applications formally instituted proceedings by the Court. These were then circulated to other governments which, in the opinion of the Court, ought to receive them. There then followed the fixing of dates for the submission of written proceedings which, in the practice of the Court, take the form of "Memorial" and "Counter-Memorial." The Applicants filed their Memorials which constitute one volume of the Court's proceedings. The Respondent, South Africa, made preliminary objections to the Court's jurisdiction. In December 1962, the Court having considered these objections, rejected them by eight votes to seven. The Respondent then filed its Counter-Memorial in ten volumes. The Applicants submitted a one volume Reply which was answered by the Respondent with a two volume Rejoinder.

By March 1965, the Court was able to open a series of ninety-one sittings of oral proceedings which ended in November 1965. The Court then adjourned to deliberate and prepare the decision which was given on 18 July 1966.

The Court in its judgment stated, in effect, that the two Applicants had no legal standing in the case, which was consequently dismissed. The question was whether under the mandates system, the various mandatories had any direct obligation toward other members of the League individually. The Court considered that they had not. If this general right of individual members had not been enjoyed during the period of the League, the Court considered that it certainly could not apply now. Rights could not be presumed to exist merely because it might seem to be desirable that they should. The Court, the judgment stated, was not a legislative body. Its duty was to apply the law as it found it, not to make it.

The votes of the judges were equally divided: seven-seven and the President, Sir Percy Spender of Australia, gave his casting vote in favor of the rejection of the Application. When giving its judgment, the Court follows the practice of appending dissenting opinions and separate opinions (for judges, while agreeing with a judgment, may have concurred for reasons other than those given in the judgment). In this case, each of the seven dissenting judges wrote a dissenting opinion and the President appended a declaration.

The judgment was surprising and disappointing. The surprise

may have been occasioned by the apparent reversal by the Court of its earlier decision. In 1962, the Court had overruled the objections of South Africa and stated that it had jurisdiction in the matter. In 1966, it stated that the Applicants had no standing. The Court saw no inconsistencies in the positions it took for, as it stated, ". . . it was an almost elementary principle of procedural law that a distinction had to be made between, on the one hand, the right of a court to examine the merits of a claim and, on the other, the plaintiff's legal right in respect of the subject matter of the claim, which it would have to establish to the satisfaction of the Court."

Was this all, then, as Judge Philip C. Jessup of the United States wrote in his dissenting opinion "a procedure of utter futility?" To the newcomer, this may appear so. But the voluminous proceedings of the Court provide a tremendous body of knowledge, which must surely be studied by anyone seriously concerned not only with the future of South-West Africa, but of plural societies elsewhere. To decry the role of the Court also underestimates the contribution of the dissenting opinion. In the history of the Court we find that the lively dissenting opinion has added, on occasion, as much to the body of international law as the judgment itself.

With the dismissal of the *South-West Africa* case, the question of the future of the territory was promptly taken to the General Assembly which, in an unprecedented resolution, adopted a declaration stating that the mandate was no longer in force and that South-West Africa would become the direct responsibility of the United Nations until the territory became independent. A committee was established promptly to report to a Special Session of the General Assembly in 1967 on how the United Nations should give effect to the declaration.

Certain expenses of the United Nations. In Chapter III, the advisory opinion of 20 July 1962 on the question of certain expenses of the United Nations was described in its institutional and in Chapter V in its political setting. We should now take this advisory opinion and examine, in the juridical context, how the Court came to give it.

The request was put to the Court by the General Assembly by

its resolution of 20 December 1961. By nine votes to five, the Court declared that the expenditures authorized in certain General Assembly resolutions, relating to United Nations operations in the Congo and the Middle East in pursuance of Security Council and General Assembly resolutions, were "expenses of the Organization" within the meaning of Article 17.2 of the Charter. Three judges appended to the opinion of the Court statements of their separate opinions. Five other judges appended their dissenting opinions.

The President considered that members of the United Nations were likely to furnish information on the question and set 20 February 1962 as the time limit within which the Court would receive written statements from them. Twenty members submitted statements. From 14 to 21 May 1962, the Court heard oral statements by the representatives of ten members. It then deliberated upon these statements and the material submitted to it by the Secretary-General and delivered its advisory opinion.

The General Assembly, when voting to ask the advisory opinion of the Court, had tabled before it a French amendment which would have asked the Court also for its opinion on the validity of the Security Council and General Assembly resolutions that gave rise to the expenses in question. This amendment was defeated, but the Court took note of it and did not exclude this question from its deliberations. In fact, in the oral proceedings a group of members including France, Czechoslovakia and the U. S. S. R. stated their position to the effect that if the United Nations Emergency Force was set up in violation of the Charter, there was no obligation to meet its costs.

The Court, in its advisory opinion, agreed that if an expenditure were made which was alien to the purposes of the United Nations, it could not be considered "expenses of the Organization." If the action incurring these expenses were undertaken by the wrong organ, then it would be irregular, but not necessarily improper. Also if the Secretary-General incurs financial obligations acting on authority of the Security Council or the General Assembly, the United Nations "has no alternative but to honor these engagements." The opinion at this point touched on the question of legal effects of illegal acts referred to earlier in the present chapter.

It had been argued that the Court should refuse to give an opinion because the question posed by the General Assembly was political not legal. The Court cited two of its earlier advisory opinions and one of its predecessor, the Permanent Court and found no compelling reason why it should not give an advisory opinion as it could not attribute a political character to a request which invited it to interpret a treaty provision, for the Charter is a multilateral treaty.

The Court then turned to identifying what are "expenses of the Organization." It found that neither the Charter nor the United Nations in practice had made a distinction between "administrative" and "operational" budgets. It followed that "expenses of the Organization" were not restricted to "regular expenses."

It had been argued that matters of peace and security were the concern of the Security Council and not of the General Assembly. The Court replied that the Security Council had primary but not exclusive responsibility under Article 24 of the Charter. The General Assembly was also concerned with peace and security and the powers and functions of the Security Council did not exclude the General Assembly from having powers to provide for the financing of measures designed to maintain peace and security.

The point had been raised that action in these matters could only be taken by the Security Council. The Court found that the action referred to in Article 11.2 related to enforcement action which, under Chapter VII of the Charter, was in the province of the Security Council. But the expenses arising from the General Assembly resolutions were not for coercive purposes, but to use our distinction, were for peacekeeping activities not for peacemaking.

The Court went further and examined the actual expenditures involved. The UNEF expenses did not arise from enforcement action, nor did the expenses in the Congo (Kinshasa) which arose from Security Council authorizations. Subsequent confirmation by the Security Council and the General Assembly pointed to the conclusion that the actions in the Congo did not usurp or infringe upon the prerogatives of the Security Council.

The Court summed up by pointing out that the text of Article 17.2 could lead to the conclusion that the "expenses of the Organization" were the amounts paid out to defray the costs of carrying out the purposes of the United Nations. The examination of the resolutions authorizing the expenditures led the Court to the conclusion that the question submitted must indeed be answered in the affirmative.

This is a partial summary of the advisory opinion. It is given here to show something of the processes of the Court and how it deliberates. The opinion itself and the constitutional and political appropriateness of seeking the opinion in the first place will long be discussed.

Law and politics. The Court, although its role so far has not been as significant as that of its predecessor, nevertheless has not hesitated to reach decisions which as we have seen above, have had far reaching implications for international society and the United Nations system. The question has been raised, however, whether the Court has always limited itself to legal considerations only, or whether, on occasion, the positions taken by some of the judges have seemed to reflect more the current policies of the governments of the countries of which they are nationals. It has been noted, for example, that in the *Certain Expenses of the United Nations* case, only the judge from the United Arab Republic voted against the position taken by his government. But it should be borne in mind that while the Court has wisely refused to be deterred from dealing with matters which have a heavy political content, it has also refrained from remedying deficiencies if, by so doing, it would have exceeded the bounds of normal judicial action.

The International Law Commission. One of the four standing bodies of the General Assembly, the International Law Commission, has grown in size from fifteen to twenty-five. Its members are not appointed as representatives of governments, but sit in their capacity as experts in international law. The tasks of the Commission are to give effect to Article 13.1(a) of the Charter which calls for the progressive development of international law and its codification. In spite of an activity which seems to have been somewhat desultory in its early years, the Commission has become recently the object of increased interest to international lawyers.

Progressive development of international law leads the Commission to explore those areas where existing law is fragmentary or not clear. Codification involves standardization and clarification of existing law and practice. It has not always been easy to distinguish between the twin roles of the Commission. Codification of law leads inexorably toward its progressive development. In either case, the work of the Commission is usually directed toward the preparation of drafts, which represent the degree of common ground established by legal experts of widely different backgrounds.

Not only are governments grudging in their willingness to accept sharper definitions of their legal obligations in the international community but, by the nature of the Commission's role, much of its work is bound to be subject to protracted discussion, after which it may be postponed or even abandoned. Such has been the fate of the draft declaration on the rights and duties of states, the definition of aggression and the establishment of an international criminal court. Even so, this work is not entirely fruitless as it is part of the gradual process of clarification of existing law, the identification of law that may be obsolete and the groping toward new concepts.

In the progressive development of law, one of the Commission's early tasks given to it by the General Assembly, when the Commission began work in 1949, was to prepare a draft code of offenses against the peace and security of mankind. This arose from the earlier action, in 1946, by the Assembly when it affirmed the Nuremberg principles used by the International Military Tribunal for the prosecution of the major German war criminals.

"Statelessness," which became a widespread problem for many persons displaced by World War II was also referred to the Commission, which recommended two draft conventions on the elimination or reduction of statelessness.

On the initiative of the Secretary-General, the Commission considered what procedure should be followed on reservations made by states as conditions of their adherence to or ratification of conventions. The Commission recommended a procedure which, it considered, would be most convenient for states to adopt.

The Commission has also selected topics for codification. These include arbitral procedure, referred to earlier in this chapter, consular relations, the law of the sea, diplomatic intercourse and immunities. Some of these subjects after being pursued by the Commission, as we shall see below, have led to *ad hoc* conferences being convened to conclude major international agreements.

For some years, the Commission has devoted attention to the law of treaties, a topic of lively interest to international lawyers. A law of treaties may result in the validity of certain treaties being questioned because their subject matter violates some general principles of international law. Some international lawyers question the wisdom of this as, given the fragmentary nature of much international law, the invocation of such a principle may provide a legal excuse for defaulting on international obligations by parties to treaties which have become in their eyes onerous or inconvenient. (Similar questions were raised in the League of Nations when discussion centered on the definition of aggression. Rather than serving as an instrument of the law-abiding, an accepted definition of aggression might serve as a signpost for the potential law-breaker pointing the way how to commit aggression without breaking the law.) In 1968 an international conference is to be held to consider the Commission's proposals on the law of treaties. Doubtless this aspect of the problem will be discussed.

The Legal Committee of the General Assembly. The Assembly's Sixth Committee considers a wide variety of legal subjects. Unlike the International Law Commission, the representatives of the Sixth Committee are government delegates rather than individual experts. Part of the time of the Committee is devoted to a discussion of reports submitted by the ILC, such as the law of treaties. The subjects debated, however, are extensive. For example, items discussed by the Committee during the 1967 session included—apart from the law of treaties—territorial asylum, legal aspects of friendly relations, fact finding, aggression, diplomatic privileges and immunities and technical assistance in the wider appreciation of international law. It should be emphasized that the role of the Committee in the progressive development of international law has been substantial.

Ad hoc conferences.   The fourth main arena where international law is furthered is in the *ad hoc* conference. Such meetings may be convened for the drawing up of international instruments on a wide range of matters. Others may be more modest in their scope but significant in their particular field. In 1953, for example, the International Chamber of Commerce drew the attention of the Economic and Social Council to difficulties encountered in obtaining the international enforcement of commercial arbitral awards. A League of Nations convention had been adopted concerning commercial arbitration, but its provisions needed bringing up to date, and arbitral awards which hitherto had been valid only in the country in which the award had been given, needed to be applied internationally. In 1958, the United Nations Conference on International Commercial Arbitration adopted and opened for signature a convention under which contracting states undertook to enforce arbitral awards made in the territories of other states. In the following year the Convention entered into force.

Other conferences have had much wider responsibilities and we should refer to three of them: one on the law of the sea; another on diplomatic intercourse; and the third on investment disputes.

Law of the sea.   To Hugo Grotius and others, the law of the sea was one of the less complicated matters on which to write in their treatises on international law. The sovereignty of a state extended in the sea as far as its land power could be felt. Shore batteries had a range of about three miles. The "three-mile limit" thus came to be generally accepted as the extent of a state's territorial waters. Beyond that were the High Seas. Gulfs and bays running into the territory of a single state were also commonly regarded as territorial waters even if their width at the point of junction with the sea exceeded six miles, e.g. Chesapeake Bay. Also, it was generally accepted that the littoral or "marginal sea" and its sea-bed were subject to the sovereignty of the state adjacent to it.

In more recent times, what constitutes territorial waters has been the subject of wide variation. Off-shore fishing areas have often been included in the jurisdiction of the neighboring state, and as the International Court found in its judgment on the *Anglo-Norwegian Fisheries* case, territorial jurisdiction was not a matter of legal principles only but also of the economic significance of the fishery to the two parties. Also, the adjacent sea-bed has been claimed as being under the sovereignty of a state, particularly where oil might be available in commercial quantities. The need to reach agreement on these matters was pressing and, after much preparatory work, eighty-six countries were represented at the first Conference on the Law of the Sea held in Geneva in 1958. The Conference adopted four conventions and an optional protocol which were then opened for signature.

The Convention on the Territorial Sea and the Contiguous Zone sets out criteria for delineating territorial waters, establishes rules for the right of innocent passage and sets out the conditions under which this right can be exercised or suspended. The Convention on the High Seas sets out the conditions under which the freedom of the high seas may be exercised. The Convention on Fishing and the Conservation of the Living Resources of the High Seas contained regulations on the conservation of marine resources and a procedure for the settlement of fishing disputes. The Convention on the Continental Shelf concerns the sea-bed and the exploitation of its resources such as oil and pearls. The optional protocol is the legal underpinner to these conventions, providing for the compulsory settlement of disputes that might arise from them by recourse to the International Court, by conciliation or arbitration.

A second conference was convened in 1960 to continue the consideration of questions left unsettled by the first conference. These included the breadth of territorial waters and the extent of fishing limits. The conference failed to adopt, by one vote, a convention permitting states to claim six miles of territorial waters, and six additional miles of fishing zone. Practice continues to vary; for example, the United States adheres to the traditional three miles, and the U. S. S. R. claims twelve.

Diplomatic practice.   In 1815 at the Congress of Vienna, after twenty-five years of revolutionary wars and the Napoleonic Imperium, the European powers drew up a peace settlement that was not to suffer a major breakdown for one hundred years. Advantage was taken of the occasion to tidy up a number of international matters that were in urgent need of attention. Many different practices had been allowed, some of them rusty with age, and to some medieval cobwebs still clung. At Vienna, a new set of ground rules were drawn up and adopted. Surprisingly liberal and enlightened in approach, in spite of the then gathering clouds of obscurantism, the *Règlement* of the Congress drew up new rules for diplomacy and brought into being standards and practices which are adhered to today. Nevertheless, to take another look at these matters every 150 years would seem called for in a rapidly changing world, even though the forms of diplomacy have not changed that much.

After careful preparation under the auspices of the International Law Commission, the United Nations Conference on Diplomatic Intercourse and Immunities met in Vienna in 1961. Eighty-one countries were represented. A convention entitled *The Vienna Convention on Diplomatic Relations* was there adopted and opened for signature. Its fifty-three articles cover practically every important aspect of diplomatic relationships between states. The Convention entered into force in 1964 when twenty-two instruments of ratification or accession had been received by the Secretary-General. Two optional protocols to the Convention were also adopted at Vienna dealing with supplementary diplomatic matters and these also entered into force in 1964.

Investment disputes.   An increase in the international flow of private as well as of public capital is generally considered as one way in which to assist underdeveloped countries in accelerating their economic growth. Potential investors, however, have often been deterred from investing in the under-developed countries due to a feeling of uncertainty regarding the repatriation of their earnings and worry that their holdings may be the object of expropriation without adequate compensation. Some under-developed countries, while recognizing the need for capital, are often startled by what they consider to be unreasonable demands for guarantees, or the high level of return expected by the foreign investor. Various proposals have been discussed in the United Nations and elsewhere on how to improve the climate for international investments and to develop greater measures of mutual confidence between the investor and the recipient country.

As an attempt toward promoting an improved climate for the flow of international private capital, the World Bank Group, whose activities are described in Chapter XI, has taken the techniques of arbitration referred to earlier and has extended them to cover international investment disputes in an extremely novel way.

After three years of preparatory work including consultations at a series of regional preparatory meetings with government legal experts in Africa, Latin America, Europe and Asia, a convention on the settlement of investment disputes between states and nationals of other states was opened for signature by all members of the World Bank. The convention entered into force on 14 October 1966. Its title is descriptive if cumbersome. The new treaty establishes in Washington an international center for the settlement of investment disputes. It is under the control of an administrative council composed of representatives of the contracting states. Its chairman is the President of the World Bank.

The novelty of the convention lies in the provisions for arbitrating investment disputes not between states, which are the traditional objects of international law, but between states and foreign investors who are nationals of other states (which, of course, are parties to the convention). A dispute between such individuals and a state may be submitted to the international center for arbitration. Arbitral awards are to be binding not only on the parties but are to be recognized by all contracting states. As an alternative to arbitration, the parties may apply to the center for a conciliator in which case due consideration must be given to his findings.

It is significant that the breaking of new ground in international law should be under the sponsorship not of a legal body but of a major international financial institution. For, as we may find, recent innovations in international law have emerged, not exclusively from legal organs in the United Nations system, but also from the work of the political and economic organs.

Crossing the Rubicon. An original feature of the 1966 *South-West Africa* case and one of considerable significance to the development of both international law and the United Nations system was the presentation of the Applicants' case by Ernest Gross, an American lawyer. Whether or not South Africa had contravened its "sacred trust" as mandatory to promote the well-being of the peoples involved by introducing *apartheid* into the territory was not in question. ". . . the value judgment of the organized international community whether *apartheid* is 'good or bad' has already been made," he stated. "It has been made by the organized international community acting and speaking through the competent organs." Gross was referring to the many resolutions of the General Assembly and other political bodies which have repeatedly condemned this practice.

This can be cited, with the *Expenses* case, as an occasion on which the Court had been asked to base its judgment not so much on the facts as submitted in evidence, as on the legal norms which may be derived from United Nations resolutions. We are not concerned whether the Court, if it had taken judgment, would have followed this argument. Our purpose is rather to focus attention on the emergence of customary international law through the political and economic organs of the United Nations.

Custom emerges from usage. Gradually, or quite quickly, individual practices or standards become widely, if not uniformly, adopted. It would be difficult to point out at what precise moment usage becomes custom. As the noted international lawyer, Sir John Fischer-Williams put it, "The Rubicon between usage and custom is crossed silently and in the night." It might be stated, however, that the two requirements of customary law are that it should be extensively practiced and that there should be a general conviction that there is a legal obligation to follow the practice.

The sources of international law are not many. To those who seek an enhanced role for international law, the actions, resolutions and the debates of the United Nations and the specialized agencies provide a quarry from which can be hewed occasional nuggets of customary law. In many situations it may be possible to derive a "common standard of right" which is such an essential ingredient of law. These normative standards may be found in the work on human rights which is discussed in some detail in the following chapter. The General Assembly resolutions on Algeria, Hungary, *apartheid* and on the treatment of peoples of Indian origin in South Africa have played a similar role. United Nations decisions on domestic jurisdiction, on the use of peacekeeping forces and on statehood, although mainly political in content, have a legal ingredient which has contributed to customary law.

The legal component emerges with greater clarity in the activities of the United Nations in international trade, international commodity agreements, fiscal and financial policy, and transport and communications. To find additions to customary international law, we must seek increasingly among the decisions, actions and resolutions of the United Nations or its agencies. An excellent example of how this law does develop can be found in the recent actions of the United Nations regarding outer space.

The need to develop rules for the peaceful use of outer space has been a subject of concern in the United Nations since the nineteen fifties. The prospect that the moon might become the object of a power scramble, in the same way Africa was in the nineteenth century, was a frightening if distant prospect. The 1959 Antarctica treaty served as a basis for much of the discussion. This treaty provides that Antarctica shall be used only for peaceful purposes and shall have no military bases. It opens up the whole area to inspection by parties to the treaty.

In 1961 the General Assembly adopted its first resolution on the establishment of a regime for outer space, taking analogous international law and the principles of the Charter as guides. A committee on the peaceful uses of outer space then concerned itself with formulating basic legal principles on this subject. Members made their views known on rights and obligations of exploration, the use of space vehicles and space stations, the landing on celestial bodies and assistance to cosmonauts and spaceships, including liability for space vehicle accidents. A second resolution was unanimously adopted by the General Assembly in 1963.

The legal norms which emerged from these discussions provided the basis for the treaty on outer space, which entered into force late in 1967. The treaty prohibits the placing of nuclear weapons or other weapons of mass destruction in orbit, on the moon, or on other celestial bodies. It forbids claims to sovereignty on the moon and the planets, and ensures that all celestial stations are open to inspection. The treaty requires the prompt and safe return of cosmonauts to their native lands but holds the owners of space vehicles liable for any damage caused by them. The success of this endeavor which had such unlikely chances at the beginning may now encourage the Organization to explore similar possibilities for the adoption of an international regime for the ocean floor, before military and commercial aspirations extend international tensions to deeps which have so far been the exclusive preserve of science fiction.

Public international law traditionally has been the sum of rules accepted by states as determining their conduct towards each other and towards each other's subjects. We have seen in this chapter how international law develops through actions of judicial bodies, positive agreement expressed in multilateral conventions, and in usage, when it is sufficiently generally acceptable to give rise to custom. But with the emergence of the United Nations system and of other international bodies outside the United Nations, a new branch of international law is developing which applies to the international institutions themselves.

In an important advisory opinion in 1949, the *Reparations for Injuries* case, the Court affirmed the international personality of the United Nations. This represented an early recognition of the status of the United Nations not only in regard to its members but in the international community. From its beginnings, however, the United Nations had entered into agreements with the Specialized Agencies (see Table 4 in Chapter XI, p. 247); its members were usually parties to the United Nations Convention on Privileges and Immunities; and the United Nations had concluded a headquarters agreement with the United States.

Today, the United Nations Development Program has concluded a host of technical assistance agreements and Special Fund basic agreements to provide the legal basis upon which assistance is made available to the economically developing countries. Special agreements have also been concluded to provide for international administrative personnel under the OPEX scheme which is discussed in Chapter XII (p. 270).

The peacekeeping operations in many different parts of the world, described in Chapter V, have required carefully drafted and delicately negotiated agreements regarding the use and presence of United Nations forces. International trade agreements, United Nations sponsored common market treaties such as those now in force in Central America, and the vast array of international economic, commercial, transport and communications, social welfare and emergency relief operations agreements involving directly international institutions, have now given rise to a considerable body of precedent and interpretation which has become generally recognized as law.

We began this chapter with a reference to Marx and his half-truths. We might now return, if not to him, to the philosophical speculations of his time. The political philosophy of the nineteenth century was distinguished from the leisurely speculations of the Enlightenment of the eighteenth century by a sense of urgency. After the revolutionary turbulence that had engulfed much of the world for more than a generation, Comte, Cousin, Hegel and Marx in their different ways sought to provide an active, normative discipline. These nineteenth century positivists tried not so much to explain the world as to change it.

A generation after World War II, as we shall see in Chapter X, there is developing an awareness of an international economy and a sense of common responsibility for it. In a more inchoate way we saw, in Chapter V, how the growth of mutual confidence can result in the first steps toward arms control. A high official of the International Labor Office, Wilfred Jenks, in his writings has shown us how, as the international community is knit tighter together with the extending functions of the United Nations and its associated agencies, it is possible to discern, in those widespread and continuous activities, the glimmerings of what one day may become a common law of mankind. Given the historic role of the jurist even before Grotius in the development of international society, could we not look to our lawyers for the new international positivists?

Chapter IX

A GREAT
WILD GOOSE CHASE?

. . . nothing has done more harm to the Organization in general . . . than the great wild goose chase after human rights. No country is innocent in this matter, neither the United States, which pressed at San Francisco for human rights provisions in the Charter, nor the Soviet bloc, which exploited them with a magnificent indifference to the beams in their own eyes, nor the Latin-Americans, who found here ideal nourishment for their rhetorical appetites, nor the Anglo-Saxons, who, false to their tradition of realism in things liberal and humanitarian, joined with the rest in the collective admiration for the Emperor's new clothes. Thus a cowardly conspiracy developed to gloss over the inherent absurdity of an organization of governments dedicating itself to protect human rights when, in all ages and climes, it is governments which have been their principal violators. Logic and experience were thrown to the winds in extending the concept far beyond anything any court could enforce to cover anything which any state (particularly those with least respect for human dignity) happened to think desirable. When in 1948 the General Assembly gave endorsement without dissentient voice to the Declaration of Human Rights, words came as near to being emptied of meaning as at any time in the history of the Organization. When verbal promissory notes had to be changed into the harder legal currency of conventions some healthy misgivings appeared, but too late to save years of verbiage to which no end is in sight.

So wrote H. G. Nicholas in his book *The United Nations as a Political Institution* in 1959. Of the many vigorous denunciations of the work of the United Nations, this well-known attack by a distinguished writer needs to be examined. For Nicholas, while having strong views, expresses with some eloquence the opinion of many. In this chapter, we shall consider whether or not the pursuit of human rights is a great wild goose chase.

That the international community should seek to establish rights and to take steps to see that they are observed is not without precedents. In the seventeenth century, as a weary Europe turned away from religious wars, and tolerance of different sects became widespread, major international settlements, such as the Treaty of Westphalia in 1648, reflected the changing mood and included guarantees of religious rights. The tolerance foreseen by Sully in his letters to Henry IV became an accepted feature in much of the life of Western Europe.

Intervention by the Great Powers. Armed intervention to protect minorities, once a frequent occurrence, is a practice which exposes the rescuer to strong criticism. This has always been the case, particularly in situations where protection may appear to shield political motivation. In the nineteenth century, the Great Powers on several occasions intervened on behalf of racial and religious minorities in order to secure for them a measure of protection. The Orthodox Christian subjects of the Sublime Porte were the frequent objects of intervention in the Ottoman Empire by France, Great Britain and Russia. In Bulgaria, Montenegro and Syria, Christians were massacred, and the Great Powers intervened. In 1815 at the Congress of Vienna, steps were taken to guarantee civil rights to Jews in the German Confederation. Later Austria, France, Great Britain and the United States intervened to protect the Jews in Rumania. Much of this action was taken as a result of personal representation by concerned individuals. Not the least of these was Baron Hirsch, the European "Railway King" who, at the Congress of Berlin in 1878, lobbied vigorously and effectively for the protection of Jews on the European continent. In the early years of our century the Great Powers intervened in the Congo when the treatment of the Congolese by the Belgian authorities became known through the revelations of Sir Roger Casement.

With less effect did the Great Powers attempt to prevent the periodic massacre of Armenians in the Ottoman Empire over the turn of the century.

It was not until the Treaty of Versailles and the creation of the League of Nations that the rights of minorities received institutional guarantee. With the breakup of empires, particularly that of Austria-Hungary, and the subsequent creation of succession states, the principle of self-determination triumphed. The newly independent states, however, included within their frontiers many minority groups. Czechoslovakia, for example, included both Hungarians and Sudeten Germans as well as Czechs and Slovaks. The Versailles settlement made detailed provisions for the protection of such minorities. This was felt to be necessary for, in several cases, the ruling power had passed from dominant races to former minority groups which, in turn, were now rulers over population pockets comprising ethnic groups which formerly were dominant.

Treaties were devised to ensure that each new state pledged itself to give equal and fair treatment to all its subjects. The League was appointed as an international watchdog to see that these guarantees were honored. When new countries such as Iraq, Finland and the Baltic States joined the League, similar undertakings were exacted from them.

Initially, as we might expect, national pride being what it is, the countries whose minorities were under the protection of the League did not take too kindly to what was regarded as a slur on their capacity to govern justly. But in time some leaders, such as Beneš of Czechoslovakia, saw in the role of the League an opportunity to demonstrate before the international community that fair play indeed prevailed in their countries.

Twelve states came under the scrutiny of the League as part of its responsibility to protect minorities. This was exercised by the Council, whose minorities committee met in closed session to discuss allegations of infringements of minority rights. If, as a result of the discussion, matters were put to right, no further action was taken. If they were not, then the Council gave the allegation a public airing. When the prestige of the Council was high, its role on behalf of minorities was often an effective one. In its decline, the League's role degenerated to that of a mere onlooker.

"A commerce so odious." International action was most vigorous and effective when it was taken to crush the slave trade. At Vienna in 1815, the peacemakers took up the question of the slave trade, and the European powers adopted a strongly worded "Declaration Relative to the Universal Abolition of the Slave Trade." Subsequently, in 1822 at Verona, the Concert of Europe decided on immediate steps to suppress it. After 1920 international responsibility in these matters was assumed by the League and later by the United Nations. The emphasis in the League, however, was on the protection of minorities. It was not so much concerned with the broader issues of human rights. In 1919, a Japanese proposal that the Covenant should contain specific provisions relating to racial equality was not accepted, although the Covenant referred to the need for just treatment of colonial peoples and fair and humane conditions for workers.

In R. L. Stevenson's *Travels with a Donkey* he recounts, almost laconically, how he met a worker whose facial bone structure had been eaten away as he followed "the fatal calling of a maker of matches." "Phossy Jaw," was a disease that afflicted those who worked in factories where matches were made of white phosphorus. In 1906, at a conference in Berne, the first international labor conventions were opened for signature. One of them prohibited the use of white phosphorus in the making of matches. This was the first international convention directed toward safeguarding the worker. This task was taken up by the International Labor Office which on its inception in 1919 moved with vigor to impress upon governments that it was imperative that the rights of workers should be observed. In the 1920's particularly, ILO, with the dramatic leadership of Albert Thomas, led countries to adopt humane conditions and to require that employers observe decent standards of employment. Although the United States did not, until 1934, become a member of ILO, its very existence was the work of

Samuel Gompers, Professor James Shotwell and Felix Frankfurter.

An audacious innovation. At San Francisco the United Nations committed itself to an act of faith. Without defining them, and ducking the question of where they come from, members pledged themselves to promote and encourage respect for human rights and for fundamental freedoms for all without distinction as to race, sex, language or religion. These words were included in the statement of the Purposes of the United Nations (Article 1.3) and were repeated in Article 55 (c).

In a world profoundly marked by pluralism and wide cultural divergence, the provisions of the Charter regarding human rights represent an audacious innovation. These provisions call for: first, the establishment of norms and second, the building up of guarantees to protect the individual against arbitrary acts by the civil power. These, in turn, raise the question of universal intervention by the international community through the United Nations into matters which might well be regarded by its members as within their domestic jurisdiction, and thereby falling outside the scope of the United Nations.

The Charter, in Article 68, explicitly foresees the establishment by the Economic and Social Council of a commission "for the promotion of human rights." As we saw earlier in Chapter II, the Commission on Human Rights was set up as a functional commission of the Council. Under the chairmanship of Eleanor Roosevelt, it began work in January 1947. As its primary task it engaged in the preparation of a declaration of human rights in order to give substance to Charter provisions.

Stronger than all the armies of Napoleon. The work of the Commission on Human Rights culminated in the adoption by the General Assembly on 10 December 1948 of The Universal Declaration of Human Rights (see Appendix 2).

The Universal Declaration was adopted by the General Assembly appropriately enough in Paris. For it was there, on 27 August 1789, that the original Declaration of the Rights of Man was adopted to form the basis of the French constitution and to act as a beacon light for peoples everywhere. It would help us to place the United Nations declaration into focus if we look back for a moment to the adoption of its eighteenth-century precursor.

Declarations of principle are much more in the American and French traditions than the British which is, perhaps, one reason why H. G. Nicholas is somewhat allergic to the United Nations declaration. The Declaration of Rights adopted by the British Parliament after the "Glorious Revolution" of 1688 was not a clarion call to mankind to break its fetters. It was merely a restatement of the historic and legal rights of Englishmen against the Crown. Consequently it was a pragmatic, businesslike document drawn up to meet certain specific needs as seen by Parliament on the occasion of the Crown being vested in the two sovereigns, William and Mary.

The British Declaration of Rights differs considerably from the American Bill of Rights. These amendments to the American Constitution are a statement of general principles, couched in noble language drawn up not only to regulate the power of the state with regard to the individual, but as a statement of aspiration toward the good society.

The French Declaration of the Rights of Man is also a statement of general principles, but it is addressed not only to Frenchmen but to men everywhere. It was drawn up after protracted discussion by the Constituent Assembly when that body might have given priority to the more immediate and pressing tasks of government. But, like Wilson at Paris in 1919 who saw to the completion of the Covenant before turning to the urgent problems of peacemaking, the revolutionary leaders in Paris made sure that their first care was to state to the world what they were about.

The triumphant declaration of principles is one thing: to turn them into harder legal tender quite another. In fact the revolutionaries found them increasingly inconvenient. When we consider what followed in France, we might with some truth state that there was never in national history a greater disparity between principle and practice.

The utopian vision. The Universal Declaration of Human

Rights adopted by the General Assembly, in addition to a lengthy preamble, is composed of thirty articles laying down civil, political, economic and even social and cultural rights. The Declaration was adopted unanimously by the fifty-eight members represented at that session of the General Assembly. Forty-eight voted in favor, two were absent and eight abstained. The abstentions were from Arab states and South Africa.

In its articles the Declaration sets forth basic rights and fundamental freedoms to which all men and women everywhere in the world are entitled without discrimination. The civil and political rights follow those of the Declaration's illustrious French predecessor. These include the right to life, liberty and security of person; freedom from servitude and slavery, from arbitrary arrest and detention; the right to a fair trial by an independent and impartial tribunal; the right to be presumed innocent until proved guilty; the inviolability of the home and secrecy of correspondence; freedom of movement and residence; and the right to own property.

The Declaration enlarges further on the right to a nationality: the right to marry and found a family; freedom of thought, conscience and religion; freedom of expression and opinion, and freedom of peaceful assembly and association. The Declaration includes the right to vote and to participate in government. It goes on to encompass what for many must seem to be far-reaching social and cultural rights including the right to social security, to work, to an adequate standard of life, to education and to participation in the cultural life of the community.

In proclaiming the Universal Declaration, the General Assembly spoke of it as "a common standard of achievement for all peoples and all nations." The General Assembly did not state that it was a common standard *of* all peoples and nations but *for* all peoples and nations. It is a noble statement of aims to which all should aspire, and as such it reveals the United Nations in its utopian role.

The twilight zone. What is the Declaration? Is it law? Is it just another resolution unanimously adopted? Whatever it is, it is a great human document which cannot be disregarded. The civil, legal and political rights for the fortunate may be taken for granted.

They are part of the fabric of society and can only be laid aside or suspended in times of national emergency. But nowhere are all the rights and freedoms listed in the Declaration guaranteed. For example, equal pay for equal work, holidays with pay and social security are not to be encountered in any community as automatic rights, but as a product of the economically-advanced society which also has a particular social outlook.

The Declaration is neither legally nor technically binding. A resolution of the General Assembly is not in itself an enactment of law. It is not a treaty. Does this matter? After all, human rights exist and are furthered in a wider framework than that which the law by itself can provide. By its Declaration the General Assembly had completed one of the tasks implicit in the Charter, which was to establish norms. This having been done the United Nations needs to ensure that these rights and freedoms are not only furthered but safeguarded.

"The harder legal currency." The United Nations is still on the long, hard road which leads from the Declaration to the codification of its provisions to make them lawful and binding upon members. Following the adoption of the Declaration, the Commission on Human Rights turned its attention to the preparation of draft covenants. These the Economic and Social Council sent to the General Assembly in 1954.

Ten years later, the General Assembly, mainly in its Third Committee (Social and Humanitarian), was still engaged in the conversion of the Declaration into international instruments. It was agreed that there should be two such treaties: the Covenant on Civil and Political Rights and the Covenant on Economic, Social and Cultural Rights. Although as late as 1963 the General Assembly reaffirmed its belief that final adoption of the draft International Covenants on Human Rights was urgent and essential for the universal protection and promotion of human rights, it was not until 1966 that the conventions were adopted.

Both these covenants contain a preamble, general provisions, substantive articles, measures for implementation and final clauses. The preambles and final clauses are very similar in both covenants.

The substantive articles of the Covenant on Civil and Political Rights are taken from the relevant articles of the Declaration, as are the substantive articles of the Covenant on Economic, Social and Cultural Rights.

There is a significant difference between the obligations to be assumed by the parties to the covenants. For the Covenant on Civil and Political Rights, states which become parties to that Covenant would undertake immediately to respect and ensure the rights laid down. Where these rights were not effective immediately, the state concerned would take steps to give effect to them. The obligations are less stringent for parties to the Covenant on Economic, Social and Cultural Rights. The rights embodied in this instrument would be achieved progressively through legislative and other action to the maximum of the available resources of each party.

The provisions for ensuring implementation of the provisions of the covenants also are somewhat different. For civil and political rights, a Human Rights Committee would be created to which a state, party to the Covenant in question, could complain if it considered another party was not meeting its obligations. Possibly drawing on the experience of the League Council's minorities committee, it is considered that the Human Rights Committee should be mainly a fact-finding body which could, if necessary, make available its good offices to the states concerned. If a satisfactory solution were not reached, either state could bring a case before the International Court of Justice.

Consistent with the less onerous provisions of the covenant on Economic, Social and Cultural Rights, the arrangements for their implementation would not be so exacting. Compliance with the provisions of this covenant would be the object of periodic reports to the Economic and Social Council.

As has been noted earlier, the ambitious list of rights and freedoms which was accepted as a statement of aspirations in 1948 looks rather different when converted into legal obligations. This, to some extent, was resolved when the General Assembly in 1952 decided to separate civil and political rights from the rest by having two draft instruments. The civil and political rights might well receive wider acceptance once they stand by themselves. But the wide range of even these rights, however variously they might be interpreted in different cultural settings, may give many states cause to approach the covenant with reserve.

Along the hard road from Paris, the drafters of the covenants have found that the going has been made harder by picking up along the way bits and pieces for inclusion which did not form part of the original Declaration. Such additions as an article on the rights of the child or another concerning freedom from hunger are probably generally acceptable. The main difficulty has been encountered with the wish of the majority of members to include in the covenants a statement on the right of peoples to self-determination. This right would give to peoples freedom to determine their political status and freely to pursue their economic, social and cultural development. Moreover, such a right provides that peoples may freely dispose of their natural wealth and resources. Thus the drafters have been drawn into the anti-colonial discussion, and the covenants have become a vehicle of colonial emancipation. It was the addition to the preamble of each draft covenant of an article on the right of peoples to self-determination that more than any matter lengthened the debate on the draft instruments.

Cause to reflect may also be found in the arrangements for ensuring implementation. The Charter provisions excluding matters within the domestic jurisdiction of a member from coming within the scope of the United Nations, except when such matters might be a threat to the peace, have been heavily eroded as the United Nations has evolved. In fact, we have seen how, if enough members feel strongly enough, issues of domestic jurisdiction go by the board. The General Assembly in 1952 and 1953 made its views known on the alleged presence of forced labor in Eastern Europe. The treatment of persons of Indian and Pakistani origin in South Africa and the whole question of *apartheid* as practiced there have been matters on which the General Assembly has been most vociferous. Not only have niceties of domestic jurisdiction been disregarded, but also when a matter was *sub judice* the General Assembly has acted. This occasion was in 1963 when political prisoners were on trial in South Africa and the General Assembly requested the government "to abandon the arbitrary trial . . . forthwith. . . ."

While many members might be prepared to contribute to a diplomatic consensus condemning what to them may be an arbitrary and cruel act, it is unlikely that a government would be prepared to adhere to an international instrument that would give any other party to the treaty a right to bring to international attention (and possibly an international tribunal) allegations that it was defaulting domestically in not complying with obligations entered into internationally. Regardless of their willingness to expose themselves to this kind of situation, many states with a federal structure such as Australia, Canada, India and the United States might encounter considerable constitutional difficulty in assuming, federally, obligations which may be more within the purview of their constituent states. The two conventions, by early 1968, had received more than thirty ratifications.

Wider observance. Simultaneously with the codification of the Declaration, the United Nations has continued to work on a broad front towards the wider observance and furtherance of human rights. The Declaration itself has been the spearhead of this effort and we should review how the Declaration has found its way into international and national life.

The Declaration made its international debut when it featured in the preamble to the Japanese Peace Treaty signed in San Francisco in 1951. When the territorial dispute over Trieste and the surrounding area was finally resolved between Italy and Yugoslavia with France, Great Britain and the United States underwriting the settlement, the Special Statute of 1954 stated that the provisions of the Declaration would apply to the populations concerned.

When, in 1950, former Italian Somaliland was placed by the United Nations under Italian trusteeship for ten years, the Declaration featured in the trusteeship agreement; and in 1960 when the Trust Territory joined with the British Somaliland Protectorate to form the Republic of Somalia, the new constitution stated that the provisions of the Declaration would be adopted as far as practicable.

Many of the new constitutions which have been drawn up since 1948, if they do not make specific reference to the Declaration, are in many cases profoundly influenced by it. The constitution of Libya (1951) and the constitutional arrangements for Eritrea (1952) show the influence of the Declaration. Beginning with the 1956 statute to provide for an "Autonomous Republic of Togoland," many constitutions such as that for the Republic of Guinea (1958) and the Cameroons (1961) affirm their attachment to the Universal Declaration of Human Rights. Since then, twelve African states, formerly under French administration, have similarly expressed their adherence in the preambles to their constitutions. When, in 1962, the former Belgian Trust Territory of Ruanda-Urundi achieved independence as Rwanda and Burundi, their constitutions referred to the inspiration of the Declaration. The constitutions of Nigeria (1960), Sierra Leone (1961) and Uganda (1962) contain a bill of rights which can be traced to the influence of the Declaration, as can the Preamble to the constitution of Tanzania. It will come as no surprise that the United Nations experts charged with the task of drafting a federal constitution for Congo (Kinshasa) in 1962 included a bill of rights based on the provisions of the Declaration.

The African example has been followed elsewhere in the world. In Europe, court decisions have shown how the Basic Law of the German Federal Republic has been based on the Declaration, and the 1958 French Constitution in its preamble included reference to the Declaration with its own 1789 Declaration of the Rights of Man. The constitutions of Cyprus (1960), of Jamaica, and of Trinidad and Tobago (both 1962) contain references to fundamental rights which are embodied in the Declaration.

In both municipal and international law, the Declaration has not been cited very often for reasons related earlier. In the lower courts of the United States, the Declaration has been cited on a few occasions as well as in the Penal Chamber of the Supreme Court of the Netherlands. Belgian, Italian and Filipino courts have

also cited the Declaration. The International Court has never referred to the Declaration in a judgment or an opinion. Such references as have been made were made in dissenting opinions only.

Genocide. While the Declaration was the spearhead, action
was taken by the United Nations in other and more specific ways
to carry out the tasks implicit in the Charter. In 1946, with the
horror of the concentration camps and mass deportations still fresh
in the minds of many, the United Nations acted swiftly to bring
the crime of genocide (a word uncoined in 1945) under international law.

The Convention on the Prevention and Punishment of the
Crime of Genocide was adopted by the General Assembly in 1948
and entered into force in 1951. It condemns all acts with intent
to destroy, in whole or in part, a national, ethnic, racial or religious
group as such. As its title implies, the Convention is designed not
only to prevent, but also to punish such acts. All who are guilty
must be punished, "whether they are constitutionally responsible
rulers, public officers or private individuals."

A growing body of international legislation. Several other international conventions on specific matters bearing on human rights
have entered into force in recent years. The Convention Relating
to the Status of Refugees and the Convention Relating to Stateless
Persons entered into force in 1954 and 1960 respectively. The old
1926 League convention on slavery and the slave trade was replaced
by a new convention in 1956, covering also institutions and practices resembling slavery. This Supplementary Convention on Slavery,
the Slave Trade, and Institutions and Practices Similar to Slavery
entered into force the following year.

Not all such instruments enter into force. Three draft conventions on freedom of information and another on the status of stateless persons have not been completed. In such cases, the General
Assembly may embody their provisions in a resolution or adopt
them in the form of a declaration as in the case of the Declaration
of the Rights of the Child and the draft Declaration on the Right
of Asylum.

The record of achievement is impressive, particularly when

joined with that of the ILO which, together with the United Nations, has studied questions relating to forced labor. In 1957 the International Labor Conference adopted a Convention on the Abolition of Forced Labor. In 1948 it adopted the Freedom of Association Convention and the Right to Organize, and in 1949, the Right to Organize and Collective Bargaining Convention.

Women.   The Commission on the Status of Women has been successful in drafting international conventions concerning themselves. The Convention on the Political Rights of Women was the first of the conventions of the United Nations relating to human rights to enter into force. This was in 1952. The Convention on Consent to Marriage, Minimum Age for Marriage and Registration of Marriages adopted in 1962 by the General Assembly came into force in December 1964. This latter convention, while not having any enforcement provisions, has been the object of a resolution in the Economic and Social Council. It calls on the states which are parties to the convention to report to the United Nations on the measures they take to adopt its provisions.

A living document.   When Hammarskjöld remarked that the Universal Declaration had "acquired an authority and growing importance," he was drawing attention to the way the Declaration, drawn up and adopted at a very dark period in international life in 1948, had become widely recognized and increasingly adopted in the following years. Pope John's *Pacem in Terris* (1964) refers to its influence. The Charter of the Organization of African Unity of 1963 refers to the Declaration as providing a solid foundation for peaceful and productive cooperation. The European Convention of Human Rights and the machinery established by it are drawn directly from the United Nations Declaration. Within the United Nations its influence permeates the house. The 1960 General Assembly Declaration on the Granting of Independence to Colonial Countries and Peoples represents a major development as far as the Declaration is concerned, and requires us to reconsider the binding nature of the Declaration itself.

An occasion for individual appeal.   ILO has for many years had an efficient machinery to deal with individual petitions regarding alleged infringements of trade union rights. Similar but less effective arrangements were set up by the Economic and Social Council to receive petitions in the United Nations from individuals concerning allegations of infringements of human rights. Many thousands are addressed annually to the Secretary-General. They are referred to the governments concerned and to the Commission on Human Rights.

Action programs. Some members, such as the United States, for domestic reasons encounter difficulty when it comes to being parties to the growing body of international conventions in human rights. The United States has not become a party, for example, to the Genocide Convention. This does not mean that they are less concerned with them. The United States has sought to express its own interest by fostering action programs by which the United Nations through its technical assistance, advisory and expert services can assist countries in the observance and furtherance of human rights. A first step was taken in 1955 when, at the invitation of the outgoing government of Costa Rica, a distinguished international mission observed the elections in that country. It reported favorably upon them and made some suggestions for improving the electoral law. A modest program, but carefully administered, can have a far-reaching impact in countries expressing a willingness to participate.

Some Scandinavian countries and, in 1965, the United Kingdom have found that with the increase in the responsibilities and authority of the public service, situations arose where civil authority on occasion transgressed civil rights. To ensure that these are redressed, Parliament has appointed an Ombudsman. He is a distinguished individual with considerable independence and extensive influence. Allegations of infringements of civil rights, which by their nature cannot find redress too appropriately in a court of law, may be addressed to him. These are examined promptly and matters are put to right speedily should his findings suggest that the individual has been wronged. Many countries are now examining the Scandinavian experience with a view to making similar appointments.

The proposal of the Philippines delegation at San Francisco that there should be appointed a United Nations Attorney-General to see that the human rights provisions of the Charter were observed is again being examined. If human rights are furthered not so much by the law but by their being pursued within a wider social framework, where social attitudes rather than the law as such determine behavior, is there not a case for the international Ombudsman rather than for an international attorney-general?

Discrimination and minorities. One of the most active subsidiary bodies of the Commission on Human Rights is its subcommission on the Prevention of Discrimination and the Protection of Minorities. It has studied collectively, and through *rapporteurs* usually selected from among its members, the status of human rights throughout the world. The emphasis in the subcommission work is on the prevention of discrimination rather than on the protection of minorities. This tends to point up a difference between the United Nations and the League. Today we are concerned with human rights; yesterday—albeit at a much lower level of significance—with the protection of minorities. But should minorities today be completely excluded from the purview of the United Nations? Perhaps they should; for viewed through nationalist spectacles, heterogeneity is often assumed to be homogeneity. And for the international community to place under special and public scrutiny the condition of minorities would be to give international recognition to their existence, and thus possibly introduce domestically and internationally divisive influences.

Chapter X

MORE ECONOMIC
THAN SOCIAL

It was largely due to the representations of the smaller powers that at San Francisco the Economic and Social Council was elevated to the status of a Principal Organ. In 1939, the League of Nations' Bruce Committee, making recommendations for the improvement of the League's machinery, had proposed that an economic and social council be established. Special attention could be given by such a body to furthering international economic and social cooperation. At Dumbarton Oaks only the United States had shown special interest in giving such a body prominence in the new international organization.

Happily the Charter in its final form reflected the recommendations of the Bruce Committee in this respect. The Charter included the Economic and Social Council as a Principal Organ with its own major substantive functions, as well as broad responsibilities for coordinating the activities of the various technical and specialized agencies already in existence or for which plans were already being made. In the present chapter, we shall discuss the first of these responsibilities: In Chapter XI, the second.

Article 55 of the Charter states the objectives of the United Nations in furthering international economic and social cooperation. Articles 57–59 describe the Council's responsibilities in drawing the specialized agencies into a relationship with the Council and in coordinating their activities. Articles 61–72 spell out the composition, functions and powers, and procedure of the Council.

Compared with it's coordination provisions, the Charter is almost laconic when it comes to describing how the Economic and Social Council was to carry out its own substantive and formidable responsibilities. It is empowered to make or initiate studies on international economic, social and related matters and may make recommendations on them to the General Assembly. The Council may also prepare draft conventions for submission to the General Assembly, and convene international conferences on matters within the Council's competence.

In its early, formative period, the Council erected an elaborate framework within which to pursue its tasks. In addition to its own committees (economic, social coordination, non-governmental organizations, etc.), it embarked upon not only a functional decentralization of its activities, but a regional one as well. Each one of these functional and regional commissions, as they were created, became a center of initiative for the proliferation of activities.

The venturer into a labyrinth, however intrepid, enters at his peril, unless he has studied the ground plan beforehand. We should do this now before we examine the work and achievements of the United Nations in furthering international economic and social cooperation and providing a center for the harmonization of national policies.

Functional commissions. Beginning with the Economic, Employment and Development Commission and its subcommissions, the Council moved rapidly to establish functional commissions for statistics, transport and communications, population, social matters, the status of women, narcotic drugs and, in 1954, for international commodity trade. (The Commission on Human Rights and the Commission on the Status of Women, having been discussed in the preceding chapter, are not included in references in the present chapter.) These bodies, which initially met annually, are composed of government representatives whose qualifications are given a perfunctory scrutiny by the Council. The commissions' tasks are generally to consider those matters within their terms of reference and to advise the Council on what recommendations it should make concerning them.

While these commissions provided useful service in the early days of the Council in identifying problems and proposing what action should be taken regarding them, the commissions did not fully meet the changing needs of the Council. The wide range of subjects covered by a commission often exceeded the collective competence of the representatives, however well qualified. In other bodies the discussions too often mirrored the debates in the Council proper. After ten years of experience the Council, as part of a vigorous streamlining exercise, discontinued some of the functional commissions and placed others on a biennial cycle of meetings, so as to enable the Secretariat to make more effective preparation for them.

The Transport and Communications Commission was discontinued. This Commission had continued much valuable work originated by the League of Nations. But it was not always easy for a representative to bring special technical competence to bear on such a wide range as, say, the transportation of dangerous goods, the pollution of sea water by oil, road signs and signals, and ocean freight rates. Also, the Economic Commission for Europe assumed much responsibility for inland transport matters and, with the creation of the Intergovernmental Maritime Consultative Organization (IMCO), maritime matters were transferred to the new Specialized Agency.

Narcotics. One commission which has not diminished in importance over the years, because of the increasing quantities and widening range of narcotic drugs illicitly entering international trade, is the Commission on Narcotic Drugs, and we can use this as an example of a functional commission at work.

Once upon a time there was no difference between the licit and illicit trade in harmful drugs. Warren Hastings, the first Governor-General of British India, in surely an imperishable dictum, stated "Opium is a pernicious article of luxury for use in foreign commerce only." Today, the world's licit demand for narcotic drugs is known and catered to. But the illicit trade is large and is directed toward the United States and a few other countries where the illegal use of habit-forming drugs is a source of continuing anxiety.

The Commission is concerned with all kinds of narcotic drugs.

Those that are the subject of widespread smuggling are raw opium and its opiates (such as morphine and heroin), cocaine and cannabis (Indian hemp). Other drugs are more localized in their use, such as the chewing of the coca leaf in the Andes. More recently, the introduction of synthetic drugs, which are habit-forming, has extended the scope of the Commission's work.

In 1909 at Shanghai the first international conference on narcotic drugs met. The first international convention in these matters was drawn up at The Hague in 1912. In 1920 the League of Nations began to take the first steps in its attempt to establish an international control system. Several international conventions entered into force under the auspices of the League, which was entrusted to supervise past and future agreements on controlling the drug traffic through its Advisory Committee on the Traffic in Opium and Other Dangerous Drugs, a body, incidentally, in which the United States participated actively.

In 1925, the Permanent Central Opium Board was established. It continued in operation until 1965. Its tasks were to examine the statistics submitted to it by governments, to estimate the volume of the traffic in opium, and to identify areas where opium was being accumulated and where leakages might occur. The Board was empowered to recommend that sanctions be applied against recalcitrant countries. This weapon was seldom used, but the knowledge that such quasi-legal measures were at the disposal of the Board was efficacious in itself. The procedure supervised by the Board was that an exporter of opium could only do so with a license issued by his government. This application would, in each case, have to be accompanied by an import certificate issued by the government of the importing country.

The effect of these measures was to divert the traffic in opium to countries either outside the control system or to those where the administration was either too venal or inefficient to apply the necessary measures. The international control system, in any case, was limited to the requirements of opium for medical purposes.

In 1931, a further convention established the Drug Supervisory Body. Meeting twice a year, this four-member body made projections of the world's opium needs and then assigned production quotas to the producing countries. In the event of noncompliance, the Drug Supervisory Body informed the PCOB which then took action. There were, therefore, two bodies, one supervisory and the other administrative, set up by the League under its Advisory Committee on the Traffic in Opium and Other Dangerous Drugs.

This Committee became the United Nations Commission on Narcotic Drugs. Its representatives are drawn from the main drug-producing countries and those that are the main targets of the illicit traffic. In twenty years it has introduced a more positive approach to the control of narcotic drugs. Advisory services to governments on improving their control systems, assistance in introducing alternative crops in areas where income is mainly derived from growing drug-producing crops, and closer relations with the International Criminal Police Commission on the identification of smugglers—all have played their part.

Additional international conventions have been adopted. But of greatest importance has been the untangling of the accumulation of international legislation with the drafting of the Single Convention on Narcotic Drugs which entered into force in 1964. The PCOB and DSB were replaced by the International Narcotics Control Board. While the convention extends control to the cultivation of plants which contain the raw materials of certain drugs, the legislation is realistic in that it provides for the progressive outlawing of such drugs over a period of fifty years.

Expert bodies. Not every functional commission has had such a colorful history, although others have been extremely effective. The Statistical Commission, for example, less obtrusive in its work, has given guidance on the assembling and dissemination of statistics in accordance with the various classifications it has led the world to adopt.

The Economic and Social Council, nevertheless, has turned increasingly to the convening of *ad hoc* committees, or groups of experts for specific purposes, rather than relying on the functional commissions. Where expert opinion is required, the Secretary-General is asked to bring together experts, often acting in their individual capacity, to advise on what action may be needed on certain matters. The first group of this kind was the one whose 1949 report, National and International Measures for Full Employment, provided the mainspring for much of the Council's activity in this area of its responsibilities. This pattern of work, more flexible, more economical, and much more specialized, has tended to overlay that of the functional commissions.

Regional commissions. In any global organization, there are bound to be regional tendencies. We saw something of these proclivities during the war years in the making of the Charter. As the United Nations developed, the regional tendencies developed almost entirely in the economic rather than the political sphere. They were encouraged, not by the Great Powers as had at one time seemed possible but by the small powers, particularly those that were economically underdeveloped and relatively new to membership in the United Nations. The regional economic commissions have attracted a great deal more attention than any of the Council's other subsidiary bodies, and have been a more satisfactory forum for the discussion of economic problems of the underdeveloped countries, if for no other reason than that they felt that they were not so overshadowed by the Great Powers who, in several cases, were not included in the commission's geographical scope.

ECE, ECAFE, ECLA, ECA. In 1947, with Gunnar Myrdal as its first Executive Secretary, the Economic Commission for Europe was established with its staff housed in the *Palais des Nations* in Geneva. The Economic and Social Council created this Commission to facilitate the reconstruction of Europe, to raise the level of economic activity of European countries and to strengthen their economic relations. The Marshall Plan followed soon afterwards, leaving the Commission with only residual reconstruction responsibilities. Through its main committees and a host of working parties and technical groups, however, the Commission has worked constantly towards a pooling of economic and technical experience, a sharing of common problems and a center where European cooperation in practically every economic sector could be furthered, even in the harshest days of European political differences.

The Economic Commission for Asia and the Far East (ECAFE) was established by the Council in the same year with its staff based eventually in Bangkok. Under the auspices of the Commission, which like that of ECE meets annually, economic experience has been shared and useful technical work accomplished, particularly through its Bureau of Flood Control. As an outgrowth of the activities of the latter, the massive effort to develop the resources of the lower Mekong River, with large-scale bilateral and international financial and technical support, has been a landmark of ECAFE's activities. The harnessing of this experience and competence to the proposed major international program for the reconstruction and development of Southeast Asia, could open the way for a happier future for the peoples of this area.

Of more immediate significance, however, is the Asian Development Bank, which opened its doors in 1966, with its head office in Manila. The Bank was established as a result of initiatives taken by the Commission.

In the following year (1948) the Economic Commission for Latin America, based in Santiago, Chile, was established. Meeting biennially the Commission has emerged as the main center of economic competence and experience in South and Central America. It has provided advanced training for Latin American economists and, through its trade committees and working parties, has formulated the concept of a Latin American common market and has fostered its development, as well as the economic integration of the Central American republics.

In 1958, the Economic Commission for Africa held its first session in Addis Ababa, where it is now based. Serving a continent where most countries have only recently become independent, the Commission provides a forum for examination of common problems and the sharing of experience. Its work is directed toward providing the new countries with the services, assistance and training in economic development, planning and related matters, of which African members find themselves in such urgent need.

The African Development Bank, with its head office in Abidjan, Ivory Coast, was established in 1965 as a result of the Commission's activities. It is now fostering other regional African programs, including the development of an African telecommunications system to supplement the overloaded Africa-Europe circuits established as part of the old colonial links with the metropolitan powers.

The regional commissions served by secretariats, whose members to a large extent are recruited from the regions they serve, have naturally developed strong regional ties. Recent representation in the Economic and Social Council and the General Assembly have forced increased recognition of these centrifugal tendencies to a point where decentralization of development programs has had to take place, requiring some major administrative adjustments in the headquarters Department of Economic and Social Affairs of which the regional secretariats form a part.

NGOs. The relationships of the Council extend to private groups, termed by the Charter "non-governmental organizations." For the most part, they are international associations such as the International Chamber of Commerce, World Federation of Trade Unions, religious bodies and smaller national groups with special interests. The Charter foresees a two-way system of consultations between the Council and the NGOs but the Council has only occasionally availed itself of the opportunity.

The role of these organizations in raising matters in the Council, however, and in unobtrusive lobbying, has been significant. Private groups have always played their part at international gatherings. The Charter simply gives recognition to this and institutionalizes the ways in which this cooperation can take place.

The Council and the General Assembly. To complete our examination of the framework for economic and social cooperation, a reference should be made to the place of the General Assembly. As in the case of other Principal Organs, the Council's role has not been enhanced by the lack of precision concerning the responsibilities of the General Assembly. The Charter requires that the Council shall perform such functions within its competence in carrying out the recommendations of the General Assembly. It may, with the Assembly's approval, perform services at the request of the members of the United Nations and at the request of the Specialized

Agencies. It shall also perform other functions as are specified in the Charter or as may be assigned to it by the Assembly.

The General Assembly established two committees, one to deal with economic and financial items, and the other with social and humanitarian items. As the membership of the General Assembly came to include an increasing number of economically underdeveloped countries who use the Assembly as a forum for making their needs known, the Council, with a membership which has kept a modicum of balance between the developed and the underdeveloped, has been frequently overshadowed by the Assembly whose debates have been characterized by a greater sense of urgency.

The setting in which the Council and its related bodies have evolved is different from and considerably more complex than that envisaged by the Charter. As we have seen, the language of the Charter and the preparatory activities leading to its adoption, clearly established economic and social cooperation as one of the main components in the global strategy to establish peace and security in the postwar world. Those responsible for drafting the Charter accepted, almost without discussion, the theory that war had economic causes and that their elimination was a prerequisite to peace. Fortunately this argument is now purely academic. It has become academic as a result of various interrelated forces at work in the world, which have caused the United Nations to give great prominence to economic and social cooperation, particularly to assistance in the development of the economically developing countries.

Of greatest significance is the persistence of the economically developing countries in forcing recognition by the developed countries of their responsibilities to assist in the process of economic development, and to enable the less developed to participate in world trade on more equitable terms. To a large extent these countries, which now comprise an overwhelming majority of the United Nations membership, have been bypassed by the industrial revolution, and their economic condition, in spite of their own efforts and reinforced though they have been with external support, has not to any marked degree improved. The awareness of the widening gap between economic growth rates in the developed countries and more modest rates of growth or even the relative stagnation of the economies of many of the underdeveloped countries, has resulted in a groundswell of informed opinion whose voice now dominates the proceedings, not only of the economic organs of the United Nations, but of many of its other bodies as well.

Just as social change in the nineteenth century was dominated by an interplay between the forces unleashed by the industrial revolution and the forces of nationalism generated by the American and French revolutions, in the twentieth century the development of the economically underdeveloped countries is inextricably bound up with the movement toward the emancipation of colonial and other dependent peoples, which has been discussed in Chapter VI. Political equality and independence cannot be pursued in isolation from considerations of economic viability.

To accelerate the process of involvement of the richer nations, there have been socialist allegations that governments and commercial interests of the "free enterprise" economies deliberately confine the primary "raw material" producing countries in a condition of economic dependency. This gadfly applied to the necks of the developed countries has been an irritant, but it has acted as a spur to the richer countries to respond more readily to the condition of the poor.

Partly as a result of these pressures upon the economically advanced countries of Western Europe and North America, there has developed a lively sense of collective responsibility for furthering the welfare of the underdeveloped, particularly those who are new arrivals on the international scene. But domestic pressures have also made themselves felt. Here, as elsewhere, motives may be mixed: self-interest, both political and economic, a strong sense of moral responsibility as well as colonial relationships transmuted on independence into ties of a different nature—all play their domestic part in changing the climate of opinion.

Finally, in the organs of the United Nations, in keeping with the spirit of the Charter, there has been a deliberate movement fostered by the Secretariat, directed toward the acceptance of the concept of a world economy and with it, too, a systematic effort to establish a sense of common responsibility for its well-being and development.

These forces, sometimes clamorous, permeate debate and deliberation, not only in the economic organs of the United Nations, but in practically every meeting of the Organization, whatever the subject, whether it be on disarmament or on human rights. They provide the economic and political realities in the face of which the economic bodies of the United Nations have evolved.

The work cycle. The work of the Economic and Social Council and, with appropriate variations, that of its functional, regional and other subsidiary bodies, falls into four main categories. The cycle of work begins with the collection and analysis of basic information about the world economy. Statistical and demographic yearbooks provide a continuing flow of basic data. The highly professional *World Economic Survey* and the regional economic studies provide the basic economic analyses.

These and other reports enable the economic organs to identify the basic problems of the world economy and to make, with an increasing measure of success, concerted attempts to overcome them. Problems of the world economy, such as the stimulation of the international flow of private capital, the adoption of effective measures relating to land reform or increasing agricultural productivity, the need to increase international liquidity, to bring about a degree of stability in the prices of primary commodities entering international trade or to mitigate the effects of a downward trend with compensatory measures, are a few examples.

This process involves what is termed "the confrontation technique" which calls for the periodic examination of government economic policies. This technique makes it possible to identify the secular trends in the world economy and the need to harmonize national policies in the long-term interests of the world community.

In this way national awareness of the world economy and of a common responsibility for it is strengthened. On the basis of this awareness, international agreements, action programs and other common measures can be devised, fostered or encouraged.

Such an elaborate and sophisticated pattern of enquiry, deliberation and action in the economic organs of the United Nations did not develop overnight. As with national experience, international economic cooperation in the United Nations has been the product of trial and error, patience and hard work.

In the early years, the economic bodies passed through what might be termed the Platonic period. During these years the Secretariat, at the behest of the Council, collected information from governments through such devices as—in the spirit of the times— the full employment questionnaire. The economic studies which were based upon them were presented as a setting for discussion. This may not seem to represent any marked achievement in itself, but it is unlikely that in the interwar period, governments would have been prepared to report to an international body in detail on their national economic condition and the policies they intended to follow. Least of all, it is unlikely that they would have been prepared to participate in international debate under public scrutiny. Today such reporting is routine.

In this period also the functional commissions and the *ad hoc* groups of experts, such as the one that in 1951 produced the report, Measures for the Economic Development of Underdeveloped Countries, helped to identify the basic problems of the world economy and laid down the strategy of attack on them, in anticipation of the day when action could be taken. In these ways the substratum of knowledge and awareness of the problems and what to do about them were built up. Also, and this was an almost imperceptible process, through the debates, tedious and time-consuming though they may have seemed, there developed a growing awareness on the part of national representatives of a concept of an international economy, and of a common international responsibility for it. Today this is axiomatic. But if we consider the economic, commercial and fiscal policies of the interwar period, when economic problems were exported onto the backs of weaker countries, competitive tariff and other protective measures and jockeying for position on the world's exchange rates were commonplace, we can see how much we have moderated our international behavior in favor of the world's interest.

How the Council and the General Assembly led the way to the

first breakthrough to action programs in 1948 with a modest technical assistance program, leading to the United Nations Development
Program in 1966, is the subject of Chapter XII. We should now
consider the developing role of the United Nations, not so much in
aid as in trade.

A dead letter. Of the many specialized agencies projected
in the postwar period, one failed to come into being: the International Trade Organization. The attempts to implement piecemeal
the provisions of the Havana Charter, which provided for this Organization, were a continuing feature of the work of the United
Nations economic organs concerned with world trade until 1964,
when the United Nations Conference on Trade and Development,
enlivened—indeed revolutionized—the whole approach of the
United Nations to international trade problems.

When planning for the postwar world, those concerned (including the economists of the League Secretariat, who continued their
work at Princeton during the war) were naturally conditioned in
their thinking by the breakdown in world trade relations that had
been a feature of the interwar period. To prevent a recurrence and
in order to reestablish multilateral trade, the Economic and Social
Council began, almost from its inception, to prepare for the U. N.
Conference on Trade and Employment which, in 1947 and 1948,
met in Havana. The Charter adopted there was the blueprint for
the International Trade Organization. Of the fifty-two countries
that adopted it, only two, Australia and Liberia, ever deposited their
instruments of ratification.

The Havana Charter represented the highest common denom-
inator between diverse and often contradictory interests. It laid
down a regime for international economic behavior reaching far
beyond the immediate problems of international trade. The Charter
included in its scope full employment, economic development, commercial policy, tariffs, customs practices, primary products and restrictive business practices.

However, the Organization failed to come into existence mainly
because the major trading and commercial countries turned their
backs on ITO, as they had failed to establish for themselves voting

rights similar to those obtained at Bretton Woods (see p. 256). Also, few countries, on reflection, were prepared to accept wholly the doctrine of multilateralism propounded in the Charter at a time when quantitative and other restrictions were being increasingly imposed.

The Havana Charter itself remained a dead letter, but its concepts and concerns permeated the thinking of all United Nations economic organs where trade problems were given an airing. In the Economic and Social Council and elsewhere attempts were made piecemeal to refine and implement the provisions of the ill-fated Charter. Economic development, as we have seen, came to be the main concern of the Economic and Social Council. Although it occasioned much debate and the attention of several expert bodies, measures concerning restrictive business practices did not command the necessary broad degree of support among the major trading partners in the Council. Greater success, however, was achieved in the lowering of tariffs and in the stabilization of the prices of selected commodities entering international trade.

GATT. In 1947, as part of the preparatory negotiations for the Havana Conference, a multilateral contract, the General Agreement on Tariffs and Trade (GATT), was adopted embodying the tariff concessions negotiated during the preparatory discussions for the Havana Conference. Neither an agency, nor, strictly speaking a part of the United Nations, GATT remained a series of agreements serviced by an executive secretary, and a small staff who have maintained administrative links with the United Nations. GATT has made a modest contribution to the freeing of international trade from quotas and tariffs. Through the annual meetings of the contracting parties in Geneva, it has established a code of good international conduct by limiting the use of quantitative restrictions. It has also served as a useful forum for international trade consultations as well as for trade disputes for which a Panel of Complaints was established.

Of greatest significance has been the "binding" of tariffs. As a result of a series of marathon trade negotiations in Geneva, 1947, Annecy, 1949, Torquay, 1957 and annually at Geneva, thousands of agreements, initially negotiated on a bilateral basis, were adopted to reduce duties on individual items and "binding" other duties against increase. Moreover, GATT extended these reciprocal concessions to almost all the contracting parties. By the nineteen sixties such arrangements affected the value of half of the total world trade.

Many loopholes necessarily existed in these arrangements and, in many instances, there was a reluctance, particularly on the part of European countries, to enter into trade agreements that might disturb domestic recovery measures. Waivers were so frequently granted that, in several cases, they substantially reduced the effectiveness of the agreements themselves. The emergence of regional free trade areas posed special problems for the contracting parties. But the chief weakness of GATT was the absence of most of the economically underdeveloped countries, who suffered most from this piecemeal implementation of the Havana Charter. They saw only marginal advantage in participating in tariff agreements without the accompanying provisions regarding commercial policy, economic development and commodity price stabilization.

The Kennedy Round, which began in 1963 and reached its climax in 1967, was not only a major departure for GATT but it was also the most important development to take place in international trade since World War II. The Kennedy Round was not a traditional conference where tariff reductions were negotiated as a result of item-by-item bargaining. It was, in effect, a world trade conference where massive non-tariff as well as tariff obstacles to world trade were removed by taking each major group of industries in turn and agreeing to across-the-board liberalization measures. On industrial items this has led to a reduction in tariffs of between 35 and 50 percent.

Of great significance was the understanding reached on the elements of a world food grains agreement. This may now open the way for the creation of a multilateral food grains authority, possibly under the United Nations, which would transfer food surpluses on a continuing basis to the countries where population increases raise Malthusian anxieties.

For the first time, socialist countries of Eastern Europe participated in the GATT negotiations and the economically developing countries, though disappointed with the outcome as far as their need for introducing preferential tariffs were concerned, gained increased recognition of the special problems they faced when attempting to participate in an expansion of world trade. In 1968 at the second United Nations Conference on Trade and Development held in New Delhi, the developing countries were able to discuss what the Kennedy Round had left undone as far as their special interests are concerned.

Commodity trade. The most intractable world trade problem is undoubtedly the stabilization of international prices of primary commodities entering international trade. Not only are they subject to violent cyclical oscillation, but the secular trend of the prices of many of them are due to varying demand conditions on the part of the manufacturing countries who are their traditional importers. The experience of the primary producing countries, in many cases, had led them to the conclusion that their participation in international trade was not based on the classical concept of comparative advantage, but rather of "absolute disadvantage."

International commodity agreements have remained the province of the United Nations for which the Interim Coordinating Committee for International Commodity Arrangements (known for having the longest title and the smallest membership of any United Nations body) and, in 1954, the Committee on International Commodity Trade were established. International agreements were concluded and periodically renewed, under United Nations auspices, for wheat, tin, sugar, coffee and olive oil. For other commodities, such as cocoa, lead and zinc, working parties, composed of both producers and consumers, have met to consult on the adoption of stabilization measures. For yet others, United Nations and FAO studies on commodity problems have provided information and analysis on current problems and prospects. Proposals for more broadly based compensatory financing schemes for a whole range of commodities entering international trade are now attracting attention in the economic organs of the United Nations, and have recently provided the basis for an International Monetary Fund "facility" in this field.

Under new management. The turbulent debates of the first United Nations Conference on Trade and Development held in 1964, focused attention sharply on world trade problems, particularly those affecting the economically underdeveloped countries, many of whom were entering the world community as independent states for the first time.

The setting for the conference was one in which the majority of the governments represented there were of economically underdeveloped countries. They saw a world economy in which trade was increasing substantially, but their share in the increase was proceeding at an appreciably lower rate than that of the developed countries. Between 1950 and 1962, the underdeveloped countries share of world trade had declined from one-third to one-fifth. Moreover, the terms of trade were becoming increasingly unfavorable to them. The trade surpluses they had enjoyed in 1950 had vanished and, by 1962, their total trade deficit amounted to some $2.3 billion. In addition, their payments, in 1960, for dividends and interest on foreign investments and loans, as well as for invisible items, amounted to $3.3 billion.

Faced with this situation, with every indication that the "trade gap" would widen still further, the Conference called for new and vigorous measures to stimulate the developing countries' trade, to stabilize international commodity prices and to take other related measures.

The machinery, subsequently devised by the General Assembly on the recommendation of the Economic and Social Council, was to make the Conference an organ of the United Nations. It is to meet triennially and is to be composed of members of the United Nations or of its Specialized Agencies. Its permanent organ is the Trade and Development Board composed of fifty-five members. A new feature in the development of economic organs is the arrangement by which members are elected from among different groups. At present, Group A comprises twenty-two Afro-Asian countries (and Yugoslavia); Group B, eighteen Western free enterprise economies; Group C, nine Latin American; and Group D, six Socialist countries. The Trade and Development Board has four subsidiary committees dealing with invisible trade items (i.e., rendering or paying for services, rather than selling or buying goods), and with financing related to trade, commodities, manufacturing and shipping.

The Secretariat is headed by a Secretary-General, currently Raul Prebisch, a former executive-secretary of the Economic Commission for Latin America. At the end of 1965, after a period of uncertainty, it was decided to establish UNCTAD's Headquarters in Geneva.

The method of work follows the pattern of addressing recommendations on trade and related matters to members. This is followed by enquiry and public report on the action taken to implement these recommendations. Already, steps have been taken to implement the findings of the 1964 Conference and, in 1965, the Conference on Transit Trade of Landlocked Countries adopted a convention that has already been signed by twenty-nine countries on the trading rights of landlocked countries. In 1965, the international tin agreement was the first of such international agreements to be renegotiated under the auspices of UNCTAD.

Economic and social. An ambassador, on introducing his country's newly arrived and rather dapper representative on the Economic and Social Council to the Permanent Representative of the United States, is reported to have said, "May I introduce our representative on the Economic and Social Council? He is, I fear, somewhat more social than economic."

While this may have been true, the reverse is the case of the Council itself: it is more economic than social. For while the world economy is held together by commerce, trade and finance, similar social ties do not bind so effectively. But in another sense, the opportunities for furthering international cooperation are much greater socially than in matters economic. For the most part, social problems confronting countries today are very similar. A sharing of experiences and the elaboration of common measures to overcome these problems are becoming increasingly important to countries, be they developed or underdeveloped economically.

Breeding and feeding. Ever since the Black Death swept Europe in the fourteenth century, decimating the population and thus presaging the end of feudalism, we have been alarmed alternately by fears of under-population and of over-population. In the eighteenth century, Malthus, fearing an over-populated world, foresaw one in which food production increased by arithmetical progression while population increased by geometrical progression, unless held back by the "natural checks" of war, famine, pestilence and disease. Fortunately, his guesses were wild. England and subsequently the continents of Europe and North America experienced an industrial revolution made possible by a great increase in population shortly after his gloomy projections appeared. In fact, the process of economic growth from "take-off" to "self-sustaining" development usually results in a tripling of population before the claims of prosperity divert us from increasing our progeny, and population increases taper off.

Nevertheless, Latin America and Asia are areas where population increases are so rapid as to nullify increases in productivity. Unless economic growth is to be of no account due to expanding populations, measures may need to be introduced as long as they do not conflict with cultural or religious attitudes.

Changes in breeding and feeding habits, as they touch the most important moments in our lives, are naturally greeted with more emotion than analysis. The Population Commission and the Secretariat have done much to publish demographic statistics, identify population trends and show the way to a more meaningful discussion of these problems.

The city teaches a man, so the ancients would have it; but now the man must teach the city. The increase in urban living throughout the world is proceeding at double the rate of population increase. As poor families in the United States have found, it is less uncomfortable to be ill-fed, ill-housed and unemployed in the city than in the countryside. All over the world in Shanghai, Tokyo,

Calcutta, Caracas, Lagos and Rio, the steady stream of people comes to the towns and subtopias (as Sir Lewis Casson has called the shanty towns and *bidonvilles*) generating as they do social and possibly also political problems.

How to slow this trend to the towns by bringing urban amenities to rural areas, and how to plan for and control the growth of cities without congestion, acute social dislocation, and epidemics, are problems common to every country. Through the Social Commission (of ECOSOC) and its subsidiary bodies, these problems are being identified and action programs, to assist countries in need of assistance in tackling them, are devised.

Anomie. Durkheim, in his studies, dwelt on the loss of social cohesion in the individual and the anti-social behavior to which it gave rise unless understood and controlled. Now it is not so much the individual as the group, particularly in societies experiencing a measure of prosperity, that is of concern. The alienation of many, particularly the young, has led to increasing juvenile delinquency and crime. This is another social phenomenon, common to nearly all countries, calling for new approaches to the problem of crime and the treatment of the offender. Here again the Social Commission can provide a center where experience can be shared, and the best talents available can come from all over the world to discuss measures most likely to repair this loss of social cohesion.

Twenty years on. One of the purposes of the United Nations, as stated in Chapter I of the Charter, is to achieve international cooperation in solving international economic problems and to serve as a center for harmonizing the actions of nations in the attainment of these common ends. The aspirations of the governments meeting in San Francisco in 1945 have not yet become a universal reality, but remarkable progress has been made in spite of (and possibly, in certain situations, because of) the political climate of the postwar world, until recently, not being conducive to international cooperation or the harmonization of economic policies.

From out of the labyrinth of economic and social bodies created by the Economic and Social Council and regardless of the uncertainty of the Council's role *vis-à-vis* the General Assembly, great strides have been made. In the first place governments have come to accept the concept of a world economy and, with it, there has emerged a sense of collective responsibility for its well-being and development. Considerations of short-term national economic interest have been influenced, to a degree, by a sense of international responsibility, as a result of the deliberations of the Economic and Social Council and the General Assembly.

The earlier experience of attempting to implement piecemeal the provisions of the Havana Charter, and the lack of balance in existing trade agreements, has been overtaken by the impressive show of unity of purpose on the part of the underdeveloped countries in creating UNCTAD. Teething troubles are inevitable, but in the midst of them, the new body has built up an offensive against secular trends in world trade and has created the beginnings of a new economic framework for world trade and payments.

The emergence of what might be termed a new sense of international economic solidarity was facilitated, then fostered, by the United Nations. A start was made with the identification of world economic and social problems and opportunities. That the economic and social organs were not condemned to endless debate without any tangible outcome acted as a spur to fresh efforts as confidence grew in the capacity of the United Nations to administer large-scale programs, regardless of political differences among its members. As we shall see in Chapter XII, the building of the United Nations Development Program on the experience of EPTA and the Special Fund, with the possibility of its being enlarged to embrace further responsibilities including, in the minds of many members, that of a capital development fund opens up a new series of opportunities for international economic cooperation.

Before we can examine these developments, however, we need to place in perspective the structure and functions of the United Nations family as a whole. In Chapter XII we will return to these and other international action programs.

Chapter XI

A COMMONWEALTH
OF AGENCIES

The origins of the constellation of agencies which comprise the United Nations system are three-fold: one theoretical, one practical and the other historical.

Pascal's orders. Many of the United States and British officials responsible for setting up the postwar machinery of international economic and social cooperation were bemused by the concept of "functionalism." Just as Pascal had postulated three orders, the political, the scientific and the religious, each subject to separate laws and different disciplines, so the negotiators at Bretton Woods, Hot Springs, Philadelphia and elsewhere saw a separation of the political from the technical. The United Nations was to be principally, but not exclusively, a political body. International technical cooperation would be thus insulated from the harsher political pressures of international life and carried forward by technical agencies. The World Health Organization would enable public health officials, doctors and their associates to work together to discuss international health problems. The World Meteorological Organization would further cooperation in the study of climatology and so on, while the United Nations dealt primarily with political problems.

The supporters of this approach were reinforced in their views by the actual course of events. President Roosevelt, possibly recalling the withdrawal of support from President Wilson after World War I, was not anxious to wait until after the end of hostilities to set up the machinery of international cooperation, but wanted to assemble and begin operating the system piecemeal while the battles were still raging and there still remained a semblance of Great Power unity.

The beginnings. By the time the United Nations entered the picture, therefore, the landscape was already occupied by agencies such as the International Bank for Reconstruction and Development and the International Monetary Fund. These had joined the older agencies, the Universal Postal Union, the International Telecommunications Union and the International Labor Organization which had emerged from the twilight of wartime. In addition, the preparatory work to establish the United Nations Educational, Scientific and Cultural Organization, as well as other specialized agencies, was well advanced.

So, instead of a relatively centralized machinery, such as that of the League, the United Nations found itself at the center of a decentralized—even dispersed—system with the Economic and Social Council saddled with the tasks of entering into agreements with the specialized agencies and then of coordinating their activities. How the Council, after an initial attempt to carry out its functions in these respects, came to delegate them to the Secretary-General and how, through the apparatus of the Administrative Committee on Coordination, the beginnings of a systematic approach was made to this work will be recounted toward the end of the present chapter.

We will now discuss the development of the United Nations system beginning with the United Nations' own emergency agencies following through to the specialized agencies.

UNRRA. A generation ago the battle lines, as they rolled back in Europe, left in their wake destruction, devastation and dislocation. One of the most pressing problems, in the midst of every kind of problem, was coping with feeding, repatriating or resettling millions of refugees. Much of the relief operation was carried out by voluntary agencies and by governments themselves. But husbanding and supporting the total effort was the United Nations Relief and Rehabilitation Administration (UNRRA), which came into being in 1943 and continued until its activities began to taper off in 1949.

Supplied, and for the most part staffed and led by the United States, UNRRA was a remarkable international relief effort. At the peak of its activity it was directed by Herbert Lehman and, in its final stages, by Fiorello LaGuardia, the former Mayor of New York City, under whose dynamic, if erratic, leadership many civil servants, destined to rise high in the service of the United Nations and the Specialized Agencies, had their first experience of international organization and international public service.

The mantle falls . . . Realizing that displaced persons and refugees remained a major problem of the aftermath of the war and in anticipation of the closing down of UNRRA, the General Assembly, in 1946, approved the establishment of an International Refugee Organization to take over the resettlement or repatriation of displaced persons. A Preparatory Commission for IRO met in 1947, and IRO itself took over from the Commission in 1948 entering into an agreement with the Economic and Social Council in the same year, thus becoming a Specialized Agency of the United Nations.

During its short and politically turbulent life, IRO provided assistance to 1,600,000 refugees; it resettled 1,000,000 and many were repatriated to their own countries. IRO was liquidated in 1951. But, in 1949, the General Assembly had vested responsibility for the international protection of refugees, on the termination of IRO, in the High Commissioner for Refugees whose statute was adopted in the following year for an initial period of three years.

The Office of the United Nations High Commissioner for Refugees began operations in 1951. It is headed by a High Commissioner nominated by the Secretary-General and elected by the General Assembly. UNHCR has its Headquarters in Geneva where the Arctic explorer, Fridtjof Nansen once lobbied on behalf of the refugees of World War I.

The main function of the Office is to provide international protection for refugees falling within its purview. It seeks a permanent solution to their problems by assisting in their voluntary repatriation, their integration within the country offering them asylum or their resettlement elsewhere. Outside its scope are the Palestine refugees, or refugees whose country of asylum offers them legal protection, such as refugees from eastern Germany who have found homes in the German Federal Republic.

The Office has been prolonged for terms of five years. There would seem to be no end to its work. It inherited not only many refugees from World War II, but even residual pockets of them from World War I. To those were added refugees from Algeria who fled to Morocco and Tunisia. More recently, Uganda has offered asylum to refugees from the Congo (Kinshasa), Rwanda and Sudan.

Special problems have emerged requiring special programs. It was found hard to resettle the very old, the infirm and the handicapped and to absorb them into new surroundings. Sweden led the way in receiving many of these. Emergency programs have had to spring into action, such as the one to receive, in 1956 and 1957, refugees from Hungary when more than one per cent of the total population of that country moved into Austria and Yugoslavia. UNHCR, under the direction of the General Assembly, also makes available its "good offices" to assist in finding solutions for refugees such as those now crowding Hong Kong.

UNHCR is an integral part of the United Nations. The staff of the High Commissioner is appointed by the Secretary-General. The budget is voted by the General Assembly, although the High Commissioner's programs, for which he obtains the approval of the thirty-member Executive Committee of the High Commissioner's Program, is financed by voluntary contributions from governments and private groups. In World Refugee Year (1959–60) a determined effort was made with increased contributions and intensified programs to reduce the numbers of refugees.

Palestine refugees. Immediately following the conflict in Palestine, the General Assembly, in 1948, set up a relief fund for the refugees. In the following year the Assembly established the United Nations Relief and Works Agency for Palestine Refugees in the Near East (UNRWA) which since has provided protection, shelter, health services and basic rations for more than two million refugees, many of whom are now of the second generation.

Palestine refugees are maintained in camps in Jordan, Gaza, Lebanon and Syria. Now, in addition to bringing relief to them, the Agency has developed vocational training programs designed to make the refugees self-supporting.

As with UNHCR, the Agency is continued for several years at a time and its status is reviewed by the General Assembly annually. The Commissioner-General of UNRWA is appointed by the Secretary-General and the Agency's budget is voted by the General Assembly. The Commissioner-General is assisted by an Advisory Commission comprising representatives of Arab governments in the Middle East, Belgium, France, Turkey, the United Kingdom and the United States. The outbreak of fighting in 1967 greatly increased the number of refugees, particularly in Jordan.

Korean reconstruction. To channel assistance to the people of the Republic of Korea, the General Assembly, in 1950, established the United Nations Korean Reconstruction Agency (UNKRA) Before it was wound up in 1959, about $150 million of emergency relief and reconstruction assistance had been made available from thirty-nine countries. This assistance brought a measure of relief to the people of that war-devastated country as well as an opportunity for many to start on the long road back to reconstruction.

UNICEF. The oldest and best known of the agencies of the United Nations is UNICEF, the United Nations Children's Fund. (The "I" was for "International," and the "E" was for "Emergency," but while the initials remain unchanged, the title has now been shortened.)

UNICEF was created by the General Assembly in 1946. Controlled by an Executive Board comprised of thirty members, it reports annually to the Economic and Social Council and to the General Assembly. Its Executive Director is appointed by the Secretary-General in consultation with the Executive Board.

Voluntary contributions from governments, private groups and individuals (including children at Halloween) enables UNICEF to support schemes where there is a special emphasis on child welfare. These programs are jointly sponsored by the host governments and also usually involve the United Nations, or FAO or WHO.

There are five main areas of assistance under UNICEF. It has supported health projects directed towards reducing diseases of children, such as yaws, leprosy, intestinal infections and malaria. Through school-feeding and other nutrition programs, support is given to bring about an improved diet, particularly where protein deficiencies cause widespread debilitation and undernourishment. Increasingly, assistance is given for vocational training so that young people may have a better start in life. Family and child welfare services are also supported and, finally, emergency aid to areas stricken by famine or any other natural disaster helps to take the strain off the local relief services.

Of the agencies in the United Nations system, two have been awarded Nobel Prizes: UNHCR and UNICEF. Both bodies are organs of the United Nations and like UNRWA, they operate within the framework of the United Nations proper. These agencies follow a similar pattern. Their budgets are (for the most part) controlled by the United Nations General Assembly and their funds are subject to the United Nations Controller's procedures. The chief administrative officer is appointed by the Secretary-General subject to confirmation by or following consultation with another Principal Organ or subsidiary body. A consultative committee of a small number of UN members advises the chief officer and reviews the progress of the work.

We shall return to the pattern of administration and control in these organs later in the chapter.

The smaller technical agencies. The Universal Postal Union and the International Telecommunication Union are the oldest of the agencies. After World War II, their work expanded in scope and took on a new gloss.

UPU, through its Consultative Commission on Postal Studies, has been able to provide guidance and assistance in the improvement and extension of postal services throughout the world, particularly in those countries which have only recently achieved independence.

ITU has taken in its stride the shifts in interest and emphasis in international cooperation as new inventions have transformed communications. Through its consultative committees on telegraph and telephones, and on radio, international standards are adopted and the new improvements in these fields are made known. Of considerable importance is the allocation and registration of radio frequencies, by which the congestion of radio bands has been reduced. Now, the adoption of international standards in space and the allocation of frequencies for space use have become increasingly significant.

In fact, we are not far from a worldwide telecommunication system. This could be made possible through a synchronous orbit system which would require three satellites above the Equator orbiting eastward at the same speed the earth orbits westward. Such satellites placed around the Earth could ensure complete telecommunications links everywhere except for the unfortunates living at the North and South Poles. The presence of ITU to facilitate international discussions of such matters hastens their development.

A sister agency to UPU and ITU is the World Meteorological Organization. Its precursor was the International Meteorological Organization established in 1878, comprising the directors of various meteorological services. In 1947, at the conference of directors of national meteorological services meeting in Washington, the World Meteorological Convention was adopted which provided for the establishment of WMO which came into existence in 1951.

WMO seeks to facilitate international cooperation between national meteorological systems and to promote collaboration between climatologists. The extent of this agency's interest has now expanded beyond weather forecasting to the use of climatology in water resources development and crop protection. In spite of its burgeoning membership and increasing responsibilities, WMO remains modest in size with a modest budget—a welcome trend against Parkinson's Law on the nature of organizations which causes them to expand more rapidly than their usefulness increases.

In Chicago, in 1944, a new convention was drawn up by the International Civil Aviation Conference. It provided for the establishment of the International Civil Aviation Organization which came into being in 1947. Its aims are to foster the planning and development of international civil aviation and to develop the principles and improve the techniques of international air navigation.

Through ICAO, the facilities for airports, navigational aids, search and rescue and air traffic control have been improved through the adoption of international standards, and assistance to countries in complying with them. The weather ships in the North Atlantic maintained by nineteen nations covering the busiest international air routes have been set up through ICAO. The almost universal introduction of jet aircraft on international routes since 1956 has involved ICAO in additional responsibilities for introducing new safety standards and minimum operating procedures.

Public international law, as it applies to civil aviation, has been extended by ICAO through the fostering of such conventions as the International Recognition of Rights in Aircraft, Damage Caused by Foreign Aircraft to Third Parties on the Surface, as well as by protocols bringing up to date parts of the Warsaw Convention of 1929 which still remains the main instrument of international law regarding civil aircraft.

The last of the smaller technical agencies is the Intergovernmental Maritime Consultative Organization which came into being in 1959. IMCO is concerned with facilitating cooperation and the exchange of information on all technical matters concerning ocean shipping. The convention to establish IMCO was opened for signature in 1948 to those states with maritime interests. Twenty-one such states had to ratify the convention and, of those, seven had to have one million gross tons of shipping registered before the convention entered into force. This was delayed because of the wariness with which some of the larger carrying nations regarded IMCO's possible involvement in such delicate commercial matters as ocean freight rates.

In the interval, the United Nations acted as caretaker of much of the work which subsequently was taken over by the new agency. Its work now includes maritime safety, navigation efficiency, preventing oil pollution of the sea, tonnage measurements and the revision of the international code of signals. IMCO is the depository of such international instruments as the 1954 Convention on Prevention of Pollution of the Sea by Oil and the 1960 International Convention for Safety of Life at Sea.

IAEA, Vienna. President Eisenhower in an address before the General Assembly in 1953, proposed that a world body should be created to further international cooperation in the peaceful uses of atomic energy.

Although not a specialized agency, the International Atomic Energy Agency is an autonomous intergovernmental organization under the aegis of the United Nations. In 1957, the year the Agency came into being, an agreement to this effect was approved by the General Assembly and IAEA's General Conference.

Comprising a General Conference, a Board of Governors and a Secretariat, the Agency collects and publishes information on the peaceful uses of atomic energy. It has expert bodies to consider such questions as safety measures in the handling of radioactive substances. More recently, under the United Nations Development Program, IAEA has assumed responsibility for a small number of projects using radiation techniques and isotopes as tracers in agricultural experimental schemes.

The more ambitious proposal for IAEA to act as an international broker for fissionable materials has not yet been realized. A start has been made, however, in carrying out international inspection of nuclear plants to ensure that they are safe and their activities are not diverted to military purposes. Such modest beginnings could be of great significance as the international political climate improves, for they will enable the agency to test the principles and procedures of what might become an international safeguards system as nuclear plants proliferate.

This brief rundown on the technical agencies reveals that they have certain shared characteristics. All of them owe their existence to an international convention. Membership was open to states rati-

Table 4

UNITED NATIONS SPECIALIZED AGENCIES

Title	Abbreviation	Agreement entered into force with the United Nations	Headquarters
International Labor Organization	ILO	1946	Geneva
Food and Agriculture Organization of the United Nations	FAO	1946	Rome
United Nations Educational, Scientific and Cultural Organization	UNESCO	1946	Paris
World Health Organization	WHO	1951	Geneva
World Bank Group:			Washington
International Bank for Reconstruction and Development	IBRD	1947	Washington
International Development Association	IDA	1961	
International Finance Corporation	IFC	1957	
International Monetary Fund	IMF	1947	Washington
International Civil Aviation Organization	ICAO	1947	Montreal
Universal Postal Union	UPU	1948	Berne
International Telecommunication Union	ITU	1949	Geneva
World Meteorological Organization	WMO	1951	Geneva
Intergovernmental Maritime Consultative Organization	IMCO	1959	London
International Atomic Energy Agency (IAEA is not technically a specialized agency but "an agency under the aegis of the United Nations")	IAEA	1957	Vienna
International Refugee Organization (IRO was liquidated in 1951)	IRO	1948	Geneva

fying or adhering to the international instrument establishing the agency (with the exception of IMCO which only maritime countries may join).

An assembly, general conference or congress of all the members meets not more frequently than once a year or less frequently than every five years. Such an assembly sets policy, adopts the budget and decides upon the program of work. A smaller executive body or council is elected by the assembly to act on its behalf between assembly sessions. The secretariat of the agency is headed by a chief administrative officer appointed or elected by the assembly. Exactly where the dividing line lies between the director-general and the executive body varies between agencies and, possibly, also between directors-general.

A global agency with great responsibilities and obligations, by its very nature, stands in danger of becoming a victim of the contemporary fad, the latest panacea or, being carried away by the size of the tasks that lie before it, runs the risk of dissipating its talents and resources by trying to do too much too soon. Worse still, it might become blinkered by its own doctrines or "philosophy," thus limiting its vision and thereby losing contact with the world around it. Fortunately, these agencies have retained that compact and competent look and jaunty air which comes with a trim and well run ship.

Labor, Geneva. Table 4 listing the specialized agencies is headed by the International Labor Organization as it was the first to be associated with the United Nations. Established in 1919, the Constitution of ILO formed part of the Treaty of Versailles.

ILO was founded to advance the cause of social justice. In 1944, the Declaration of Philadelphia was adopted and subsequently was annexed to the ILO Constitution. This statement, agreed to at the wartime Conference in Philadelphia, gave ILO a fresh look and in the noble sentiments of the time, and perhaps also of the place, declared that all human beings have the right to pursue both their material well-being and their spiritual development in conditions of freedom and dignity, economic security and equal opportunity.

Unique among the agencies, ILO members are represented not

only by government officials but by employers' and workers' representatives as well. ILO has a tripartite structure. The International Labor Conference, the main deliberative body, meets annually in Geneva and each national delegation is composed of two government delegates, one employer's delegate and one worker's delegate. The Executive Committee is the governing body, meeting three or four times a year. It is composed of twenty government members, ten employers' and ten employees'. Ten of the members are drawn from the major industrial countries.

Elected by the Conference, the governing body appoints the Director of ILO (since 1946, the Director-General), screens the budget, considers policy questions and determines the work programs. These fall, for the most part, into three broad categories: the elaboration of the International Labor Code, technical cooperation and labor studies.

Almost from its inception, ILO has worked to improve labor conditions by drawing up draft conventions on labor and other matters. These are designed to become part of each government's own legislation. When such conventions are ratified, they become part of the domestic law and practice of the country concerned. No government is bound by such a convention, but is bound to bring the convention's provisions to the attention of its own legislative bodies. If a government ratifies a convention, it is required to report periodically on the implementation of its provisions. If it does not, then it still is expected to report on its position concerning ratification. In this way collective pressure can be brought to bear on the recalcitrant governments by ILO.

In addition to the conventions, now 124 in number, ILO also adopts recommendations which, while not subject to ratification, are set up as guidelines for national action. Taken together the conventions and recommendations add up to an impressive code of international law and practice with a built-in review mechanism. The nineteen twenties might be regarded by some as the heroic period of ILO in providing international leadership. Since World War II, however, the Organization has extended its activities beyond protective legislation relating mainly to the worker, and has broadened its activities into promoting economic and social standards, and, as we have seen in Chapter IX, into furthering human rights.

Not content with assisting governments in labor matters, ILO has entered fresh fields such as vocational technical training for industry, improving industrial management, accelerating rural development and supporting special social programs such as those for the Andean Indians. Most of this work was made possible through the availability of technical assistance funds and, beginning in 1959, Special Fund project support.

ILO's programs are buttressed by its being a worldwide center of competence in labor matters. In 1962, so that its collective experience could be drawn on more effectively, an International Institute for Labor Studies was created within ILO to serve as a staff college in labor and social policy.

ILO is the oldest of the larger agencies and its present Director-General, David Morse, a former United States Assistant Secretary of Labor, appointed in 1948, has the longest tenure of all the present chief administrators. In the United Nations system, therefore, the role of ILO in safeguarding traditions and upholding standards in institutional and staff questions is of considerable importance.

Agriculture, Rome. During the biennial conference of the Food and Agriculture Organization of the United Nations, a lecture is now given in honor of F. L. MacDougall, an Australian, who convinced President Roosevelt of the need to have a world agency which would speed the plough and help to grow more food, catch more fish, use forests wisely and improve animal husbandry. Such an agency would raise living standards, keep the land fertile, conserve the world's resources and improve nutrition. It would also help to stabilize international commodity trade in agricultural products.

When Gulliver tried to explain to the King of Brobdingnag why men were honored, the King brusquely informed him that in Brobdingnag a man was honored if he could make two blades of grass grow where one grew before. This spirit which prevailed in Swift's land of giants motivates FAO today as it did in 1943 at Hot Springs,

Virginia where the United Nations Conference on Food and Agriculture established a commission which drafted the constitution for FAO.

The structure of the agency, which came into being in 1949, follows what should be, by now, a familiar pattern. A conference composed of all members meets every other year. The council of twenty-seven governments is appointed by the Conference to supervise FAO's work in between its sessions. The staff is headed by a director-general who is elected for four-year terms by the Conference.

FAO through its studies, surveys and expert bodies keeps the world food situation under continuing review. It has large technical programs in land and water development, plant production and protection, animal production and health, forestry and fisheries, with smaller programs in nutrition, rural institutions and education. Funds for action programs are derived mainly from the United Nations Development Program to which reference is made in the following chapter. As was discussed in the previous chapter, FAO has joint responsibility with the United Nations for the World Food Program.

Agriculture remains, however, the world's economic laggard and the lessons are stark in their significance. In underdeveloped countries, progress in agricultural production sets the pace in the growth process, for that sector employs more than half of the working population. Also, the output of the farmer is only one-third that of his counterparts in other sectors of the economy. At the same time, food consumption absorbs a large part of increases in income. In the face of rising populations, in the underdeveloped countries, food consumption is rising more rapidly than increases in agricultural production. In spite of the efforts of nations and international agencies, the poorer countries are becoming increasingly dependent on imported foodstuffs for which they have little foreign exchange to pay.

The brightest spot is the fishery sector. Here expansion is rapid. Where a country has access to marine resources there is no rent to pay, few institutional obstacles, and no land reform needed.

Once the techniques of harvesting the fishery resources have been acquired and the catch has been preserved or processed and marketed, a high quality protein food is available. The success here points to failure elsewhere and it is perplexing. But the development of industrialized fisheries and the impact made, with international assistance, in this sector can be examined with a view to trying out these methods in agriculture where pivotal scarcities persist.

UNESCO. International understanding would surely be enhanced if the citizenry of nations could, as Chaucer's Clerke of Oxenford, gladly learn and gladly teach. It was probably in this spirit that one 1945 London conference for the establishment of an educational, scientific and cultural organization drafted the constitution of UNESCO. A preparatory commission was also created which made the link between that conference and the organization which came into being in the following year.

UNESCO's constitution requires it to promote collaboration between nations through education, science and culture as a contribution to peace and security. Its structure comprises a General Conference, an Executive Board and a Secretariat headed by a Director-General.

Members of the United Nations may automatically become members of UNESCO. The admission of others is more elaborate. A state not a member of the United Nations can be elected by a two-thirds majority vote of the General Conference upon the recommendation of the Executive Board, provided that the Economic and Social Council has concurred.

As its title suggests, UNESCO's work program is broad—collecting, analyzing and disseminating information in education, science and culture. Much of this work is carried out by its secretariat, but UNESCO plays host to a large number of expert groups drawn from all over the world, and fosters international associations of scientists and others such as the International Biological Program and the International Indian Ocean Expedition.

UNESCO now projects its work program on a ten-year basis. In this way, future planning is possible for such major programs as those supporting primary education in Latin America, anti-illiteracy campaigns and furthering scientific investigation into the possibilities for developing arid and semi-arid regions, which make up more than a third of the land surface of the world. As with the activities of FAO, the action programs of UNESCO are now to a large extent those of the United Nations Development Program.

Health, Geneva. A proposal made at the San Francisco Conference that there should be a Specialized Agency for health led, in 1946, to a conference in New York to draft a constitution for the World Health Organization and to establish an interim commission which could set up house for the new agency and, on an interim basis, handle the residual tasks of the League of Nations in health matters as well as those of UNRRA. In 1948, the WHO constitution, being ratified by a sufficient number of states, entered into force.

WHO's objective is simply the attainment by all peoples of the highest possible level of health. Members of the United Nations become members of WHO by accepting its Constitution. States not members of the United Nations are admitted by a simple majority vote of the World Health Assembly. Associate members—usually dependent territories—may also be admitted. This is also a membership feature of several of the other postwar Specialized Agencies.

Unique among the Specialized Agencies, WHO is highly decentralized in its operations. In addition to the World Health Assembly, an Executive Board and a Secretariat, the agency has six regional offices which enjoy a considerable degree of autonomy. Most of the larger Specialized Agencies have regional or branch officers but the heads of the WHO regional offices are not appointed by the Director-General, but elected by the World Health Assembly. In this way, the regional directors and their offices are given a special status. The regional offices for the Americas is the Pan American Sanitary Bureau in Washington. The others are: South-East Asia—New Delhi; Eastern Mediterranean—Alexandria; Western Pacific—Manila; Africa—Brazzaville; and Europe—Copenhagen.

The international tasks of WHO are directed mainly toward

establishing and adopting international standards and facilitating international cooperation in health. The monumental work of the *International Pharmacopoeia* as well as other publications establishes international medical standards. The adoption of international sanitary and international quarantine regulations has brought national and international legislation up to date. The international epidemic warning system relays radio-telegraphic broadcasts daily from Geneva based on notifications of outbreaks received from national health services.

Under the aegis of WHO, medical research programs are coordinated. For example, eight countries in Africa, Asia and Latin America are conducting research into the control of bilharziasis. This disease tends to spread as new irrigation systems are developed. The adoption of effective and economic control measures is consequently urgent.

Operational programs are aimed at the main fatal or debilitating diseases. Malaria, tuberculosis, yaws, leprosy and virus diseases are the object of joint programs with government health services, as well as with other international bodies such as UNICEF. The relationship of such programs to population increase and economic development programs is now more widely understood. WHO works increasingly in closer contact with other international assistance programs.

Bretton Woods.   While forty-four nations were represented at the United Nations Monetary and Financial Conference which met at Bretton Woods, New Hampshire, in 1944, it was essentially an Anglo-American negotiation, particularly as much of the preparatory work had been carried out by Harry Dexter White for the United States and Lord Keynes for the United Kingdom.

There is one thing all economic projections have in common: they are always wrong. White and Keynes were determined to prevent a recurrence of the economic and financial disasters of the previous postwar period. They planned for a postwar world where there would be a return to economic stability with a high level of employment; a return to free trade and a rapidly expanding world economy in which the underdeveloped countries would share. The immediate problem of repairing the ravages of war would take about five years with the assistance of UNRRA and to some extent that of the International Bank for Reconstruction and Development. With the exception of the maintenance of full employment in most of the highly industrialized countries, none of these optimistic prognostications proved anywhere near the mark.

The Articles of Agreement for the International Monetary Fund were drawn up at Bretton Woods and represented a compromise between the positions taken by White and Keynes. We must look at these briefly because they are not only of historical interest, but have a new relevance in the present discussions on the future of IMF (International Monetary Fund).

The International Bank for Reconstruction and Development was also founded at the Bretton Woods Conference. After an uncertain start, it has now become the most formidable and successful of the Specialized Agencies. When the negotiations were over, Lord Keynes was reported to have remarked "We should have called the Fund 'the Bank,' and the Bank 'the Fund'." This comment is not intended to confuse, but to suggest the intricacies of the negotiations which gave rise to these two agencies and to hint at the difficulty involved in reducing twenty-one years of international financial transactions to a handful of paragraphs.

A central banker's central bank. Lord Keynes presented a plan for a Clearing Union which would be a kind of central banker's central bank. Overdraft facilities to the amount of $25 billion would enable countries with short-term deficits in their balance of payments to draw on this facility. In the event of a major economic setback, the Clearing Union would be able to create credit without asking its members to make supplementary contributions. Members could, nevertheless, appreciate or depreciate their currencies when necessary but by not more than five per cent of par value.

The concept of unlimited liability that lay behind Keynes' proposals was too much for the United States Treasury to stomach. The more conservative White proposals provided for a stabilization fund to which members would contribute. Thus, there would be a currency pool upon which members could draw under certain

circumstances and subject to the permission of the Fund's authorities in the event of an emergency. The currency pool would be
in the amount of $5 billion, and there would be no provision for
its expansion or for massive intervention in the event of a severe
depression.

A compromise was reached which is reflected in the Articles of
Agreement of IMF. The Fund was to set the par values of the
currency of its members. Exchange depreciation up to ten per cent,
without having first to obtain the permission of the Fund, was
accepted. For a further depreciation the permission of the Fund
had to be obtained. The total assets of IMF were to be $8 billion
and a system of weighted voting was introduced so that members
had voting power in proportion to their quota contributions. The
funds of IMF would be drawn on by a member purchasing from
the pool the foreign exchange needed to tide over a balance of
payments deficit, paying for this foreign exchange with its own
currency. Also a member could obtain the agreement of the Fund
to a standby arrangement whereby it could make such a drawing
in case of need. This latter process was designed to restore confidence in a currency which was approaching difficulty.

The Fund helped to replace the chaos of the interwar period
with a system of orderly currency management. It has provided a
forum for consultations on currency questions and a world center
where advice and guidance could be obtained in these matters. The
days of competitive devaluation, jockeying for position on the
world's exchange rates and of exporting one's economic problems
onto the backs of weaker trading partners were over.

The problems of the postwar world, however, were too big for
the Fund to handle by itself. Massive United States support under
the Marshall Plan was needed to restore Western Europe. There
has been no return to international equilibrium. The economies of
the underdeveloped countries, for the most part, remain stagnant
with a long-term unfavorable shift in their terms of trade. Monetary and trade restrictions persist in many countries, delaying a
return to multilateralism.

Discussions on reforming the Fund now center on the need to increase international liquidity. By "international liquidity" is meant the stocks of gold and other internationally accepted means of payment, particularly the dollar and the pound sterling which are the main international "support" currencies. To these can be added readily available credit through the IMF or friendly central bankers. It is now generally agreed that these reserves are not sufficient to permit most countries to take the expansionary steps needed to benefit their own economies, as well as to ensure a continued expansion of the world economy as a whole.

A country may need large liquid assets for three main reasons: (a) to finance domestic expansion and the tooling up needed; (b) to meet serious fluctuations in the balance of payments arising from abrupt shifts in the terms of trade or large capital movements; and (c) to offset short-term speculation against the currency, often termed "hot money."

These problems afflict the developed as well as the under-developed countries and they become more acute when the United States, in an effort to reduce its own balance of payments deficit, reduces its outflow of dollars. If world trade is to continue to expand at between four to six per cent a year, then liquid assets need to expand at a rate greater than the present one per cent, and they need to be made more generally available. International liquidity discussions continue, and center on a proposal to liberalize the Fund's practices concerning drawing rights, and on a variant on the original Keynesian proposal to create liquidity without calling for additional subscriptions.

The Board of Governors of the Fund meets once a year, but the Fund has in residence a Board of Executive Directors which is responsible for the conduct of the operations of IMF. The Board appoints a Managing Director who acts as Chairman of the Board and Chief of the operating staff.

The World Bank Group. The twin of the Fund is the World Bank whose Articles of Agreement were also adopted at Bretton Woods. Both agencies have their offices on H Street, NW, in Washington, which are appropriately linked by a bridge and a basement tunnel. All powers are vested in the Board of Governors, the annual meeting of which is held jointly with the Fund.

The Board of Governors has delegated most of its powers to the eighteen Executive Directors, resident in the Bank, who hold regular meetings. As in the case of the Fund's Board of Executive Directors, five of the Directors are appointed by the five members having the largest number of shares of capital stock (in the Fund it is the five with the largest quotas) and the rest of the Directors are elected by the remaining members. The President of the Board is elected by the Executive Directors and serves as their Chairman. He is responsible for conducting the business of the Bank and is the head of the staff.

In addition to the International Bank for Reconstruction and Development, there are now two affiliates, the International Finance Corporation and the International Development Association. Taken together they comprise the World Bank Group.

IBRD. The authorized capital of IBRD, originally $10 billion, is now $24 billion. Only one-tenth of its subscribed capital has been paid in, the balance remains on call. Only a small proportion of the Bank's capital is used for loan operations. Funds for lending are raised by borrowing on the capital market. This is done by selling its bonds. As of the end of 31 March 1968 the Bank's funded debt outstanding amounted to about $3,400,000,000. The Bank also sells part of its loans thus recovering funds for further lending. These are sold to banks and to other institutional investors.

As its title implies, IBRD lends for reconstruction and for development. In its early years lending was directed toward reconstruction in Europe. In 1947, $497 million was lent for this purpose. Now, loans are almost entirely for development. By 31 March 1968, the Bank had made 537 loans totalling about $11,200,000,000 in 77 countries and territories.

Loans are made subject to the recipient government's guarantee. The Bank does not compete with the private money market but lends only whenever favorable terms are not obtainable on that market. Loans are usually for twenty-five years and the interest charged is about five and a half per cent including the Bank's commission of one per cent.

The Bank is exhaustive in its examination of loan applications. Wide-ranging studies of the whole economy, its structure, trends and future prospects are included. Such loans are based exclusively on economic and not political considerations. Intensive economic and technical feasibility studies of the project itself are carried out. When a loan agreement has finally been signed, the Bank retains supervision over much of the construction and keeps a close watch on the project after completion through frequent on-the-spot visits.

As a result, no country has ever defaulted on a Bank loan. The standing achieved by a country in obtaining credit from IBRD, though an exhausting process, gives the country a higher financial rating in the world's money markets and is tantamount to being given a seal of approval on its economic and financial policies.

With success has come respectability. And with respectability the freedom to experiment. The Bank now has an Economic Development Institute which serves as a staff college for bankers, development planners and other government officials. It has a Development Advisory Service which provides financial and economic advisers to governments.

Development diplomacy. The Bank has also entered into diplomatic negotiations where there is a financial or development component. Its first attempt to negotiate a settlement over the Anglo-Iranian oil dispute failed. Its role, however, in clearing the Suez Canal in 1957 and, in the following year, reaching a financial settlement between the United Arab Republic and the Suez Canal Company as well as with the United Kingdom were triumphs for the then President of IBRD, Eugene Black, if not for the Bank itself.

The Indus waters dispute was successfully negotiated over a period of nine years. In the eighteen nineties under the British Raj, the Punjab was irrigated by a complex system of canals. Ninety million people now live in this huge, highly productive grain bowl. In 1947 the line between India and Pakistan was drawn right through the middle of this great development area. The Indus waters immediately were the source of contention. Beginning in 1951, the sorting out of this imperial legacy began. In 1960, in the presence of the Bank, the Indus Waters Treaty was signed.

IFC. The International Finance Corporation is an affiliate of the Bank with the same Board of Governors, Executive Directors, and the President of the Bank serves as Chairman of the Board of Directors of IFC.

The creation of IFC was first proposed by the United Nations General Assembly. It came into existence in 1956 to lend, without government guarantee, to private enterprises in the underdeveloped countries. It can participate in the equity of such enterprises, invest in capital shares, make conventional loans or a combination of these. It can also assist in underwriting share offerings to other investors. Investments are small, usually in the region of one and a quarter million dollars and are made, for the most part, to industrial enterprises.

IDA. The International Development Association, established in 1960, has many of the features of the proposed SUNFED, the debate on which is discussed in the following chapter. While IDA has its own funds, the staff and organizational structure is the same as that of the World Bank of which it is an affiliate.

From its members' subscriptions, IDA provides "soft" loans, i.e. on terms less stringent than regular Bank loans. Credits are arranged for a fifty-year term. Amortization begins after a ten-year period. After then, one per cent is repayable annually for ten years and three per cent annually for thirty years. IDA charges a three-fourths of one per cent commission.

IDA loans are aimed at improving the economic infrastructure of the underdeveloped countries. This includes transportation, irrigation, electric power and telecommunications. The role of IDA is becoming increasingly important as the external debt burden of many of the underdeveloped countries reaches a ceiling and makes further borrowing on commercial terms increasingly difficult.

The stars in the constellation. The larger specialized agencies also share many characteristics. As the smaller technical bodies, they owe their origin to a convention or other international instrument such as the Articles of Agreement of IMF. While sufficient ratifications were being deposited to bring the convention into force, an interim commission usually was responsible for the preparatory arrangements.

In those agencies which came into being after the United Nations was created, members of the United Nations have almost automatic membership rights. For non-members of the United Nations, more elaborate admission arrangements are followed. These agencies, too, have annual or biennial conferences of the total membership, but much of the authority is vested in the smaller executive bodies. In the agencies established at Bretton Woods, the membership and voting rights are more complicated than in other agencies. Furthermore, the Chief Administrative Officer is also Chairman of the Executive Board, thus occupying positions of very special authority.

The United Nations system is one chiefly characterized by the concept of functional autonomy. Each agency has its own membership which, with the exception of IMF and IBRD, is greater than that of the United Nations. Each one has its own constitution, organization, staff and budget. It draws for support on the government ministry concerned. FAO has its link with the Minister of Agriculture, WMO with the national meteorological office and so on. In a certain sense, each agency is the collectivity of all the ministries directly concerned. WHO is, in a way, the corporate expression of the ministries of health of its members. Also, with separate headquarters in different cities not only are lines of communication long but the setting in which they are located makes, over the years, its own impression.

The Economic and Social Council was given the task of coordinating the activities of the Specialized Agencies. In order to do so, it first had to draw them into a relationship with the Council. This it did through a series of agreements. They were negotiated on a basis of equality.

The experience of the United Nations in economic and social cooperation was recounted in the previous chapter. The stages through which the Specialized Agencies have passed in the same period show considerable similarity. The process of developing the institutional structure, of fact-gathering, analysis and identification of problems and the eventual emergence of each agency as a center of competence in those matters of direct concern to it follows a pattern similar to that of the United Nations.

After the formative period, operational programs developed. These were made possible partly by the budgets of the agencies themselves, in some cases through undertaking joint programs financed by UNICEF, but for the most part by drawing on funds from the Expanded Program of Technical Assistance and, more recently, by acting as executing agencies for projects supported by the United Nations Special Fund. There are other sources of operational financing, including the practice of setting up trust funds by which a country can arrange for an agency to act as steward of a fund to run a program in its own country.

The accumulation of responsibilities has led to an overlay of programs to which has been added an increasing burden of operational responsibilities. This has led to a strain being placed on the resources of the agencies as well as to the need to make administrative and psychological adjustments. It calls for great flexibility and resilience to be at home equally in the library, the conference hall and the operations room. Yet all these are vital. Without the constant study and analysis of experience, it is not possible to generalize and apply the experience gained in one place to another. Without periodic consultation and sharing of experience between governments, the international secretariat will drift away from its membership. And if the agency cannot be an effective tool of development, it may eventually be bypassed and disregarded.

Coordinating a constellation. The difficulties to be encountered by the Economic and Social Council in coordinating the activities of the Specialized Agencies may have been foreseen by the Preparatory Commission of the United Nations which, in 1946, requested the Secretary-General to establish a coordination committee composed of himself and the administrative officers of the agencies. This body held its first meeting in 1947 and, in 1948, it became the Administrative Committee on Coordination.

From its inception, the ACC was chaired by the Secretary-General and its meetings were attended by the directors-general of the Specialized Agencies. The position of the Secretary-General was and remains that of *primus inter pares,* working with the heads of the agencies in a spirit of collegiality.

On administrative matters, the ACC and its subsidiary committees and working parties have, to some extent, been successful. Although the ACC failed to establish a form of budget and an audit procedure common to all the agencies and, in certain countries, to establish common facilities for regional or branch offices of the United Nations and the agencies, for salaries, pensions, allowances and many other housekeeping arrangements, administrative policies and practices were, to a large degree, harmonized.

Although political considerations can seldom be far away from the minds of the members of the ACC—any more than they can be from any public servant—the Committee has rarely taken positions on political issues. After being consulted in 1950, by the then Secretary-General, the ACC gave its support to Lie's Twenty-Year Peace Program and issued a statement urging an early solution to the political difficulties then confronting the Security Council due to the absence of the representative of the U. S. S. R. from that body. Perhaps, on the basis of this experience, the ACC has since been prudent, if not reserved, about making its views known on political issues although, on occasion, individual directors-general continue to consult the ACC on political matters.

The main work of the ACC has centered on the furtherance of economic and social cooperation through the avoidance of overlapping activities and needless duplication of effort. Few, if any, activities on the international plane are the exclusive concern of the United Nations or of one specialized agency. A measure of consultation on who is to do what is almost always desirable whatever the outcome. On basic economic and social studies, the examination of commodity trade problems, transport and communications, the conservation and utilization of resources and on refugees—in fact, on any questions where the interests of agencies or of the United Nations converge—consultation at the formative stage of the exercise became, if not mandatory, at least a hallmark of good bureaucratic behavior.

Consultation is one thing; concerted action is something quite different. When the ACC was asked to make its views known to the Economic and Social Council on the methods of financing a cooperative program—the Expanded Program of Technical Assistance—the Secretary-General had to report the lack of agreement on the establishment of a single common fund. The compromise arrangement is described in the following chapter.

Nevertheless, closer working relationships began to develop for two reasons. As action programs developed, the dangers of excessive duplication of effort became apparent and the harmonization of agency activities began to take place. Shared operations, for example, between FAO and WHO in the control of diseases which afflict man and animals, or joint investigations by the United Nations, ILO, UNESCO and FAO into community development problems, became commonplace. As more became known about development problems, it became increasingly clear that programs pursued along lines delimited by an agency's institutional competence in almost all cases were doomed to failure.

The second reason was an institutional one. With the creation of the Special Fund, a central policy-making body controlling a single fund, while prudently obtaining agency advice on technical matters, vigorously took decisions on how the agencies could be used in the overall strategy of development. They would then be retained to play their part. The United Nations Development Program, inaugurated in 1966, presents fresh opportunities for the adoption of a new and bold strategy of development with the Specialized Agencies enjoying an enhanced role, but one in which jurisdictional niceties and concerns of functional autonomy may be expected to cease to be of paramount importance.

Full circle. The proliferation of specialized agencies cooperating with the United Nations within the framework of agreements negotiated by them with the Economic and Social Council would now seem to have ended. Instead, the trend is towards the establishment of new bodies within the United Nations proper where they enjoy a degree of administrative autonomy. Their staffs are part of the United Nations Secretariat and their governing bodies elected by the Economic and Social Council or the General Assembly under terms of reference laid down by those Principal Organs.

The process began with the Special Fund, developed with the establishment of UNCTAD, the United Nations Development Program and the United Nations Industrial Development Organization (UNIDO). There is nothing new about this trend. As we saw at the beginning of this chapter, the early United Nations agencies such as UNICEF, UNHCR and UNRWA followed the same pattern. The experience of these agencies has shown how such diverse programs can be administered successfully from within the same house, yet enjoy an independence which enables them to make their own impressive contribution to the furtherance of the interests of the international community.

Though more flexible in terms of membership than the United Nations, several of the Specialized Agencies are more limited with respect to the actual members who participate. If there is any general criterion which can be observed regarding qualification for participation in the Specialized Agencies, it is that their entry is conditioned upon their being able to contribute to the purposes of the agency in question. Membership is often not restricted to states but includes in some cases, dependencies, Trust Territories and, in the case of the Universal Postal Union, a single postal administration. Even so, universality is not observed as fully as it is in the United Nations. In some agencies, such as FAO, several of the socialist countries including the U. S. S. R., do not participate. Neither are they members of the World Bank Group, nor IMF, preferring to keep their multilateral financial arrangements outside the Bretton Woods organizations.

Within the United Nations system, therefore, there is a wide variety of Specialized Agencies fashioned differently so as to tackle best their different functional responsibilities. As the needs of the world community increase and change, the Specialized Agencies may need to adjust to these changing requirements. The United

Nations Organization itself has shown, with what seemed like a rigid constitution, how it has adapted to the rapidly changing needs of a rapidly changing world. Although there may be little interest in increasing the number of the Specialized Agencies, there are, under periodic consideration, proposals for their reorganization and reallocation of function.

Chapter XII

THE REVERSED
SWIFTIAN THEORY

The action of the General Assembly, in 1948, setting in motion the beginnings of a United Nations technical assistance program to assist the economically underdeveloped countries, was destined to revolutionize the work and operations, not only of the United Nations but of practically all the Specialized Agencies as well. Having seen, in Chapter X, something of the works and machinery of economic and social cooperation in the United Nations and, in Chapter XI, of the structure of the other members of this far-flung family of international agencies, we should now trace the experience of the United Nations system working in harness for the welfare and development of the international community.

In 1948, the times could have hardly seemed less conducive to starting international action programs, with the Berlin airlift and other crises demanding attention. But in that year $350,000 was voted to provide for a United Nations Technical Assistance Program. In voting this small amount to start a modest program, the General Assembly provided some initial guidance on how the program was to be administered. Assistance could be made available only at the request of governments themselves to meet urgent needs. It should be provided completely free of political considerations. Governments of countries receiving assistance would be expected to contribute to the solution of the problems concerning which international assistance had been requested. As international programs evolved, these original criteria became embodied as basic requirements.

The debates and discussions, from which the early programs emerged, were mainly concerned with the short-term transitional problems of India and Pakistan and other countries which had just become independent. The dimensions of the problems of the under-developed countries and the need to mobilize massive international support to assist these countries in overcoming them was not fully comprehended; this was to come later.

An "expanded program." In 1949, the Economic and Social Council established the Expanded Program of Technical Assistance, in which the whole United Nations family would participate, drawing on extra-budgetary funds contributed voluntarily by governments which were members of the United Nations or of the Specialized Agencies. The climate of opinion changed almost overnight with the speech made by President Truman in 1950, in which he enunciated under "Point IV" of that statement the need to provide large-scale assistance to the underdeveloped countries and the role of the United Nations in channelling much of that assistance. The discussion was immediately raised to a higher level of significance.

"EPTA," as it came to be known, was designed to bring the technical competence of the United Nations and the Specialized Agencies to bear in a cooperative program of assistance to be placed at the disposal of the economically underdeveloped countries. In this way, a major program could be launched in an attack on poverty, disease, ignorance and economic backwardness.

Assistance would be provided in every sector of the economy as a result of the rapidly accumulating experience in the United Nations and the family of Specialized Agencies. Planning in economic development and the organization of public services; vocational and management training and trade union activities; agriculture, including fishery, forestry and animal husbandry; education; public health and disease control; and the development of transport and communications, including civil aviation—all of these were considered areas in which support could be provided.

The forms in which such support was made available were aimed at the transfer of skills from the developed to the underdeveloped; this called for the services of highly qualified experts with the ability to work alongside their opposite numbers in the developing countries and to transfer the skills to them. Fellowships were also made available so that advanced training could be provided abroad to limited numbers of the "counterparts," as the opposite numbers in the assisted countries were called, so that they could, on their return, take over from the international experts.

Contributions in usable currencies were voluntarily pledged on an annual basis at a Pledging Conference held every year, usually during the period of the General Assembly.

The Economic and Social Council set up the Technical Assistance Committee (TAC) as a standing body to oversee the new program. The central coordinating body was the Technical Assistance Board (TAB), comprising the administrative heads of the technical assistance programs of the United Nations Technical Assistance Administration and of the Specialized Agencies. This body was presided over by the representative of the Secretary-General who, in 1952, became, full time, the Executive Chairman of the Board. Such was the machinery established to run the new program, which began operations in 1950.

To facilitate the handling of requests for assistance and the coordination and supervision of the support provided to governments, many of the agencies in countries where they had larger programs appointed their own mission chiefs. With the increasing impact of the Expanded Program, Resident Representatives of the Technical Assistance Board were appointed by the Executive Chairman to provide overall coordination on the spot.

Within this framework, the Expanded Program increased in utility and grew in size, drawing on the voluntary contributions of many more governments and extending support to practically all the economically underdeveloped countries. The enlargement of the Program was not an even progression. For 1953, there was a loss of momentum as demands for assistance outstripped the resources available. This period of belt-tightening served as an opportunity to review and improve the techniques and administration of technical assistance. In 1956, country programming techniques were adopted by which the requirements of each country were projected, on the basis of which the total program was shared between the United Nations and each of the Specialized Agencies participating in EPTA. A Contingency Fund was set up to be administered by the Executive Chairman to meet requests for assistance which were not foreseen when the country programs were formulated. Eventually, biennial programming was adopted and the role of the Resident Representative strengthened. Thus, a degree of stability was introduced together with some much needed flexibility in meeting the needs of developing countries, particularly those that were becoming independent in increasing numbers.

Under the lee of the United Nations Technical Assistance Program, a new and still small program designed to transfer senior administrators to the service of the developing countries had its beginnings. In a world where nationalism was not so virulent, there was nothing odd about a national of one country serving the government of another. Hugo Grotius, it will be recalled, served as the Ambassador of Sweden to France. Earlier, Marco Polo was the Governor of a Chinese province. Today, this would scarcely be possible. But the experience of the Expanded Program had pointed up the urgent need for governments to strengthen their administrations, particularly because in the underdeveloped countries, as elsewhere in the world, government functions had broadened and the public sector had widened.

In 1958, drawing initially upon regular program funds, then subsequently on EPTA funds, an experimental program was approved by the General Assembly called OPEX (Operational, Executive and Administrative Personnel). The United Nations was able to provide senior administrators to the civil services of the developing countries as a short-term measure to strengthen their administration in key areas, particularly that of economic planning and execution. Such civil servants received local salaries but their additional emoluments and travel costs were met from technical assistance funds.

Financing. In the identification of the world economic problems, in the debates of the Economic and Social Council and in the Economic and Financial Committee of the General Assembly, the financing of economic development rapidly became the central issue. The international flow of private capital had shrunk to a trickle compared with, say, such movements in the period before 1914. Lending by the International Bank for Reconstruction and Development, however, had extended to the economically developing countries and had steadily increased in volume. But this was lending at commercial rates and by the early nineteen sixties the external debt burden of many countries had reached a point where further international borrowing on these terms did not seem feasible. In the nineteen fifties, in any case, this kind of financing did not reach down in sufficient quantities to the economic infrastructure of the underdeveloped countries. The mock lament of Mark Twain: "Oh! what a pity there is never enough money in the world" came to have a more sardonic ring.

Normally, the financing of the capital costs of basic services, such as schools, hospitals and communications, is undertaken by the government from tax revenues, or local financing through the bond market. In most of the underdeveloped countries, because income per head is so low, the marginal propensity to consume is high and there are little or no savings for investment. As a partial measure to fill this void, in 1952, a committee of nine experts appointed by the Secretary-General recommended the establishment of a Special United Nations Fund for Economic Development (SUNFED) which would provide grants-in-aid and long-term, low interest loans for the financing of the economic and social infrastructure of the underdeveloped countries. An initial capital of 250 million dollars was called for. Supported by most of the underdeveloped countries and some of the developed (notably the Netherlands), the proposal was opposed by most of the economically developed.

The opposition stemmed from the concern of the potentially major contributors over the high levels of taxation prevailing in their countries, the burden of maintaining a high level of armaments and the need to find additional support for well-tried and successful programs, such as those of technical assistance. Perhaps underlying these objections was the apprehension of the developed countries at the prospect of placing large funds at the disposal of the United

Nations where, with the developed countries being a minority in the General Assembly, the underdeveloped countries might exercise their majority vote to control a fund to which they were only likely to be marginal contributors.

The "SUNFED debate" permeated practically all the economic organs of the United Nations throughout the nineteen fifties. The establishment by IBRD of two affiliates, the International Finance Corporation (IFC) in 1956 and the International Development Association (IDA) in 1962—the latter with many of the characteristics of the ill-fated SUNFED—did little to reduce the intensity with which the proposal for a United Nations capital development fund was pursued. The debate continues in a broader context, made possible by the accumulating experience of United Nations economic organs in development programs and in the light of the changing needs of the developing countries themselves. In 1966, in the teeth of opposition by the potential major contributors, the General Assembly decided to establish a United Nations Capital Development Fund to begin operations in 1968. But the debate's most tangible contribution to date as far as the United Nations is directly concerned, was in the establishment, in 1958, of the Special Fund.

A compromise that worked.   Beginning its operations in 1959, the United Nations Special Fund represented the first major departure, since the establishment of the Expanded Program, along the road to the creation of development assistance on a large scale within the United Nations framework. Due mainly to the initiative of the Secretariat acting on behalf of the Secretary-General and in consultation with delegations with special interest or responsibility in economic development programs, the General Assembly in 1957 called for the creation of a special fund which, while it could not finance capital expenditures, would through pre-investment surveys, research schemes and training programs, make a significant impact on the development process.

The United Nations Special Fund.   In 1957 the General Assembly, therefore, appointed a preparatory committee to define the basic needs for assistance and the operational machinery required and to ask governments what they would be prepared to contribute.

The General Assembly added a thumbnail sketch of a fund that would be multilateral in character and devoted to assisting the underdeveloped countries. Control would be vested in a governing body reflecting in its membership a parity between donors and recipients. The fund would have an executive head. A link with the proposed SUNFED was preserved through the provision that, when the resources prospectively available were of the order of magnitude of $100 million, the status of the fund would be reviewed. A deadline of 1 January 1959 was set for starting operations.

The preparatory committee, using as its principal conference paper the recommendations of the Secretary-General concerning the new fund, reported to the Economic and Social Council which, in turn, forwarded the committee's proposals to the Thirteenth General Assembly together with a draft resolution for adoption.

In the words of the resolution adopted in 1958, the Special Fund was designed: "To provide systematic and sustained assistance in fields essential to the integrated technical, economic and social development of the less developed countries."

The Special Fund was to enlarge the scope of technical assistance and to concentrate on relatively large projects of high priority likely to lead to earliest results. These projects might be supported over a period of several years and should be integrated with national and other international development programs. Regional as well as national projects would fall within its scope. There should be no interference in the domestic affairs of recipients, and assistance should be so provided as to enable an early transfer of responsibilities to the countries concerned. Over a period, an even geographical spread of assistance should be maintained.

More specifically, the Special Fund should assist in the development of all economic sectors. Project support should take the form of surveys, research and training, including pilot and demonstration schemes. Special Fund support could involve expert services, equipment, supplies and services, and a limited number of fellowships for training counterpart staff abroad as an integral part of the project. Governments would be expected to contribute towards the cost of such schemes and participate actively in them.

The structure of the Special Fund was to include a Governing Council of eighteen members elected by the Economic and Social Council with the balanced participation required by the 1957 resolution. Voting would be by a two-thirds majority. Among its responsibilities was the approval of programs recommended by the Managing Director.

The somewhat elaborate provisions concerning the appointment of the Managing Director were indicative of the significance attached by the General Assembly to his role. His appointment by the Secretary-General was to be made after consultation with the Governing Council and confirmation by the General Assembly. In the Managing Director was vested the sole authority for deciding what projects should be recommended for approval by the Governing Council.

Assisted by a small staff recruited on the basis of their special competence, the Managing Director was also chairman of a small Consultative Board comprising the Secretary-General of the United Nations, the President of IBRD and the Executive Chairman of the Technical Assistance Board.

Some misplaced criticisms. Although there were some conspicuous gaps in the resolution (including how such a major development effort was to be carried out effectively), it was a most impressive act of the General Assembly in economic matters. Some differences and hesitations had featured in the negotiations. The underdeveloped countries were not satisfied with the tenuous link with the proposed SUNFED. They would have preferred elections to the Governing Council to take place not in the Economic and Social Council but in the General Assembly where their influence was greater. Most of all, they criticized the "qualified" voting arrangements whereby a two-thirds majority was required in a body half of which was composed of developed countries. Many of the Specialized Agencies, accustomed to the spirit of collegiality that prevailed in the Technical Assistance Board, were critical of being excluded from membership (although not necessarily from participation) in the Consultative Board.

The apprehensions that gave rise to those criticisms were, for the most part, misplaced. Except on one occasion—and then a procedural matter was involved—the Governing Council of the Special Fund never voted but carried out its business by arriving always at a consensus. The United Nations and its family of agencies came to have exclusive responsibility for carrying out Special Fund supported projects and their technical evaluation was always sought before decisions were taken by the Managing Director.

Many of the features of the Special Fund represent a refinement of the techniques and approaches originated in the Expanded Program. Support is not available for country programs, with the United Nations and the participating agencies assuming percentage shares of the total program, but on a project by project basis. Assistance can be projected over a number of years so that forward planning both by the governments and the Special Fund can take place without being subject to the annual pledge of funds. Government applications, as with the Expanded Program, are submitted through a single channel designated by the government—usually the Ministry of Planning—and not by individual ministries. Increased emphasis is placed on the primary role of the developing countries themselves, the assistance provided by the Special Fund serving to underpin and meet part of the foreign exchange component in the development effort. Finally, support is made available according to certain criteria laid down by the Managing Director.

A change of mood. The appointment of Paul G. Hoffman, the former Chief Administrator of the Marshall Plan, as Managing Director and, for the initial formative period, Professor (now Sir) Arthur Lewis as his deputy, resulted in an aggressive management and high standards of administrative efficiency that became a continuing feature of the direction of the Special Fund. Their bracing effect was not limited to those who worked in the Special Fund. The new approaches to development assistance called for a major tooling up throughout the United Nations family of agencies and for some psychological adjustment, not only on the part of the agencies, but also by government authorities responsible for obtaining international assistance.

Nevertheless, the Special Fund followed the pattern of work

elaborated under the Expanded Program. Funds were pledged by members of the United Nations or of the Specialized Agencies each year at the same conference where technical assistance funds were pledged. Joint administrative arrangements were established for both programs. The Resident Representatives of the Technical Assistance Board also became Special Fund agents, and their field offices were strengthened for this purpose. Close working relationships were maintained throughout, particularly in the field where technical assistance experts came to play a significant role in helping governments to identify projects suitable for Special Fund support and assisting in their formulation, evaluation and, in many cases, their eventual implementation.

A look at procedures. . . As a general framework for the provision of assistance a Basic Agreement is signed by the Special Fund with the government interested in receiving assistance. A government submits its application to the Managing Director through the Resident Representative. The submission, to be considered, has to be of a pre-investment character. If the request is within the terms of reference of the Special Fund, it will be evaluated by the staff in consultation with the United Nations, TAB, IBRD and other specialized agencies concerned. If necessary, the submission is reformulated jointly with the government, possibly drawing on the services of consultants specially retained for this purpose.

When the project has been appraised and prepared, it is reviewed by the Consultative Board and then submitted to the Governing Council as part of the program presented at one of its biannual sessions where it is approved and the required funds earmarked. Following approval, the Executing Agency, which would be the United Nations or one of the Specialized Agencies (or the International Atomic Energy Agency) retained by the Special Fund to carry out the work, will prepare a Plan of Operation for implementing the project. This is signed by the government, the Special Fund and the Executing Agency, and, after a cash payment to the Special Fund of a sum to assist it in meeting certain local expenditures, the project starts. From government contributions, held in liquid form by the United Nations Controller, the funds required for the project by the Special Fund are then disbursed.

A systematic review of the progress of the project takes place throughout the period of Special Fund support. Consultations take place toward the end of the project on the timely transfer of responsibilities to the participating governments including, in certain cases where follow-up investment is proposed, the services of a financial adviser.

. . . and policy. The Special Fund aims at supporting projects designed to attract (or underpin) investment or to raise productivity. It will not normally support schemes which call for a Special Fund involvement of less than $250,000 (the Expanded Program usually dealing with requests up to this amount). Nor can it participate in capital financing, i.e. it can assist in the feasibility surveys of a dam site—as it did for the Kainji Dam in Nigeria—but it is not permitted to participate in financing its construction.

Governments are expected to contribute to the scheme, and on an average 60 per cent of the total costs are met by them, although there is no fixed percentage, burden sharing being determined by the requirements of each project. The Special Fund, however, will not meet expenditures in local currency or provide services or equipment locally obtainable.

Within its first three months of existence, $125 million of viable project applications were received. But, because pledges for 1959 amounted to little more than $25 million, some stringent criteria had to be adopted and these continue to apply in varying degrees. With regard to surveys, the Managing Director decided to assist only those which call for intensive investigation with a likelihood of early results. Preliminary or general reconnaissance surveys were ruled out. For example, detailed soil surveys following reconnaissance conducted under other auspices, or mineral investigations based on prior studies which indicate the probable availability of mineral bearing ores in commercial quantity are preferred. The ability to apply the results have to be demonstrated. There would have to be a competent soils unit, say, in the Ministry of Agriculture to apply the soil survey, or a development corporation or commercial concern ready to exploit the mineral survey if it showed promise.

Similar criteria are applied to training schemes. The principle of only "training trainers" is followed, so that government expenditures and international participation would yield their maximum benefit. On this principle, school teachers would not be provided, but support would be made available for training school teachers through establishing or strengthening a teachers' training college. Initially, at least, emphasis was placed on post-secondary school vocational training, and only in agriculture was support provided at university levels. Here again, governments would be expected to demonstrate their willingness to maintain the institutions receiving external support at the appropriate level. To ensure that governments assumed such responsibilities, Special Fund support would be applied on a diminishing scale toward the end of the project and government involvement proportionately increased.

Finally, pure research would normally fall outside the scope of the Special Fund. Applied research would be supported if it were likely to lead to early results which would have an impact on development, preferably in a whole region. In East Africa, the rapid development of the cattle industry is predicated upon cheap and effective control of tick-borne diseases such as East Coast Fever. Scientific research to develop an East Coast Fever vaccine and of operational research to clear infested areas of tse-tse flies in Kenya are typical of applied research schemes of great urgency and potential economic significance, not only for Kenya but for other affected countries.

The proof of the pudding. The proof of the pudding is not in the eating, as we are often led to believe, but in the digestion. The impact of eight years of Special Fund support has yet to be measured. To evaluate the significance of any work in progress is always difficult; consequently, in the case of the Special Fund, anything other than an interim evaluation will have to wait.

However, in an attempt to make an interim evaluation and to show the interaction of various United Nations agencies, we have chosen the biggest and most complex of the many Special Fund projects—one which combines all aspects of United Nations development activity and one that might prove to be a *locus classicus* of how international assistance linked with determined and strenuous efforts of both the underdeveloped and the developed countries can achieve, just possibly, a complete success where success was never considered possible.

The problem. A scourge since Biblical times, the desert locust marauds all the way from Afghanistan to the Atlantic, cutting a swathe of crop destruction across southwestern Asia, the Middle East and Africa. In its path lies one-eighth of the world's population, for the most part dependent on the crops the desert locust periodically has ruined.

A swarm of the desert locust can measure five miles by twenty-three. Twenty or thirty such swarms can operate in one area at the same time, stripping vegetation and leaving the land bare. Swarms can become plagues, such as the formations that blacked out Delhi and the surrounding countryside for several days in 1961.

Locust invasions cause increased crop losses, as new areas in the countries, lying in the "high frequency belt" of desert locust activity, enter into cultivation. By 1958, the governments most affected met in Damascus with FAO to discuss what steps they might take to improve, in concert, their control measures.

No one thought—least of all the experts—that a 4,000-year-old menace could be wiped out any more than the common cold could be cured. Also the locust, knowing no frontiers and capable of ranging 700 miles or more in a matter of weeks, is a global menace and as such had to be tackled globally. Perhaps, by doing so, international control measures could reduce the total cost and introduce newer and more efficient techniques of control.

Not that no one had attempted this before. In the interwar period, both the French and British governments conducted research on how to control the pest. During World War II, to keep up food production in East Africa and the Middle East in the rear of the Allied armies fighting in the Western Desert, vigorous control measures were attempted. After the war, on the basis of this earlier experience, FAO, drawing on technical assistance funds, assisted as well as it could to coordinate control measures and to concentrate them in the most likely outbreak areas. But it had never been possible to mount a large-scale international assault on the desert locust because of the lack of funds, and the absence of a body which could bring all the countries concerned together and give them the necessary support for a concerted attack.

Strategy. When the Special Fund started work in 1959, it was confronted with the request of the governments which met in Damascus. The Managing Director informed them that he would be prepared to support a six-year project if the governments themselves were willing to pay—in addition to their own control measures—at least one-third of the total cost. Also, he informed them, there was little point in embarking upon such a long-range enterprise unless they were prepared to maintain international control operations on a continuing basis after the six-year period of Special Fund support had ended.

To the surprise of many, these conditions were found acceptable, and in addition a burden-sharing arrangement by which countries which suffered most from desert locust invasions paid the most.

With international agreement thus secured, the next step was to decide what to do. A small group representing the top scientific talent from all over the world was brought together to consider what long-range measures should be adopted. An ecological survey would be carried out to find the breeding areas of the desert locust. Field research stations would be strengthened, or new ones established to conduct field trials with new control techniques. Pest control officers would be trained in the techniques thus developed. An international flight of aircraft would carry out operational research into the efficiency and cost of low-density air spraying with different kinds of insecticide over wide areas. Finally, the international warning system centered on the Anti-Locust Research Center in London would be strengthened to become a nerve center where information on desert locust movements would be received, plotted and analyzed, and warnings sent to the countries lying in the path of locusts so that their control units could be made ready for action.

On the basis of the proposals of the scientists, the Governing Council of the Special Fund approved a project costing $3,614,000 with the governments paying for $1,400,000, the balance being obtained from the Special Fund. In April 1960, sixteen governments signed a Plan of Operation. FAO was given the task of carrying out the project as the Executing Agency of the Special Fund.

By 1964, the ecological survey had been completed. Likely breeding grounds had been studied beginning in West Africa and ending in Pakistan. Hundreds of pest control officers had received advanced training in courses held in Morocco, Ethiopia, India and Pakistan. Scientists had the opportunity, through exchange visits, to study how work was progressing elsewhere and to carry out research in the more developed research centers in Asmara, Dakar, London and Algiers. The map became dotted with field research stations across the world, and desert locust control forces were strengthened, or set up for the first time in some countries such as Afghanistan.

The reporting and forecasting network was tightened. With assistance from WMO and with regular photographic coverage from the TIROS weather satellite, the advanced warning system reached a high level of sophistication by relating meteorological data to reports of desert locust movements. Aircraft used on an international scale demonstrated how hopper bands of locusts could be totally destroyed at low cost.

During the years from 1960 to 1966, the original sixteen participants increased to forty-two thus including almost every country in Asia, Africa and the Middle East, subject to invasion. The project became the only international operation to include Israel and all the Arab countries.

Work on the ground was complemented by political activity. Regional control organizations slowly came into being. In West Africa the French-supported *Organization Commune pour la Lutte Antiacridienne* took over crop protection on an international basis. The Desert Locust Control Organization for Eastern Africa also came into being, followed by control commissions in southwestern Asia, the Arabian peninsular and finally for the Magreb countries of North Africa. By mid-1966, control organizations on a regional basis were tooled up for control purposes, the new techniques were established and training was provided in their use with an international trust fund established by FAO to maintain international cooperation on a continuing basis.

Nothing fails like success. What of the desert locust itself? As a result of several factors, the desert locust has almost completely disappeared in a trough of inactivity. Solitary locusts and occasional immature swarms are still reported but a careful watch is kept on their whereabouts. What caused this? Definitely the timely and systematic introduction internationally of the latest aerial spray techniques has played its part. The late arrival of the monsoon in Asia in 1963 and the cold winter that year in other areas also had a significant effect. Perhaps, also, for some as yet unknown biological reason, the desert locust declined in activity just as have other plagues in history.

Will governments with many claims on their limited resources, be prepared to maintain the interlocking complex of control now established or will they let their guard drop? The temptation in national treasuries will doubtless be to dismantle what would seem now to be no longer needed. The answer may lie in broadening desert locust control to other pests such as the weaver bird and the army worm, susceptible to control by the same techniques. In West Africa this has already been done. If adopted elsewhere, the experience gained can be applied in crop protection on a broader front and the apparatus maintained in readiness in case of a resurgence in locust activity.

As we have discussed in earlier chapters, in international cooperation success cannot always be measured by the extent to which the objective is achieved. Often the ancillary results, the side effects, are most significant. Even if the plagues return to swamp the control services now developed, the six years of international effort and achievement have taught many lessons and enabled a tremendous fund of experience to be accumulated in the ways governments can work together for the common good through international institutions.

The United Nations Development Program. The merger of the Expanded Program and the Special Fund in 1966 into the United Nations Development Program was a natural outcome of the earlier experience of both programs. It provides for an integrated attack instead of a cooperative one on development problems. The Technical Assistance Committee of the Economic and Social Council is merged with the Governing Council of the Special Fund to make a UNDP Governing Council of thirty-seven members. The Technical Assistance Board and the Consultative Board have been replaced by the Inter-Agency Consultative Board with an increased membership, as its title implies. The staffs have been blended with the Managing Director appointed as Administrator and the Executive Chairman as Co-Administrator of the Development Program.

Food surpluses and development. Perhaps one of the most successful aid programs of the United States has been that of food surplus disposal permitted by Public Law 480. The massive farm surpluses, maintained at an increasing cost to the taxpayer, have been drawn down and shipped to feed the hungry of other lands. Other countries, such as Canada, followed suit and, today, bilateral food aid programs have an average annual total value of some $2 billion.

After a period of debate and consultation in the United Nations and FAO, the General Assembly and the FAO Conference jointly established, in 1962, a World Food Program for an experimental period of three years beginning in 1963. Under the direction of its governing body, the Intergovernmental Committee, and vigorous administration by A. H. Boerma, its Executive Director, the World Food Program at the end of 1965 was placed on a continuing basis.

The Program, in effect, is PL 480 internationalized with global participation. Its resources for the initial period were nearly $100 million in commodities, cash and services pledged voluntarily by some seventy governments.

As long as they do not disturb normal patterns of trade or price stability, commodities may be shipped at the request of the recipient governments. Much assistance has been devoted to emergency food needs. Faced with natural disasters such as earthquakes, hurricanes, floods and droughts, twenty-five countries have received surplus foods. Assistance has gone to countries acting as hosts to refugees. Uganda, for example, is housing refugees from three neighboring countries and is receiving regular shipments of food surpluses.

While food aid is made available in such emergencies, as well as for school and special feeding programs, the World Food Program has, as it major aim, not relief, as such, but development. In large-scale resettlement schemes the introduction of commodity surpluses can lighten the burden of cost to the government and relieve the newly-settled farmer of anxiety over his early harvests. Where labor is diverted to industrial development or major construction schemes, food may be used as a partial substitute for wages in cash; 116 such development programs have received an underpinning wedge of food aid during the three-year trial period.

The problems of administering an international commodity surplus program, on a global scale, in the interest of the economically developing countries are considerable. The application of counterpart funds accumulated from the sale locally of food surpluses may pose special problems if food aid is applied on a massive scale. Fortunately the Program has been administered with a flexibility rare in international administration, with considerable freedom of action given to the Executive Director who is permitted by his governing body to allocate up to $100,000 of surpluses without prior authorization. On the basis of the initial three-year experience, both the United Nations and FAO agreed at the end of 1965 to put the Program on a continuing basis. At the Pledging Conference held at the same time, forty-four governments made commitments for 1966 totalling more than $208 million.

Both the United Nations and FAO recognized that as experience is accumulated, careful study of the role of food aid in the development process should be undertaken. At present, both bilateral and international programs of this kind are needed in the face of the relative failure—in spite of great efforts—of the agricultural sector in the developing countries. In the long-run such countries have no alternative but to increase their domestic food supply. In such cases food aid can serve as a timely diversion, enabling countries to determine their development policies free from the pressures of recurrent food deficit. Others, such as India, are unlikely to be able to feed themselves entirely from their own resources at least in this century. For them, food shipments should be programmed on a long-term basis.

The "Development Decade." The nineteen sixties have been designated by the United Nations as the "Development Decade." A target has been set up for a five per cent annual growth rate for the underdeveloped countries and the diversion of one per cent of the national income of the developed countries to the development needs of the underdeveloped. At midpoint the United Nations has been taking stock in debates of unprecedented frankness.

The results of the "Development Decade" so far are not heartening. The growth rate has not been near the target rate, and increases in population in many countries nullify much of the growth that has taken place. Furthermore, there has been no net increase in the volume of development assistance. Development programming and the ways in which external aid can be most effective is considerably more complex than was thought. Pivotal scarcities in the agricultural sector are difficult to overcome. The acceleration of industrialization in the underdeveloped countries by drawing on the "pool of technology" of the developed countries presents unforeseen difficulties.

These problems are probably better understood in United Nations bodies than anywhere else, but international programs, on which they could have a direct impact, comprise only a fraction of total aid. India, for example, is the greatest recipient of external assistance; but less than one per cent comes through international sources. Also, the complexity of the problems and the long-term nature of their solution are only now becoming known. Both government and international officials have tended on occasion to be dazzled by the short-term success of the Marshall Plan in bringing about Western European recovery, or of the rapid economic growth of Japan, and to generalize from this experience. Economic and social factors were present in such cases which suggest that this experience has little bearing on the problems of the developing countries.

In spite of the immensity of the tasks which are now becoming apparent, if the purposes of the Charter are to be fulfilled, there are encouraging signs within the United Nations organs themselves. The tools of analysis of world economic problems have improved. There is a rapidly accumulating body of international experience and competence in development matters. The techniques of confrontation by which national policies can be harmonized in the international interest have been refined. As a recognition of this process, governments are prepared to embark upon such discussions with increasing confidence. New bodies, such as the Advisory Committee on the Application of Science and Technology to Development, for instance, are drawing together experienced scientists and administrators with international reputations, to consider how the main development obstacles can be overcome.

A semantic footnote should be added. In the early years of the United Nations, the economically less developed countries were termed "undeveloped." In the 1950s they were termed "economically underdeveloped." In the spirit of the 1960s we now use the term "economically developing." The changes in terminology reflect the gradual shift in attitude and approach to development problems indicative of the changing climate of opinion from a negative to a more positive approach on the part of the international community.

A similar development can be seen in the changing role and significance of international programs. Let us recall a rhyme of Dean Swift.

> So, naturalists observe, a flea
> Hath smaller fleas that on him prey;
> And these have smaller fleas to bite'em,
> And so proceed *ad infinitum.*
> Thus every poet, in his kind,
> Is bit by him that comes behind.

This observation would now seem to be reversed. From very small beginnings in a United Nations technical assistance program, the Expanded Program developed. This was overtaken by the United Nations Special Fund. In turn the United Nations Development Program has emerged. This trend will continue possibly with a larger United Nations capital development fund and, in time, a multilateral food grains authority. No one likes being bitten by what comes behind, least of all administrators. But the process is unavoidable, as the international community is increasingly involved in such programs, as experience is accumulated, and the collective competence of the United Nations family of agencies begins to have its full impact.

Chapter XIII

THE SOCIAL COSMOS

The avid Pogo fan may recall the trouble Mr. Owl got into when he ran a bathing beauty contest. When questioned by "Miz" Beaver on the title with which he intended to endow the winner, he replied "Miss Cosmos." Cosmos, Mr. Owl explained, was not in this case a plant, but implied the universe in perfect order; in other words "Miss Universal Harmony."

"Jus' like a man . . . you gonna throw a bunch of females in a contest 'bout which is pertiest an' you expects Universal Harmony?"

One does not need to be a Pogo addict to see what "Miz" Beaver was driving at, nor, indeed, to see the relevance of the comment to our study. In our international society the well-informed and the well-intentioned strive toward the establishment of a social cosmos—a universe in perfect order.

That this will never be achieved is not important. The social cosmos is a myth, the pursuit of which leads international society to seek the paths of peace and mutual understanding and accommodation. The economist sees nothing strange in applying his talents to steering the economy towards a state of equilibrium. He knows he will not achieve this, but he is not concerned with equilibrium as such, but with the optimum use of the scarce resources at his disposal, and the concept of equilibrium is a useful device for him to use. And just as the economist now sees the need for introducing increasingly sophisticated techniques of economic planning and control in pursuit of his unattainable aim, so the social cosmologist—for that is what he is—has striven toward a social cosmos by depending increasingly upon institutionalized forms of international cooperation.

We began by postulating the nation-state. It is not, as we might be in some danger of assuming, the author of all our international troubles. It is merely the vehicle of a social group. Lacking it we would not have been able to develop that degree of social cohesion without which there would be little order, less law and little art. Within the state men have, more or less, learned to live in peace if not always in prosperity. The Aristotelian "will towards society" which serves well for the state, however, does not yet extend to the planet as a whole. It consequently is taking us longer to learn how states can live in peace with one another.

Of monkeys and men. Forty years ago, if we were studying international society, in all likelihood we would have been influenced by the Marxian argument that conflict between rival capitalisms was inevitable as economic power came to be concentrated in fewer and fewer hands. We would have been assured that this was the nature of the beast.

Twenty years ago, with the lessons of the nineteen thirties forcibly brought home to us by the ruins, death, destruction and dislocation of World War II, we probably would have sought to understand international conflict as originating in the wickedness of evil men, and the indolence of good men in not acting to contain evil until it was too late to avoid a holocaust. We might well have reached the conclusion, had we had an earlier brush with Freud, that dictators were the product of angry father complexes; the indolent, the result of late weaning practices; and there lay the roots of our troubles.

If we are aggressively "lowbrow" we would, in any age, possibly settle for the concept that "You can't change human nature." Whether from Original Sin or from some dark, ineradicable, destructive force in each of us, we all have to have our spot of bloodletting. And with this hackneyed saying, we would sit back and let others do our thinking for us.

Very recent studies of the behavior of wild howler monkeys,

gibbons, langurs, Japanese monkeys and other primates in their natural habitats are leading us to reconsider not only our views on *their* social organization, but to think on how their behavior might have a bearing on our own.

We have come a longer way in our two million years than, say, the ant has in his fifty million. The ant continues to live a totalitarian life, organized for total war in which he indulges until he is either enslaved or exterminated. Only a few species have developed to the point where they have a settled agriculture with a relatively peaceful domestic existence.

When man began to be man in primitive food-gathering groups two million years back, his life may not have been unlike that of the primates whose behavior we now observe. To our surprise we find here that nature is not, as Tennyson assured us, "red in tooth and claw," but ordered and peaceful. Among primates, violence is almost universally rare. Primates of the same species live in peace. Each band has a recognized territory, recognized feeding grounds, sleeping areas and migration routes. Within the common domain of the band, rights prevail and these are assured by careful restraint and highly sophisticated patterns of behavior depending in turn upon an elaborate social structure. Amicability exists between as well as within bands. Violence has hardly any place in primate society.

Strength—or power as it is now called—is not used. Prestige, which is an expression of strength, is all that is needed. A band of howler monkeys when in need of demonstrating its strength just howls; so does the band confronting it. The band that makes the least noise takes the hint and withdraws from the field. Such a violence-less society calls for elaborate skills of social evasion and mutual understanding of a kind we have yet to acquire in ours. Primates do seem, indeed, to have developed these social skills. The techniques employed, such as avoidance and redirection of aggressiveness in the more powerful, or the distraction of the strong by pseudo-sexual activity on the part of the weak, may have familiar overtones, but such tactics may have little relevance to our present study.

Although, at first sight, violence has no role in primate society, violence does certainly occur, but only when society itself breaks down. Violence is a manifestation of social stress with which primate society is inadequate to deal. Lack of social space, or to use a more acceptable but more inaccurate term, "population pressure," causes tensions which result in dislocation of the society and the degeneration into violence. Overpopulation is not the only cause of social disintegration. It can happen when bands find there is no scope for exploratory know-how or other naturally developed talents, initiative, versatility and enterprise, or that their surroundings become unfamiliar, or they have to cope with new training methods or new tool kits. Consequently, friends become fractious and relatives rivals. Under social stress leadership degenerates into dictatorship and produces meaningless violence.

We are beginning to have a glimmering of what is involved for us here. The student of Ekistics (human settlement) at the Doxiadis Planning Institute in Athens may now spend as much time being trained as a physical planner in grasping the implications of the "human bubble" (our version of the primates' "social space") as he does in learning how to devise cheap and efficient sewerage for the megalopolis. Within the state we need to understand the need for restraint, understanding and good neighborliness in order to live peacefully; how to preserve tradition yet permit innovation; and how to keep our vision of a better society at the same time as we doggedly plod forward, exploiting opportunities as they occur. If this is true of the city or of the state, it is true even more of international society.

Thucydides, who was a soldier as well as an historian, was the first to point out that conflict is a sign of stress in society. We have had to study primates to find out that what he observed in the Peloponnesus was probably true. But having taken the trouble through a fresh approach to throw new light on an old problem, where does this lead us? We need to develop an increased awareness and understanding of the nature of international society and of the tools at our disposal to shape it more effectively.

If the city is founded upon wisdom, so is the world. But how is the necessary degree of worldly awareness and worldly wisdom to be acquired, for without it we cannot, with any degree of certainty, study how international organizations can develop in the service of international society. It is unlikely that this could ever be achieved by education in the formal sense, for that remains perhaps the last great bastion of unrepentant nationalism or of local interest. Even in Switzerland, education remains the jealously guarded cantonal, not federal, preserve.

Habits of thinking and acting in the international interest have to be acquired. For as Pascal considered, there is no belief that cannot be induced by custom (or any concept that cannot be destroyed by it). The international institution itself has to assume the principal role in custom-inducing. This does not call for the constant refurbishing of the "image" of the institution, but by the institution seeking at all times to make a concrete contribution to the development of international society. Like the Stoics, we need to prove movement by walking.

In thinking about the way ahead for international society and the developing role of its institutions, there are three points which, although they have been touched upon before, deserve underlining.

The double legacy. Almost all of us are heirs to the concept, developed from Sophocles to Dante, of the supreme value of the individual and of the importance of justice and love (*philos*). This sanctifies not peace and submission, but revolution and upheaval in society. From Antigone onwards, the heroes or heroines have been in this tradition. We are also heir to the Roman legacy of order and law, by which social stability is of greater importance than any individual. Although it is sometimes difficult to see this through the misleading haze of conflicting ideology, the principal task of the international institution, whatever the aspect of international life with which it deals, is to strive to accommodate these forces and to harmonize them. Economic bodies, for example, are perennially concerned with maintaining economic stability at the same time as stimulating economic growth. The continuing process of striving to reconcile conflicting national economic interests and, at the same time, to accelerate the expansion of the world economy concerns everyone, for no one, however powerful, is entirely immune from its effects.

The early writers on international organizations were mainly interested in stability. The first international bodies, established in the nineteenth century, were designed to assist in the process of economic development throughout the world in the wake of the industrial revolution. The League of Nations was an upholder of order, although it could have been an instrument of change. The Charter may have been drawn up to bring order to the post-war world with the Great Powers enjoying a special position, but the Organization became very quickly a vehicle for rapid political, economic and social change.

The breaking of the bonds of restraint has its hazards. It is undesirable that international society should experience another Goa. At the same time, those who miss the so-called international stability of the past may be falling into the habits of old men no longer in a hurry. This kind of looking back to a golden age happens in one way or another in every generation. Plato in 421 B.C. grumbled, as did Aristophanes and even Thucydides (who should have known better), about the popular decline in standards since the days of Pericles, the evaporation of values, the new society prey to self-seekers who put private interest above public duty. Still, it was an age that produced Socrates. There is a tendency to romanticize about our history; after all, states as well as individuals tend to practice selective amnesia about their pasts.

The illusion of finality. We should take heed, however. There is nothing inevitable about progress, as Lord Acton would have found had he lived to see the trenches in 1917. Today the scientist, the historian and the theologian can join hands with Teilhard de Chardin who could ask, "Is life going anywhere?" and find comfort in the answer, "No!" History is not progress, but process: there is thus the equal possibility of regression as there is of progression. This is as true of international society and its institutions as of any other form of human activity.

There is, nevertheless, in all of us, an inner craving to be assured of the final outcome whether it is in the search for the ultimate weapon, a final settlement, or a foreign policy to end all foreign policies. The widespread assurance in the Middle Ages of the Last Judgment gave rise to no such longings. But from Descartes on this has been always present. Pascal describing the intellectual pursuits of the Mersenne circle—frequented by Hobbes in his exile—summed up this aspiration with great eloquence:

"We burn with the desire to find a firm foundation and a final constant basis whereon to erect a tower rising into infinity."

The Divine Comedy. The Charter of the United Nations eschews firmly the notion of finality which, for international society, would take the form of effective world government. But the Charter does embody the cosmological vision of an ordered society where universal justice prevails, aspiring always to a transcendental law.

Dante saw history as an immense and divinely ordained pattern. Man's understanding is finite, but the depth and dimensions of God's will are infinite. Dante had a vision of a cross-section of this. He saw a landscape occupied by human figures to whom had been entrusted a free will. This left mankind free to use its talents for good or for ill. But under the conflict and confusion which resulted, there existed the eschatological vision of an ordered society where universal justice presided. He thought he saw the partial fulfillment of this vision in the order of the Roman Empire which he wished to see re-created.

Dante's dream has a new relevance 700 years after his birth. The United Nations, in addition to being a hard-bitten operating organization, is also the expression of the eschatological vision. It is the living embodiment of the aspirations of many millions for an ordered international society where law may prevail and where change might take place peacefully. This vision is to be found in the opening words of the Charter:

"We the peoples of the United Nations determined to save succeeding generations from the scourge of war, . . ."

The extent to which we may be disillusioned about anything depends on the extent of our initial illusions. Disillusionment with the United Nations system can be avoided if we separate in our minds, on the one hand, the functions of the system and the extent to which they are carried out effectively and, on the other hand, the lofty aspiration and high hopes within which the United Nations system has its being.

Appendix 1

CHARTER OF THE UNITED NATIONS

[*Articles* 23, 27 and 61 are revised]

WE THE PEOPLES OF THE UNITED NATIONS DETERMINED

To save succeeding generations from the scourge of war, which twice in our lifetime has brought untold sorrow to mankind, and

To reaffirm faith in fundamental human rights, in the dignity and worth of the human person, in the equal rights of men and women and of nations large and small, and

To establish conditions under which justice and respect for the obligations arising from treaties and others sources of international law can be maintained, and

To promote social progress and better standards of life in larger freedom,

AND FOR THESE ENDS

To practice tolerance and live together in peace with one another as good neighbors, and

To unite our strength to maintain international peace and security, and

To ensure, by the acceptance of principles and the institution of methods, that armed force shall not be used, save in the common interest, and

To employ international machinery for the promotion of the economic and social advancement of all peoples,

HAVE RESOLVED TO COMBINE OUR EFFORTS
TO ACCOMPLISH THESE AIMS

Accordingly, our respective Governments, through representatives assembled in the city of San Francisco, who have exhibited their full powers found to be in good and due form, have agreed to the present Charter of the United Nations and do hereby establish an international organization to be known as the United Nations.

Chapter I
PURPOSES AND PRINCIPLES

Article 1

The Purposes of the United Nations are:

1. To maintain international peace and security, and to that end: to take effective collective measures for the prevention and removal of threats to the peace, and for the suppression of acts of aggression or other breaches of the peace, and to bring about by peaceful means, and in conformity with the principles of justice and international law, adjustment or settlement of international disputes or situations which might lead to a breach of the peace;

2. To develop friendly relations among nations based on respect for the principle of equal rights and self-determination of peoples, and to take other appropriate measures to strengthen universal peace;

3. To achieve international cooperation in solving international problems of an economic, social, cultural, or humanitarian character, and in promoting and encouraging respect for human rights and for fundamental freedoms for all without distinction as to race, sex, language, or religion; and

4. To be a center for harmonizing the actions of nations in the attainment of these common ends.

Article 2

The Organization and its Members, in pursuit of the Purposes stated in *Article* 1, shall act in accordance with the following Principles.

1. The Organization is based on the principle of the sovereign equality of all its Members.

2. All Members, in order to ensure to all of them the rights and benefits resulting from membership, shall fulfill in good faith the obligations assumed by them in accordance with the present Charter.

3. All Members shall settle their international disputes by peaceful means in such a manner that international peace and security, and justice, are not endangered.

4. All Members shall refrain in their international relations from the threat or use of force against the territorial integrity or political inde-

pendence of any state, or in any other manner, inconsistent with the Purposes of the United Nations.

5. All Members shall give the United Nations every assistance in any action it takes in accordance with the present Charter, and shall refrain from giving assistance to any state against which the United Nations is taking preventive or enforcement action.

6. The Organization shall ensure that states which are not Members of the United Nations act in accordance with these Principles so far as may be necessary for the maintenance of international peace and security.

7. Nothing contained in the present Charter shall authorize the United Nations to intervene in matters which are essentially within the domestic jurisdiction of any state or shall require the Members to submit such matters to settlement under the present Charter; but this principle shall not prejudice the application of enforcement measures under Chapter VII.

Chapter II
MEMBERSHIP

Article 3

The original Members of the United Nations shall be the states which, having participated in the United Nations Conference on International Organization at San Francisco, or having previously signed the Declaration by United Nations of January 1, 1942, sign the present Charter and ratify it in accordance with *Article* 110.

Article 4

1. Membership in the United Nations is open to all other peaceloving states which accept the obligations contained in the present Charter and, in the judgment of the Organization, are able and willing to carry out these obligations.

2. The admission of any such state to membership in the United Nations will be effected by a decision of the General Assembly upon the recommendation of the Security Council.

Article 5

A Member of the United Nations against which preventive or enforcement action has been taken by the Security Council may be suspended from the exercise of the rights and privileges of membership by the General Assembly upon the recommendation of the Security Council. The exercise of these rights and privileges may be restored by the Security Council.

Article 6

A Member of the United Nations which has persistently violated the Principles contained in the present Charter may be expelled from the Organization by the General Assembly upon the recommendation of the Security Council.

Chapter III
ORGANS

Article 7

1. There are established as the principal organs of the United Nations: a General Assembly, a Security Council, an Economic and Social Council, a Trusteeship Council, an International Court of Justice, and a Secretariat.

2. Such subsidiary organs as may be found necessary may be established in accordance with the present Charter.

Article 8

The United Nations shall place no restrictions on the eligibility of men and women to participate in any capacity and under conditions of equality in its principal and subsidiary organs.

Chapter IV
THE GENERAL ASSEMBLY

COMPOSITION

Article 9

1. The General Assembly shall consist of all the Members of the United Nations.

2. Each Member shall have not more than five representatives in the General Assembly.

FUNCTIONS AND POWERS

Article 10

The General Assembly may discuss any questions or any matters within the scope of the present Charter or relating to the powers and functions of any organs provided for in the present Charter, and, except as provided in *Article* 12, may make recommendations to the Members of the United Nations or to the Security Council or to both on any such questions or matters.

Article 11

1. The General Assembly may consider the general principles of cooperation in the maintenance of international peace and security, including the principles governing disarmament and the regulation of armaments, and may make recommendations with regard to such principles to the Members or to the Security Council or to both.

2. The General Assembly may discuss any questions relating to the maintenance of international peace and security brought before it by any Member of the United Nations, or by the Security Council, or by a state which is not a Member of the United Nations in accordance with *Article* 35, paragraph 2, and, except as provided in *Article* 12, may make recommendations with regard to any such question to the state or states concerned or to the Security Council or to both. Any such question on which action is necessary shall be referred to the Security Council by the General Assembly either before or after discussion.

3. The General Assembly may call the attention of the Security Council to situations which are likely to endanger international peace and security.

4. The powers of the General Assembly set forth in this Article shall not limit the general scope of *Article* 10.

Article 12

1. While the Security Council is exercising in respect of any dispute or situation the functions assigned to it in the present Charter, the General Assembly shall not make any recommendations with regard to that dispute or situation unless the Security Council so requests.

2. The Secretary-General, with the consent of the Security Council, shall notify the General Assembly at each session of any matters relative to the maintenance of international peace and security which are being dealt with by the Security Council and shall similarly notify the General Assembly, or the Members of the United Nations if the General Assembly is not in session, immediately the Security Council ceases to deal with such matters.

Article 13

1. The General Assembly shall initiate studies and make recommendations for the purpose of:

a. promoting international cooperation in the political field and encouraging the progressive development of international law and its codification;

b. promoting international cooperation in the economic, social, cultural, educational, and health fields, and assisting in the realization of human rights and fundamental freedoms for all without distinction as to race, sex, language, or religion.

2. The further responsibilities, functions, and powers of the General Assembly with respect to matters mentioned in paragraph 1(b) above are set forth in Chapters IX and X.

Article 14

Subject to the provisions of *Article* 12, the General Assembly may recommend measures for the peaceful adjustment of any situation, regardless of origin, which it deems likely to impair the general welfare or friendly relations among nations, including situations resulting from a violation of the provisions of the present Charter setting forth the Purposes and Principles of the United Nations.

Article 15

1. The General Assembly shall receive and consider annual and special reports from the Security Council; these reports shall include an account of the measures that the Security Council has decided upon or taken to maintain international peace and security.

2. The General Assembly shall receive and consider reports from the other organs of the United Nations.

Article 16

The General Assembly shall perform such functions with respect to the international trusteeship system as are assigned to it under Chapters XII and XIII, including the approval of the trusteeship agreements for areas not designated as strategic.

Article 17

1. The General Assembly shall consider and approve the budget of the Organization.

2. The expenses of the Organization shall be borne by the Members as apportioned by the General Assembly.

3. The General Assembly shall consider and approve any financial and budgetary arrangements with specialized agencies referred to in *Article* 57 and shall examine the administrative budgets of such special-

ized agencies with a view to making recommendations to the agencies concerned.

Article 18

1. Each member of the General Assembly shall have one vote.

2. Decisions of the General Assembly on important questions shall be made by a two-thirds majority of the members present and voting. These questions shall include: recommendations with respect to the maintenance of international peace and security, the election of the nonpermanent members of the Security Council, the election of the members of the Economic and Social Council, the election of members of the Trusteeship Council in accordance with paragraph 1 (c) of *Article* 86, the admission of new Members to the United Nations, the suspension of the rights and privileges of membership, the expulsion of Members, questions relating to the operation of the trusteeship system, and budgetary questions.

3. Decisions on other questions, including the determination of additional categories of questions to be decided by a two-thirds majority, shall be made by a majority of the members present and voting.

Article 19

A Member of the United Nations which is in arrears in the payment of its financial contributions to the Organization shall have no vote in the General Assembly if the amount of its arrears equals or exceeds the amount of the contributions due from it for the preceding two full years. The General Assembly may, nevertheless, permit such a Member to vote if it is satisfied that the failure to pay is due to conditions beyond the control of the Member.

PROCEDURE

Article 20

The General Assembly shall meet in regular annual sessions and in such special sessions as occasion may require. Special sessions shall be convoked by the Secretary-General at the request of the Security Council or of a majority of the Members of the United Nations.

Article 21

The General Assembly shall adopt its own rules of procedure. It shall elect its President for each session.

Article 22

The General Assembly may establish such subsidiary organs as it deems necessary for the performance of its functions.

Chapter V
THE SECURITY COUNCIL

Article 23

1. The Security Council shall consist of fifteen Members of the United Nations. The Republic of China, France, the Union of Soviet Socialist Republics, the United Kingdom of Great Britain and Northern Ireland, and the United States of America shall be permanent members of the Security Council. The General Assembly shall elect ten other Members of the United Nations to be non-permanent members of the Security Council, due regard being specially paid, in the first instance to the contribution of Members of the United Nations to the maintenance of international peace and security and to the other purposes of the Organization, and also to equitable geographical distribution.

2. The non-permanent members of the Security Council shall be elected for a term of two years. In the first election of the non-permanent members after the increase of the membership of the Security Council from eleven to fifteen, two of the four additional members shall be chosen for a term of one year. A retiring member shall not be eligible for immediate re-election.

3. Each member of the Security Council shall have one representative.

FUNCTIONS AND POWERS

Article 24

1. In order to ensure prompt and effective action by the United Nations, its Members confer on the Security Council primary responsibility for the maintenance of international peace and security, and agree that in carrying out its duties under this responsibility the Security Council acts on their behalf.

2. In discharging these duties the Security Council shall act in accordance with the Purposes and Principles of the United Nations. The specific powers granted to the Security Council for the discharge of these duties are laid down in Chapters VI, VII, VIII, and XII.

3. The Security Council shall submit annual and, when necessary, special reports to the General Assembly for its consideration.

Article 25

The Members of the United Nations agree to accept and carry out the decisions of the Security Council in accordance with the present Charter.

Article 26

In order to promote the establishment and maintenance of international peace and security with the least diversion for armaments of the world's human and economic resources, the Security Council shall be responsible for formulating, with the assistance of the Military Staff Committee referred to in *Article 47*, plans to be submitted to the Members of the United Nations for the establishment of a system for the regulation of armaments.

Article 27

1. Each member of the Security Council shall have one vote.
2. Decisions of the Security Council on procedural matters shall be made by an affirmative vote of nine members.
3. Decisions of the Security Council on all other matters shall be made by an affirmative vote of nine members including the concurring votes of the permanent members; provided that, in decisions under Chapter VI, and under paragraph 3 of *Article 52*, a party to a dispute shall abstain from voting.

PROCEDURE

Article 28

1. The Security Council shall be so organized as to be able to function continuously. Each member of the Security Council shall for this purpose be represented at all times at the seat of the Organization.
2. The Security Council shall hold periodic meetings at which each of its members may, if it so desires, be represented by a member of the government or by some other specially designated representative.
3. The Security Council may hold meetings at such places other than the seat of the Organization as in its judgment will best facilitate its work.

Article 29

The Security Council may establish such subsidiary organs as it deems necessary for the performance of its functions.

Article 30

The Security Council shall adopt its own rules of procedure, including the method of selecting its President.

Article 31

Any member of the United Nations which is not a member of the Security Council may participate, without vote, in the discussion of any question brought before the Security Council whenever the latter considers that the interests of that Member are specially affected.

Article 32

Any Member of the United Nations which is not a member of the Security Council or any state which is not a Member of the United Nations, if it is a party to a dispute under consideration by the Security Council, shall be invited to participate, without vote, in the discussion relating to the dispute. The Security Council shall lay down such conditions as it deems just for the participation of a state which is not a Member of the United Nations.

Chapter VI
PACIFIC SETTLEMENT OF DISPUTES

Article 33

1. The parties to any dispute, the continuance of which is likely to endanger the maintenance of international peace and security, shall, first of all, seek a solution by negotiation, enquiry, mediation, conciliation, arbitration, judicial settlement, resort to regional agencies or arrangements, or other peaceful means of their own choice.

2. The Security Council shall, when it deems necessary, call upon the parties to settle their dispute by such means.

Article 34

The Security Council may investigate any dispute, or any situation which might lead to international friction or give rise to a dispute, in order to determine whether the continuance of the dispute or situation is likely to endanger the maintenance of international peace and security.

Article 35

1. Any Member of the United Nations may bring any dispute, or any situation of the nature referred to in *Article* 34, to the attention of the Security Council or of the General Assembly.

2. A state which is not a Member of the United Nations may bring to the attention of the Security Council or of the General Assembly any dispute to which it is a party if it accepts in advance, for the purposes of

the dispute, the obligations of pacific settlement provided in the present Charter.

3. The proceedings of the General Assembly in respect of matters brought to its attention under this Article will be subject to the provisions of *Articles* 11 and 12.

Article 36

1. The Security Council may, at any stage of a dispute of the nature referred to in *Article* 33 or of a situation of like nature, recommend appropriate procedures or methods of adjustment.

2. The Security Council should take into consideration any procedures for the settlement of the dispute which have already been adopted by the parties.

3. In making recommendations under this Article the Security Council should also take into consideration that legal disputes should as a general rule be referred by the parties to the International Court of Justice in accordance with the provisions of the Statute of the Court.

Article 37

1. Should the parties to a dispute of the nature referred to in *Article* 33 fail to settle it by the means indicated in that Article, they shall refer it to the Security Council.

2. If the Security Council deems that the continuance of the dispute is in fact likely to endanger the maintenance of international peace and security, it shall decide whether to take action under *Article* 36 or to recommend such terms of settlement as it may consider appropriate.

Article 38

Without prejudice to the provisions of *Articles* 33 to 37, the Security Council may, if all the parties to any dispute so request, make recommendations to the parties with a view to a pacific settlement of the dispute.

Chapter VII

ACTION WITH RESPECT TO THREATS TO THE PEACE, BREACHES OF THE PEACE, AND ACTS OF AGGRESSION

Article 39

The Security Council shall determine the existence of any threat to the peace, breach of the peace, or act of aggression and shall make recommendations, or decide what measures shall be taken in accordance with

Articles 41 and 42, to maintain or restore international peace and security.

Article 40

In order to prevent an aggravation of the situation, the Security Council may, before making the recommendations or deciding upon the measures provided for in *Article* 39, call upon the parties concerned to comply with such provisional measures as it deems necessary or desirable. Such provisional measures shall be without prejudice to the rights, claims, or position of the parties concerned. The Security Council shall duly take account of failure to comply with such provisional measures.

Article 41

The Security Council may decide what measures not involving the use of armed force are to be employed to give effect to its decisions, and it may call upon the Members of the United Nations to apply such measures. These may include complete or partial interruption of economic relations and of rail, sea, air, postal, telegraphic, radio, and other means of communication, and the severance of diplomatic relations.

Article 42

Should the Security Council consider that measures provided for in *Article* 41 would be inadequate or have proved to be inadequate, it may take such action by air, sea, or land forces as may be necessary to maintain or restore international peace and security. Such action may include demonstrations, blockade, and other operations by air, sea, or land forces of Members of the United Nations.

Article 43

1. All Members of the United Nations, in order to contribute to the maintenance of international peace and security, undertake to make available to the Security Council, on its call and in accordance with a special agreement or agreements, armed forces, assistance, and facilities, including rights of passage, necessary for the purpose of maintaining international peace and security.

2. Such agreement or agreements shall govern the numbers and types of forces, their degree of readiness and general location, and the nature of the facilities and assistance to be provided.

3. The agreement or agreements shall be negotiated as soon as possible on the initiative of the Security Council. They shall be concluded between the Security Council and Members or between the Security Council and groups of Members and shall be subject to ratification by

the signatory states in accordance with their respective constitutional processes.

Article 44

When the Security Council has decided to use force it shall, before calling upon a Member not represented on it to provide armed forces in fulfillment of the obligations assumed under *Article* 43, invite that Member, if the Member so desires, to participate in the decisions of the Security Council concerning the employment of contingents of that Member's armed forces.

Article 45

In order to enable the United Nations to take urgent military measures, Members shall hold immediately available national air-force contingents for combined international enforcement action. The strength and degree of readiness of these contingents and plans for their combined action shall be determined, within the limits laid down in the special agreement or agreements referred to in *Article* 43, by the Security Council with the assistance of the Military Staff Committee.

Article 46

Plans for the application of armed force shall be made by the Security Council with the assistance of the Military Staff Committee.

Article 47

1. There shall be established a Military Staff Committee to advise and assist the Security Council on all questions relating to the Security Council's military requirements for the maintenance of international peace and security, the employment and command of forces placed at its disposal, the regulation of armaments, and possible disarmament.

2. The Military Staff Committee shall consist of the Chiefs of Staff of the permanent members of the Security Council or their representatives. Any Member of the United Nations not permanently represented on the Committee shall be invited by the Committee to be associated with it when the efficient discharge of the Committee's responsibilities requires the participation of the Member in its work.

3. The Military Staff Committee shall be responsible under the Security Council for the strategic direction of any armed forces placed at the disposal of the Security Council. Questions relating to the command of such forces shall be worked out subsequently.

4. The Military Staff Committee, with the authorization of the Security Council and after consultation with appropriate regional agencies, may establish regional subcommittees.

Article 48

1. The action required to carry out the decisions of the Security Council for the maintenance of international peace and security shall be taken by all the Members of the United Nations or by some of them, as the Security Council may determine.

2. Such decisions shall be carried out by the Members of the United Nations directly and through their action in the appropriate international agencies of which they are members.

Article 49

The Members of the United Nations shall join in affording mutual assistance in carrying out the measures decided upon by the Security Council.

Article 50

If preventive or enforcement measures against any state are taken by the Security Council, any other state, whether a Member of the United Nations or not, which finds itself confronted with special economic problems arising from the carrying out of those measures shall have the right to consult the Security Council with regard to a solution of those problems.

Article 51

Nothing in the present Charter shall impair the inherent right of individual or collective self-defense if an armed attack occurs against a Member of the United Nations, until the Security Council has taken measures necessary to maintain international peace and security. Measures taken by Members in the exercise of this right of self-defense shall be immediately reported to the Security Council and shall not in any way affect the authority and responsibility of the Security Council under the present Charter to take at any time such action as it deems necessary in order to maintain or restore international peace and security.

Chapter VIII
REGIONAL ARRANGEMENTS

Article 52

1. Nothing in the present Charter precludes the existence of regional arrangements or agencies for dealing with such matters relating to the maintenance of international peace and security as are appropriate for regional action, provided that such arrangements or agencies and their

activities are consistent with the Purposes and Principles of the United Nations.

2. The Members of the United Nations entering into such arrangements or constituting such agencies shall make every effort to achieve pacific settlement of local disputes through such regional agencies before referring them to the Security Council.

3. The Security Council shall encourage the development of pacific settlement of local disputes through such regional arrangements or by such regional agencies either on the initiative of the states concerned or by reference from the Security Council.

4. This Article in no way impairs the application of *Articles* 34 and 35.

Article 53

1. The Security Council shall, where appropriate, utilize such regional arrangements or agencies for enforcement action under its authority. But no enforcement action shall be taken under regional arrangements or by regional agencies without the authorization of the Security Council, with the exception of measures against any enemy state, as defined in paragraph 2 of this Article, provided for pursuant to *Article* 107 or in regional arrangements directed against renewal of aggressive policy on the part of any such state, until such time as the Organization may, on request of the Governments concerned, be charged with the responsibility for preventing further aggression by such a state.

2. The term enemy state as used in paragraph 1 of this Article applies to any state which during the Second World War has been an enemy of any signatory of the present Charter.

Article 54

The Security Council shall at all times be kept fully informed of activities undertaken or in contemplation under regional arrangements or by regional agencies for the maintenance of international peace and security.

Chapter IX

INTERNATIONAL ECONOMIC AND SOCIAL COOPERATION

Article 55

With a view to the creation of conditions of stability and well-being which are necessary for peaceful and friendly relations among nations based on respect for the principle of equal rights and self-determination of peoples, the United Nations shall promote:

a. higher standards of living, full employment, and conditions of economic and social progress and development;

b. solutions of international economic, social, health, and related problems; and international cultural and educational cooperation; and

c. universal respect for, and observance of, human rights and fundamental freedoms for all without distinction as to race, sex, language, or religion.

Article 56

All Members pledge themselves to take joint and separate action in cooperation with the Organization for the achievement of the purposes set forth in *Article* 55.

Article 57

1. The various specialized agencies, established by intergovernmental agreement and having wide international responsibilities, as defined in their basic instruments, in economic, social, cultural, educational, health, and related fields, shall be brought into relationship with the United Nations in accordance with the provisions of *Article* 63.

2. Such agencies thus brought into relationship with the United Nations are hereinafter referred to as specialized agencies.

Article 58

The Organization shall make recommendations for the coordination of the policies and activities of the specialized agencies.

Article 59

The Organization shall, where appropriate, initiate negotiations among the states concerned for the accomplishment of the purposes set forth in *Article* 55.

Article 60

Responsibility for the discharge of the functions of the Organization set forth in this Chapter shall be vested in the General Assembly and, under the authority of the General Assembly, in the Economic and Social Council, which shall have for this purpose the powers set forth in Chapter X.

Chapter X
THE ECONOMIC AND SOCIAL COUNCIL

Article 61

1. The Economic and Social Council shall consist of twenty-seven Members of the United Nations elected by the General Assembly.

2. Subject to the provisions of paragraph 3, nine members of the Economic and Social Council shall be elected each year for a term of three years. A retiring member shall be eligible for immediate re-election.

3. At the first election after the increase in the membership of the Economic and Social Council from eighteen to twenty-seven members, in addition to the members elected in place of the six members whose term of office expires at the end of that year, nine additional members shall be elected. Of these nine additional members, the term of office of three members so elected shall expire at the end of one year, and of three other members at the end of two years, in accordance with arrangements made by the General Assembly.

4. Each member of the Economic and Social Council shall have one representative.

FUNCTIONS AND POWERS

Article 62

1. The Economic and Social Council may make or initiate studies and reports with respect to international economic, social, cultural, educational, health, and related matters and may make recommendations with respect to any such matters to the General Assembly, to the Members of the United Nations, and to the specialized agencies concerned.

2. It may make recommendations for the purpose of promoting respect for, and observance of, human rights and fundamental freedoms for all.

3. It may prepare draft conventions for submission to the General Assembly, with respect to matters falling within its competence.

4. It may call, in accordance with the rules prescribed by the United Nations, international conferences on matters falling within its competence.

Article 63

1. The Economic and Social Council may enter into agreements with any of the agencies referred to in *Article* 57, defining the terms on which the agency concerned shall be brought into relationship with the United Nations. Such agreements shall be subject to approval by the General Assembly.

2. It may coordinate the activities of the specialized agencies through consultation with and recommendations to such agencies and through recommendations to the General Assembly and to the Members of the United Nations.

Article 64

1. The Economic and Social Council may take appropriate steps to obtain regular reports from the specialized agencies. It may make arrangements with the Members of the United Nations and with the specialized agencies to obtain reports on the steps taken to give effect to its own recommendations and to recommendations on matters falling within its competence made by the General Assembly.

2. It may communicate its observations on these reports to the General Assembly.

Article 65

The Economic and Social Council may furnish information to the Security Council and shall assist the Security Council upon its request.

Article 66

1. The Economic and Social Council shall perform such functions as fall within its competence in connection with the carrying out of the recommendations of the General Assembly.

2. It may, with the approval of the General Assembly, perform services at the request of Members of the United Nations and at the request of specialized agencies.

3. It shall perform such other functions as are specified elsewhere in the present Charter or as may be assigned to it by the General Assembly.

VOTING

Article 67

1. Each member of the Economic and Social Council shall have one vote.

2. Decisions of the Economic and Social Council shall be made by a majority of the members present and voting.

PROCEDURE

Article 68

The Economic and Social Council shall set up commissions in economic and social fields and for the promotion of human rights, and such other commissions as may be required for the performance of its functions.

Article 69

The Economic and Social Council shall invite any Member of the United Nations to participate, without vote, in its deliberations on any matter of particular concern to that Member.

Article 70

The Economic and Social Council may make arrangements for representatives of the specialized agencies to participate, without vote, in its deliberations and in those of the commissions established by it, and for its representatives to participate in the deliberations of the specialized agencies.

Article 71

The Economic and Social Council may make suitable arrangements for consultation with non-governmental organizations which are concerned with matters within its competence. Such arrangements may be made with international organizations and, where appropriate, with national organizations after consultation with the Member of the United Nations concerned.

Article 72

1. The Economic and Social Council shall adopt its own rules of procedure, including the method of selecting its President.

2. The Economic and Social Council shall meet as required in accordance with its rules, which shall include provision for the convening of meetings on the request of a majority of its members.

Chapter XI

DECLARATION REGARDING NON-SELF-GOVERNING TERRITORIES

Article 73

Members of the United Nations which have or assume responsibilities for the administration of territories whose peoples have not yet attained a full measure of self-government recognize the principle that the interests of the inhabitants of these territories are paramount, and accept as a sacred trust the obligation to promote to the utmost, within the system of international peace and security established by the present Charter, the well-being of the inhabitants of these territories, and, to this end:

a. to ensure, with due respect for the culture of the peoples concerned, their political, economic, social, and educational advancement, their just treatment, and their protection against abuses;

b. to develop self-government, to take due account of the political aspirations of the peoples, and to assist them in the progressive development of their free political institutions, according to the particular circumstances of each territory and its peoples and their varying stages of advancement.

c. to further international peace and security;

d. to promote constructive measures of development, to encourage research, and to cooperate with one another and, when and where appropriate, with specialized international bodies with a view to the practical achievement of the social, economic, and scientific purposes set forth in this Article; and

e. to transmit regularly to the Secretary-General for information purposes, subject to such limitations as security and constitutional considerations may require, statistical and other information of a technical nature relating to economic, social, and educational conditions in the territories for which they are respectively responsible other than those territories to which Chapters XII and XIII apply.

Article 74

Members of the United Nations also agree that their policy in respect of the territories to which this Chapter applies, no less than in respect of their metropolitan areas, must be based on the general principle of good-neighborliness, due account being taken of the interests and well-being of the rest of the world, in social, economic, and commercial matters.

Chapter XII

INTERNATIONAL TRUSTEESHIP SYSTEM

Article 75

The United Nations shall establish under its authority an international trusteeship system for the administration and supervision of such territories as may be placed thereunder by subsequent individual agreements. These territories are hereinafter referred to as trust territories.

Article 76

The basic objectives of the trusteeship system, in accordance with the Purposes of the United Nations laid down in *Article* 1 of the present Charter, shall be:

a. to further international peace and security;

b. to promote the political, economic, social, and educational advancement of the inhabitants of the trust territories, and their progressive development towards self-government or independence as may be appropriate to the particular circumstances of each territory and its peoples and the freely expressed wishes of the peoples concerned, and as may be provided by the terms of each trusteeship agreement;

c. to encourage respect for human rights and for fundamental freedoms for all without distinction as to race, sex, language, or religion, and to encourage recognition of the interdependence of the peoples of the world; and

d. to ensure equal treatment in social, economic, and commercial matters for all Members of the United Nations and their nationals, and also equal treatment for the latter in the administration of justice, without prejudice to the attainment of the foregoing objectives and subject to the provisions of *Article* 80.

Article 77

1. The trusteeship system shall apply to such territories in the following categories as may be placed thereunder by means of trusteeship agreements:

a. territories now held under mandate;

b. territories which may be detached from enemy states as a result of the Second World War; and

c. territories voluntarily placed under the system by states responsible for their administration.

2. It will be matter for subsequent agreement as to which territories in the foregoing categories will be brought under the trusteeship system and upon what terms.

Article 78

The trusteeship system shall not apply to territories which have become Members of the United Nations, relationship among which shall be based on respect for the principle of sovereign equality.

Article 79

The terms of trusteeship for each territory to be placed under the trusteeship system, including any alteration or amendment, shall be agreed upon by the states directly concerned, including the mandatory power in the case of territories held under mandate by a Member of the United Nations, and shall be approved as provided for in *Articles* 83 and 85.

Article 80

1. Except as may be agreed upon in individual trusteeship agreements, made under *Articles* 77, 79, and 81, placing each territory under the trusteeship system, and until such agreements have been concluded, nothing in this Chapter shall be construed in or of itself to alter in any manner the rights whatsoever of any states or any peoples or the terms of existing international instruments to which Members of the United Nations may respectively be parties.

2. Paragraph 1 of this Article shall not be interpreted as giving grounds for delay or postponement of the negotiation and conclusion of agreements for placing mandated and other territories under the trusteeship system as provided for in *Article* 77.

Article 81

The trusteeship agreement shall in each case include the terms under which the trust territory will be administered and designate the authority which will exercise the administration of the trust territory. Such authority, hereinafter called the administering authority, may be one or more states or the Organization itself.

Article 82

There may be designated, in any trusteeship agreement, a strategic area or areas which may include part or all of the trust territory to which the agreement applies, without prejudice to any special agreement or agreements made under *Article* 43.

Article 83

1. All functions of the United Nations relating to strategic areas, including the approval of the terms of the trusteeship agreements and of their alteration or amendment, shall be exercised by the Security Council.

2. The basic objectives set forth in *Article* 76 shall be applicable to the people of each strategic area.

3. The Security Council shall, subject to the provisions of the trusteeship agreements and without prejudice to security considerations, avail itself of the assistance of the Trusteeship Council to perform those functions of the United Nations under the trusteeship system relating to political, economic, social, and educational matters in the strategic areas.

Article 84

It shall be the duty of the administering authority to ensure that the trust territory shall play its part in the maintenance of international peace and security. To this end the administering authority may make use of volunteer forces, facilities, and assistance from the trust territory in carrying out the obligations towards the Security Council undertaken in this regard by the administering authority, as well as for local defense and the maintenance of law and order within the trust territory.

Article 85

1. The functions of the United Nations with regard to trusteeship agreements for all areas not designated as strategic, including the approval of the terms of the trusteeship agreements and of their alteration or amendment, shall be exercised by the General Assembly.

2. The Trusteeship Council, operating under the authority of the General Assembly, shall assist the General Assembly in carrying out these functions.

Chapter XIII
THE TRUSTEESHIP COUNCIL

COMPOSITION

Article 86

1. The Trusteeship Council shall consist of the following Members of the United Nations.

    a. those Members administering trust territories;

    b. such of those Members mentioned by name in *Article* 23 as are not administering trust territories; and

    c. as many other Members elected for three-year terms by the General Assembly as may be necessary to ensure that the total number of members of the Trusteeship Council is equally divided between those Members of the United Nations which administer trust territories and those which do not.

2. Each member of the Trusteeship Council shall designate one specially qualified person to represent it therein.

FUNCTIONS AND POWERS

Article 87

The General Assembly and, under its authority, the Trusteeship Council, in carrying out their functions, may:

a. consider reports submitted by the administering authority;

b. accept petitions and examine them in consultation with the administering authority;

c. provide for periodic visits to the respective trust territories at times agreed upon with the administering authority; and

d. take these and other actions in conformity with the terms of the trusteeship agreements.

Article 88

The Trusteeship Council shall formulate a questionnaire on the political, economic, social, and educational advancement of the inhabitants of each trust territory, and the administering authority for each trust territory within the competence of the General Assembly shall make an annual report to the General Assembly upon the basis of such questionnaire.

VOTING

Article 89

1. Each member of the Trusteeship Council shall have one vote.

2. Decisions of the Trusteeship Council shall be made by a majority of the members present and voting.

PROCEDURE

Article 90

1. The Trusteeship Council shall adopt its own rules of procedure, including the method of selecting its President.

2. The Trusteeship Council shall meet as required in accordance with its rules, which shall include provision for the convening of meetings on the request of a majority of its members.

Article 91

The Trusteeship Council shall, when appropriate, avail itself of the assistance of the Economic and Social Council and of the specialized agencies in regard to matters with which they are respectively concerned.

Chapter XIV

THE INTERNATIONAL COURT OF JUSTICE

Article 92

The International Court of Justice shall be the principal judicial organ of the United Nations. It shall function in accordance with the annexed Statute, which is based upon the Statute of the Permanent Court of International Justice and forms an integral part of the present Charter.

Article 93

1. All Members of the United Nations are *ipso facto* parties to the Statute of the International Court of Justice.

2. A state which is not a Member of the United Nations may become a party to the Statute of the International Court of Justice on conditions to be determined in each case by the General Assembly upon the recommendation of the Security Council.

Article 94

1. Each Member of the United Nations undertakes to comply with the decision of the International Court of Justice in any case to which it is a party.

2. If any party to a case fails to perform the obligations incumbent upon it under a judgment rendered by the Court, the other party may have recourse to the Security Council, which may, if it deems necessary, make recommendations or decide upon measures to be taken to give effect to the judgment.

Article 95

Nothing in the present Charter shall prevent Members of the United Nations from entrusting the solution of their differences to other tribunals by virtue of agreements already in existence or which may be concluded in the future.

Article 96

1. The General Assembly or the Security Council may request the International Court of Justice to give an advisory opinion on any legal question.

2. Other organs of the United Nations and specialized agencies, which may at any time be so authorized by the General Assembly, may also request advisory opinions of the Court on legal questions arising within the scope of their activities.

Chapter XV

THE SECRETARIAT

Article 97

The Secretariat shall comprise a Secretary-General and such staff as the Organization may require. The Secretary-General shall be appointed by the General Assembly upon the recommendation of the Security Council. He shall be the chief administrative officer of the Organization.

Article 98

The Secretary-General shall act in that capacity in all meetings of the General Assembly, of the Security Council, of the Economic and Social Council, and of the Trusteeship Council, and shall perform such other functions as are entrusted to him by these organs. The Secretary-General shall make an annual report to the General Assembly on the work of the Organization.

Article 99

The Secretary-General may bring to the attention of the Security Council any matter which in his opinion may threaten the maintenance of international peace and security.

Article 100

1. In the performance of their duties the Secretary-General and the staff shall not seek or receive instructions from any government or from any other authority external to the Organization. They shall refrain from any action which might reflect on their position as international officials responsible only to the Organization.

2. Each Member of the United Nations undertakes to respect the exclusively international character of the responsibilities of the Secretary-General and the staff and not to seek to influence them in the discharge of their responsibilities.

Article 101

1. The staff shall be appointed by the Secretary-General under regulations established by the General Assembly.

2. Appropriate staffs shall be permanently assigned to the Economic and Social Council, the Trusteeship Council, and, as required, to other organs of the United Nations. These staffs shall form a part of the Secretariat.

3. The paramount consideration in the employment of the staff and in the determination of the conditions of service shall be the necessity of securing the highest standards of efficiency, competence, and integrity. Due regard shall be paid to the importance of recruiting the staff on as wide a geographical basis as possible.

Chapter XVI
MISCELLANEOUS PROVISIONS

Article 102

1. Every treaty and every international agreement entered into by any Member of the United Nations after the present Charter comes into force shall as soon as possible be registered with the Secretariat and published by it.

2. No party to any such treaty or international agreement which has not been registered in accordance with the provisions of paragraph 1 of this Article may invoke that treaty or agreement before any organ of the United Nations.

Article 103

In the event of a conflict between the obligations of the Members of the United Nations under the present Charter and their obligations under any other international agreement, their obligations under the present Charter shall prevail.

Article 104

The Organization shall enjoy in the territory of each of its Members such legal capacity as may be necessary for the exercise of its functions and the fulfillment of its purposes.

Article 105

1. The Organization shall enjoy in the territory of each of its Members such privileges and immunities as are necessary for the fulfillment of its purposes.

2. Representatives of the Members of the United Nations and officials of the Organization shall similarly enjoy such privileges and immunities as are necessary for the independent exercise of their functions in connection with the Organization.

3. The General Assembly may make recommendations with a view to determining the details of the application of paragraphs 1 and 2 of this Article or may propose conventions of the Members of the United Nations for this purpose.

Chapter XVII
TRANSITIONAL SECURITY ARRANGEMENTS

Article 106

Pending the coming into force of such special agreements referred to in *Article* 43 as in the opinion of the Security Council enable it to begin the exercise of its responsibilities under *Article* 42, the parties to the Four-Nation Declaration, signed at Moscow, October 30, 1943, and France, shall, in accordance with the provisions of paragraph 5 of that Declaration, consult with one another and as occasion requires with other Members of the United Nations with a view to such joint action on behalf of the Organization as may be necessary for the purpose of maintaining international peace and security.

Article 107

Nothing in the present Charter shall invalidate or preclude action in relation to any state which during the Second World War has been an enemy of any signatory to the present Charter, taken or authorized as a result of that war by the Governments having responsibility for such action.

Chapter XVIII
AMENDMENTS

Article 108

Amendments to the present Charter shall come into force for all Members of the United Nations when they have been adopted by a vote of two thirds of the members of the General Assembly and ratified in accordance with their respective constitutional processes by two thirds of the Members of the United Nations, including all the permanent members of the Security Council.

Article 109

1. A General Conference of the Members of the United Nations for the purpose of reviewing the present Charter may be held at a date and place to be fixed by a two-thirds vote of the members of the General Assembly and by a vote of any seven members of the Security Council. Each Member of the United Nations shall have one vote in the conference.

2. Any alteration of the present Charter recommended by a two-thirds vote of the conference shall take effect when ratified in accordance with their respective constitutional processes by two thirds of the Members of the United Nations including all the permanent members of the Security Council.

3. If such a conference has not been held before the tenth annual session of the General Assembly following the coming into force of the present Charter, the proposal to call such a conference shall be placed on the agenda of that session of the General Assembly, and the conference shall be held if so decided by a majority vote of the members of the General Assembly and by a vote of any seven members of the Security Council.

Chapter XIX

RATIFICATION AND SIGNATURE

Article 110

1. The present Charter shall be ratified by the signatory states in accordance with their respective constitutional processes.

2. The ratifications shall be deposited with the Government of the United States of America, which shall notify all the signatory states of each deposit as well as the Secretary-General of the Organization when he has been appointed.

3. The present Charter shall come into force upon the deposit of ratifications by the Republic of China, France, the Union of Soviet Socialist Republics, the United Kingdom of Great Britain and Northern Ireland, and the United States of America, and by a majority of the other signatory states. A protocol of the ratifications deposited shall thereupon be drawn up by the Government of the United States of America which shall communicate copies thereof to all the signatory states.

4. The states signatory to the present Charter which ratify it after it has come into force will become original Members of the United Nations on the date of the deposit of their respective ratifications.

Article 111

The present Charter, of which the Chinese, French, Russian, English, and Spanish texts are equally authentic shall remain deposited in the archives of the Government of the United States of America. Duly certified copies thereof shall be transmitted by that Government to the Governments of the other signatory states.

In faith whereof the representatives of the Governments of the United Nations have signed the present Charter.

Done at the city of San Francisco the twenty-sixth day of June, one thousand nine hundred and forty-five.

[The Statute of the International Court of Justice, which forms part of the Charter, is not included.]

Appendix 2

UNIVERSAL DECLARATION OF HUMAN RIGHTS

PREAMBLE

Whereas recognition of the inherent dignity and of the equal and inalienable rights of all members of the human family is the foundation of freedom, justice and peace in the world,

Whereas disregard and contempt for human rights have resulted in barbarous acts which have outraged the conscience of mankind, and the advent of a world in which human beings shall enjoy freedom of speech and belief and freedom from fear and want has been proclaimed as the highest aspiration of the common people,

Whereas it is essential, if man is not to be compelled to have recourse, as a last resort, to rebellion against tyranny and oppression, that human rights should be protected by the rule of law,

Whereas it is essential to promote the development of friendly relations between nations,

Whereas the peoples of the United Nations have in the Charter reaffirmed their faith in fundamental human rights, in the dignity and worth of the human person and in the equal rights of men and women and have determined to promote social progress and better standards of life in larger freedom,

Whereas Member States have pledged themselves to achieve, in co-operation with the United Nations, the promotion of universal respect for and observance of human rights and fundamental freedoms,

Whereas a common understanding of these rights and freedoms is of the greatest importance for the full realization of this pledge,

Now, Therefore,

THE GENERAL ASSEMBLY

proclaims

THIS UNIVERSAL DECLARATION OF HUMAN RIGHTS as a common standard of achievement for all peoples and all nations, to the end that every individual and every organ of society, keeping this Declaration constantly in mind, shall strive by teaching and education to promote respect for these rights and freedoms and by progressive measures, national and international, to secure their universal and effective recognition and observance, both among the peoples of Member States themselves and among the peoples of territories under their jurisdiction.

Article 1. All human beings are born free and equal in dignity and rights. They are endowed with reason and conscience and should act towards one another in a spirit of brotherhood.

Article 2. Everyone is entitled to all the rights and freedoms set forth in this Declaration, without distinction of any kind, such as race, colour, sex, language, religion, political or other opinion, national or social origin, property, birth or other status.

Furthermore, no distinction shall be made on the basis of the political, jurisdictional or international status of the country or territory to which a person belongs, whether it be independent, trust, non-self-governing or under any other limitation of sovereignty.

Article 3. Everyone has the right to life, liberty and security of person.

Article 4. No one shall be held in slavery ir servitude; slavery and the slave trade shall be prohibited in all their forms.

Article 5. No one shall be subjected to torture or to cruel, inhuman or degrading treatment or punishment.

Article 6. Everyone has the right to recognition everywhere as a person before the law.

Article 7. All are equal before the law and are entitled without any discrimination to equal protection of the law. All are entitled to equal protection against any discrimination in violation of this Declaration and against any incitement to such discrimination.

Article 8. Everyone has the right to an effective remedy by the competent national tribunals for acts violating the fundamental rights granted him by the constitution or by law.

Article 9. No one shall be subjected to arbitrary arrest, detention or exile.

Article 10. Everyone is entitled in full equality to a fair and public hearing by an independent and impartial tribunal, in the determination of his rights and obligations and of any criminal charge against him.

Article 11. (1) Everyone charged with a penal offence has the right to be presumed innocent until proved guilty according to law in a public trial at which he has had all the guarantees necessary for his defence.

(2) No one shall be held guilty of any penal offence on account of any act or omission which did not constitute a penal offence, under national or international law, at the time when it was committed. Nor shall

a heavier penalty be imposed than the one that was applicable at the time the penal offence was committed.

Article 12. No one shall be subjected to arbitrary interference with his privacy, family, home or correspondence, nor to attacks upon his honour and reputation. Everyone has the right to the protection of the law against such interference or attacks.

Article 13. (1) Everyone has the right to freedom of movement and residence within the borders of each state.

(2) Everyone has the right to leave any country, including his own, and to return to his country.

Article 14. (1) Everyone has the right to seek and to enjoy in other countries asylum from persecution.

(2) This right may not be invoked in the case of prosecutions genuinely arising from non-political crimes or from acts contrary to the purposes and principles of the United Nations.

Article 15. (1) Everyone has the right to a nationality.

(2) No one shall be arbitrarily deprived of his nationality nor denied the right to change his nationality.

Article 16. (1) Men and women of full age, without any limitation due to race, nationality or religion, have the right to marry and to found a family. They are entitled to equal rights as to marriage, during marriage and at its dissolution.

(2) Marriage shall be entered into only with the free and full consent of the intending spouses.

(3) The family is the natural and fundamental group unit of society and is entitled to protection by society and the State.

Article 17. (1) Everyone has the right to own property alone as well as in association with others.

(2) No one shall be arbitrarily deprived of his property.

Article 18. Everyone has the right to freedom of thought, conscience and religion; this right includes freedom to change his religion or belief, and freedom, either alone or in community with others and in public or private, to manifest his religion or belief in teaching, practice, worship and observance.

Article 19. Everyone has the right to freedom of opinion and expression; this right includes freedom to hold opinions without interference and to seek, receive and impart information and ideas through any media and regardless of frontiers.

Article 20. (1) Everyone has the right to freedom of peaceful assembly and association.

(2) No one may be compelled to belong to an association.

Article 21. (1) Everyone has the right to take part in the government of his country, directly or through freely chosen representatives.

(2) Everyone has the right of equal access to public service in his country.

(3) The will of the people shall be the basis of the authority of government; this will shall be expressed in periodic and genuine elections which shall be by universal and equal suffrage and shall be held by secret vote or by equivalent free voting procedures.

Article 22. Everyone, as a member of society, has the right to social security and is entitled to realization, through national effort and international co-operation and in accordance with the organization and resources of each State, of the economic, social and cultural rights indispensable for his dignity and the free development of his personality.

Article 23. (1) Everyone has the right to work, to free choice of employment, to just and favourable conditions of work and to protection against unemployment.

(2) Everyone, without any discrimination, has the right to equal pay for equal work.

(3) Everyone who works has the right to just and favourable remuneration ensuring for himself and his family an existence worthy of human dignity, and supplemented, if necessary, by other means of social protection.

(4) Everyone has the right to form and to join trade unions for the protection of his interests.

Article 24. Everyone has the right to rest and leisure, including reasonable limitation of working hours and periodic holidays with pay.

Article 25. (1) Everyone has the right to a standard of living adequate for the health and well-being of himself and of his family, including food, clothing, housing and medical care and necessary social services, and the right to security in the event of unemployment, sickness, disability, widowhood, old age or other lack of livelihood in circumstances beyond his control.

(2) Motherhood and childhood are entitled to special care and assistance. All children, whether born in or out of wedlock, shall enjoy the same social protection.

Article 26. (1) Everyone has the right to education. Education shall be free, at least in the elementary and fundamental stages. Elementary education shall be compulsory. Technical and professional education shall be made generally available and higher education shall be equally accessibe to all on the basis of merit.

(2) Education shall be directed to the full development of the human personality and to the strengthening of respect for human rights and fundamental freedoms. It shall promote understanding, tolerance and friendship among all nations, racial or religious groups, and shall further the activities of the United Nations for the maintenance of peace.

(3) Parents have a prior right to choose the kind of education that shall be given to their children.

Article 27. (1) Everyone has the right freely to participate in the cultural life of the community, to enjoy the arts and to share in scientific advancement and its benefits.

(2) Everyone has the right to the protection of the moral and material interests resulting from any scientific, literary or artistic production of which he is the author.

Article 28. Everyone is entitled to a social and international order in which the rights and freedoms set forth in this Declaration can be fully realized.

Article 29. (1) Everyone has duties to the community in which alone the free and full development of his personality is possible.

(2) In the exercise of his rights and freedoms, everyone shall be subject only to such limitations as are determined by law solely for the purpose of securing due recognition and respect for the rights and freedoms of others and of meeting the just requirements of morality, public order and the general welfare in a democratic society.

(3) These rights and freedoms may in no case be exercised contrary to the purposes and principles of the United Nations.

Article 30. Nothing in this Declaration may be interpreted as implying for any State, group or person any right to engage in any activity or to perform any act aimed at the destruction of any of the rights and freedoms set forth herein.

Adopted and proclaimed by the General Assembly on 10 December, 1948.

Appendix 3

AREA AND POPULATION
OF MEMBERS OF THE UNITED NATIONS
(as of April 1967)

Name of Country	Total Area (Square Kilometres)	Population Latest Official Estimate	Date of UN Membership
Afghanistan	647,497	15,351,519	19 Nov. 1946
Albania	28,748	1,890,000	14 Dec. 1955
Algeria	2,381,741	12,101,994	8 Oct. 1962
Argentina	2,776,656	22,691,000	24 Oct. 1945
Australia	7,686,810	11,544,691	1 Nov. 1945
Austria	83,849	7,272,700	14 Dec. 1955
Barbados	430	244,962	9 Dec. 1966
Belgium	30,513	9,499,234	27 Dec. 1945
Bolivia	1,098,581	3,748,000	14 Nov. 1945
Botswana	569,581	576,000	17 Oct. 1966
Brazil	8,511,965	84,679,000	24 Oct. 1945
Bulgaria	110,912	8,229,500	14 Dec. 1955
Burma	678,033	25,246,000	19 Apr. 1948
Burundi	27,834	3,210,000	18 Sep. 1962
Byelorussian SSR	207,600	8,633,000	24 Oct. 1945
Cambodia	181,035	6,250,000	14 Dec. 1955
Cameroon	475,442	5,229,000	20 Sep. 1960
Canada	9,976,177	19,919,000	9 Nov. 1945
Central African Republic	622,984	1,352,000	20 Sep. 1960
Ceylon	65,610	11,232,000	14 Dec. 1955
Chad	1,284,000	3,360,600	20 Sep. 1960

Name of Country	Total Area (Square Kilometres)	Population Latest Official Estimate	Date of UN Membership
Chile	756,945	8,567,000	24 Oct. 1945
China	9,596,961	656,220,250	24 Oct. 1945
Colombia	1,138,338	18,067,667	5 Nov. 1945
Congo (Brazzaville)	342,000	826,210	20 Sep. 1960
Congo (Kinshasa)	2,345,409	16,166,916	20 Sep. 1960
Costa Rica	50,700	1,496,061	2 Nov. 1945
Cuba	114,524	7,832,700	24 Oct. 1945
Cyprus	9,251	604,000	20 Sep. 1960
Czechoslovakia	127,869	14,240,000	24 Oct. 1945
Dahomey	112,622	2,415,000	20 Sep. 1960
Denmark	43,043	4,758,125	24 Oct. 1945
Dominican Republic	48,734	3,749,672	24 Oct. 1945
Ecuador	283,561	5,340,813	21 Dec. 1945
El Salvador	21,393	3,036,536	24 Oct. 1945
Ethiopia	1,221,900	23,000,000	13 Nov. 1945
Finland	337,009	4,649,000	14 Dec. 1955
France	547,026	49,570,000	24 Oct. 1945
Gabon	267,667	468,000	20 Sep. 1960
Gambia	11,295	336,000	21 Sep. 1965
Ghana	238,537	7,740,000	8 Mar. 1957
Greece	131,944	8,550,000	25 Oct. 1945
Guatemala	108,889	4,645,841	21 Nov. 1945
Guinea	245,857	3,500,000	12 Dec. 1958
Guyana	214,969	646,371	20 Sep. 1966
Haiti	27,750	4,485,000	24 Oct. 1945
Honduras	112,088	2,362,817	17 Dec. 1945
Hungary	93,030	10,194,000	14 Dec. 1955
Iceland	103,000	192,304	19 Nov. 1946
India	3,044,736 [a]	471,624,100 [a]	30 Oct. 1945
Indonesia	1,491,564	100,045,000	28 Sep. 1950
Iran	1,648,000	23,428,211	24 Oct. 1945
Iraq	448,742	8,261,527	21 Dec. 1945
Ireland	70,280	2,880,752	14 Dec. 1955
Israel	20,700	2,636,300	11 May 1949
Italy	301,225	51,945,000	14 Dec. 1955
Ivory Coast	322,463	3,750,000	20 Sep. 1960

Name of Country	Total Area (Square Kilometres)	Population Latest Official Estimate	Date of UN Membership
Jamaica	10,962	1,843,298	18 Sep. 1962
Japan	369,661	99,056,326	18 Dec. 1956
Jordan	97,740	2,016,618	14 Dec. 1955
Kenya	582,644	9,643,000	16 Dec. 1963
Kuwait	16,000	467,339	14 May 1963
Laos	236,800	1,882,603	14 Dec. 1955
Lebanon	10,400	2,366,386	24 Oct. 1945
Lesotho	30,344	859,058	17 Oct. 1966
Liberia	111,369	1,083,073	2 Nov. 1945
Libya	1,759,540	1,681,730	14 Dec. 1955
Luxembourg	2,586	337,000	24 Oct. 1945
Madagascar	587,041	6,420,000	20 Sep. 1960
Malawi	119,310	4,042,412	1 Dec. 1964
Malaysia	332,632	9,403,350	17 Sep. 1957
Maldive Islands	298	97,743	21 Sep. 1965
Mali	1,201,625	4,654,100	28 Sep. 1960
Malta	316	317,465	1 Dec. 1964
Mauritania	1,030,700	1,050,000	27 Oct. 1961
Mexico	1,972,516	44,145,000	7 Nov. 1945
Mongolia	1,565,000	1,120,700	27 Oct. 1961
Morocco	445,050	13,323,000	12 Nov. 1956
Nepal	140,797	10,100,000	14 Dec. 1955
Netherlands	33,612	12,523,046	10 Dec. 1945
New Zealand	268,685	2,676,919	24 Oct. 1945
Nicaragua	130,000	1,684,666	24 Oct. 1945
Niger	1,267,000	3,433,000	20 Sep. 1960
Nigeria	923,768	56,400,000	7 Oct. 1960
Norway	324,219	3,738,000	27 Nov. 1945
Pakistan	946,716[a]	105,044,080[a]	30 Sep. 1947
Panama	75,650	1,286,700	13 Nov. 1945
Paraguay	406,752	2,094,000	24 Oct. 1945
Peru	1,285,215	12,011,500	31 Oct. 1945
Philippines	300,000	33,477,000	24 Oct. 1945
Poland	312,520	31,765,300	24 Oct. 1945
Portugal	91,971	9,228,000	14 Dec. 1955
Romania	237,500	19,105,000	14 Dec. 1955

Name of Country	Total Area (Square Kilometres)	Population Latest Official Estimate	Date of UN Membership
Rwanda	26,338	3,018,216	18 Sep. 1962
Saudi Arabia	2,253,300	6,036,400	24 Oct. 1945
Senegal	196,192	3,490,000	28 Sep. 1960
Sierra Leone	71,740	2,200,000	27 Sep. 1961
Singapore	581	1,913,500	21 Sep. 1965
Somalia	637,657	2,500,000	20 Sep. 1960
South Africa	1,221,037	18,296,000	7 Nov. 1945
Spain	504,750	32,005,210	14 Dec. 1955
Sudan	2,505,813	14,150,000	12 Nov. 1956
Sweden	449,793	7,844,000	19 Nov. 1946
Syria	185,180	5,634,263	24 Oct. 1945
Thailand	514,000	31,508,000	16 Dec. 1946
Togo	56,000	1,705,000	20 Sep. 1960
Trinidad and Tobago	5,128	975,000	18 Sep. 1962
Tunisia	164,150	4,457,862	12 Nov. 1956
Turkey	780,576	32,901,291	24 Oct. 1945
Uganda	236,036	7,551,000	25 Oct. 1962
Ukrainian SSR	601,000	45,516,000	24 Oct. 1945
Union of Soviet Socialist Republics	22,402,200 [b]	233,200,000 [b]	24 Oct. 1945
United Arab Republic	1,000,000	29,600,000	24 Oct. 1945
United Kingdom	244,030	55,039,000	24 Oct. 1945
United Republic of Tanzania	939,701	9,927,170	14 Dec. 1961
United States	9,363,353	197,807,000	24 Oct. 1945
Upper Volta	274,200	4,955,000	20 Sep. 1960
Uruguay	186,926	2,748,700	18 Dec. 1945
Venezuela	912,050	9,189,200	15 Nov. 1945
Yemen	195,000	5,000,000	30 Sep. 1947
Yugoslavia	255,804	19,829,000	24 Oct. 1945
Zambia	752,614	3,780,000	1 Dec. 1964

a. *Excluding data for Jammu and Kashmir, the final status of which has not yet been determined.*

b. *Including the figures of Byelorussian SSR and Ukrainian SSR.*

Based on tables of United Nations Student Map of the World, April 1967.

Appendix 4

SUGGESTED READING

General

Boyd, Andrew, *The United Nations: Piety, Myth and Truth,* rev. ed., Penguin Books, Harmondsworth, Middlesex, 1963.

Claude, Inis L., Jr., *Swords into Plowshares,* 3rd ed., Random House, Inc., New York, 1964.

Goodspeed, Stephen S., *The Nature and Function of International Organization,* 2nd ed., Oxford University Press, New York, 1967.

Luard, Evan (ed.), Ralph Townley *et al.,* contributors, *The Evolution of International Organizations,* Frederick A. Praeger, Inc., New York, 1966.

Manning, C. A. W., *The Nature of International Society,* John Wiley & Sons, Inc., New York, 1962.

Walters, Francis P., *History of the League of Nations,* Oxford University Press, New York, 1960.

Sachs, Moshe (ed.), *The Worldmark Encyclopedia of the Nations,* 3rd rev. ed. (formerly edited by Benjamin A. Cohen), Harper and Row, New York. Five vols., 1967.

Chapter I

Evatt, H. V., *The United Nations,* Harvard University Press, Cambridge, Mass., 1948.

Goodrich, Leland M. and Edvard Hambro, *Charter of the United Nations: Commentary and Documents,* 2nd rev. ed., Columbia University Press, New York, 1968.

Goodwin, Geoffrey L., *Britain and the United Nations,* Manhattan Publishing Co., New York, 1948.

Russell, Ruth B. and Jeannette E. Muther, *A History of the United Nations Charter, The Role of the United States 1940–1945,* The Brookings Institution, Washington, D.C., 1958.

Stettinius, Edward R., Jr., *Roosevelt and the Russians; The Yalta Conference,* ed. Walter Johnson, Doubleday & Co., Inc., New York, 1949.

Chapter II

Hobbes, Thomas, *Leviathan* (Everyman's Library, 691), E. P. Dutton & Co., Inc., New York, 1950.

Nicholas, H. G., *The United Nations as a Political Institution*, 2nd ed., Oxford University Press, New York, 1962.

United Nations, *Yearbook of the United Nations 1965*, 19th ed. United Nations, New York, 1967.

Chapter III

Bailey, Sydney D., *The General Assembly of the United Nations: A Study of Procedure and Practice*, 2nd rev. ed., Frederick A. Praeger, Inc., New York, 1964.

Hankey, Lord Maurice P. A., *Diplomacy by Conference; Studies in Public Affairs*, G. P. Putnam's Sons, New York, 1946.

Munro, Sir Leslie K., *The United Nations: Hope for a Divided World*, Holt, Rinehart & Winston, Inc., New York, 1960.

Carnegie Endowment for International Peace, *Issues Before the General Assembly*, Taplinger Publishing Co., Inc., New York (an annual publication).

United Nations Association of the United States of America, *China, the United Nations and United States Policy*, New York, 1966.

Chapter IV

Dallin, Alexander A., *The Soviet Union at the United Nations: An Enquiry into Soviet Motives and Objectives*, Frederick A. Praeger, Inc., New York, 1962.

Goodrich, Leland M. and Anne P. Simons, *The United Nations and the Maintenance of International Peace and Security*, The Brookings Institution, Washington, D.C., 1955.

Gordenker, Leon, *The U. N. Secretary-General and the Maintenance of Peace*, Columbia University Press, New York, 1967.

Chapter V

Benoit, Emile (ed.), *Disarmament and World Economic Interdependence*, Columbia University Press, New York, 1967.

Bull, Hedley, *The Control of the Arms Race*, 2nd ed., Frederick A. Praeger, Inc., New York, 1965.

Burns, Arthur Lee, and Nina Heathcote, *Peacekeeping by U. N. Forces from Suez to the Congo*, Frederick A. Praeger, Inc., New York, 1963.

Frye, William R., *A United Nations Peace Force*, Oceana Publications, Inc., New York, 1957.

Lefever, Ernest W., *Crisis in the Congo: A U. N. Force in Action*, The Brookings Institution, Washington, D.C., 1965.

Chapter VI

Chidzero, B. T. G., *Tanganyika and International Trusteeship*, Oxford University Press, New York, 1961.

Gardiner, Robert, *A World of Peoples*, The Reith Lectures, BBC, Oxford University Press, New York, 1966.

Hall, H. D., *Mandates, Dependencies and Trusteeship*, Carnegie Endowment for International Peace, Washington, D.C., 1948.

Sady, Emil J., *The United Nations and Dependent Peoples*, The Brookings Institution, Washington, D.C., 1956.

Chapter VII

Bailey, Sydney D., *The Secretariat of the United Nations*, 2nd rev. ed., Frederick A. Praeger, Inc., New York, 1964.

Foote, Wilder (ed.), *The Servant of Peace: A Selection of the Speeches and Statements of Dag Hammarskjöld*, Harper & Row, New York, 1963.

Hammarskjöld, Dag, "*The International Civil Servant in Law and in Fact*," Clarendon Press, Oxford, 1961.

Lie, Trygve, *In the Cause of Peace*, The Macmillan Co., New York, 1954.

Loveday, Alexander, *Reflections on International Administration*, Oxford University Press, New York, 1956.

Schwebel, Stephen M., *The Secretary-General of the United Nations: His Political Power and Practice*, Harvard University Press, Cambridge, Mass., 1952.

Chapter VIII

Higgins, Rosalyn, *The Development of International Law Through the Political Organs of the United Nations*, Oxford University Press, New York, 1963.

————, "The South West Africa Judgment," *International Affairs*, Vol. 42, October 1966, Oxford University Press, 1966.

Jenks, C. Wilfred, *The Common Law of Mankind*, Frederick A. Praeger, Inc., New York, 1958.

Jessup, Philip C. and Howard J. Taubenfeld, *Controls for Outer Space and the Antarctic Analogy*, Columbia University Press, New York, 1959.

Lauterpacht, Hersh, *The Development of International Law by the International Court*, rev. ed., Frederick A. Praeger, Inc., New York, 1958.

Rosenne, Shabti, *The International Court of Justice; An Essay in Political and Legal Theory*, A. W. Sijthoff, Leyden, 1957.

Shachter, Oscar, "The Relations of Law, Politics, and Action in the United Nations," Extract from: Hague Academy of International Law, *Recueil des Cours*, –2: 170–256, 1963, A. W. Sijthoff, Leyden, 1963.

Simpson, John L. and Hazel Fox, *International Arbitration*, Frederick A. Praeger, Inc., New York, 1959.

Stoessinger, J., *Financing the United Nations System*, Brookings Institution, Washington, D.C., 1964.

Cambridge Essays in International Law, *Essays in Honour of Lord McNair*, Oceana Publications, Inc., New York, 1965.

International Court of Justice, *Reports of Judgments, Advisory Opinions and Orders*, Certain Expenses of the United Nations (Article 17, Paragraph 2, of the Charter), Advisory Opinion, I.C.J. Reports 1962, p. 151.

————, South West Africa (Second Phase) Judgment, I.C.J. Reports 1966, p. 6.

Chapter IX

Cranston, Maurice, *What are Human Rights?* Basic Books, Inc., New York, 1962.

Ganji, Manouchehr, *The International Protection of Human Rights*, Libraire E. Droz, Geneva, 1962.

Jenks, C. Wilfred, *Human Rights and International Labour Standards*, Stevens and Sons, London, 1960.

Lauterpacht, Hersh, *International Law and Human Rights*, Frederick A. Praeger, Inc., New York, 1950.

Luard, Evan (ed.), *The International Protection of Human Rights*, Frederick A. Praeger, Inc., New York, 1967.

Pollack, Rosalind S., *Individual Rights and International Organization*, Smith College, Northampton, Mass., 1966.

Chapter X

Asher, R. E., *et al.*, *The United Nations and Economic and Social Cooperation*, Brookings Institution, Washington, D.C., 1957.

Hadwen, John G., and Johan Kaufman, *How United Nations Decisions are Made*, 2nd ed., Oceana Publications, Inc., New York, 1961.

Hagras, Kamal M., *United Nations Conference on Trade and Development: A Case Study in U. N. Diplomacy*, Frederick A. Praeger, Inc., New York, 1965.

Chapter XI

Black, Eugene R., *The Diplomacy of Economic Development*, Atheneum Publishers, New York, 1963.

Gardner, Richard N., *Sterling-Dollar Diplomacy*, Oxford University Press, New York, 1956.

Morris, James, *The Road to Huddersfield: A Journey to Five Continents*, Pantheon Books, New York, 1963.

Phelan, E. J., *Yes and Albert Thomas*, Columbia University Press, New York, 1949.

Weaver, James H., *The International Development Association*, Frederick A. Praeger, Inc., New York, 1965.

Chapter XII

Hunter, Guy, *The Best of Both Worlds? A Challenge on Development Policies in Africa*, Oxford University Press, New York, 1967.

Little, Ian M. D. and J. M. Clifford, *International Aid*, Aldine Publishing Company, Chicago, 1966.

Shonfield, Andrew, *The Attack on World Poverty*, Random House, Inc., New York, 1960.

Ward, Barbara, *The Rich Nations and the Poor Nations*, W. W. Norton & Co., Inc., New York, 1962.

The United Nations, *The United Nations Development Decade: Proposals for Action*, New York, 1962.

————, *The United Nations Development Decade at Mid-Point: An Appraisal by the Secretary-General*, New York, 1965.

INDEX

Some common abbreviations follow the names of agencies or organs of the United Nations. Area and population figures for member countries will be found in Appendix 3, pp. 333–36. Special abbreviations can be found in Tables 1 (pp. 106–07) and 4 (p. 247).

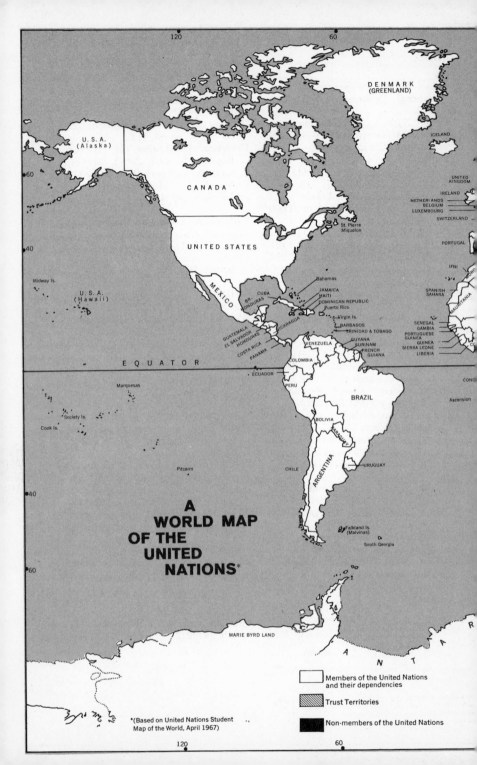

A
WORLD MAP
OF THE
UNITED
NATIONS*

*(Based on United Nations Student
Map of the World, April 1967)

Members of the United Nations
and their dependencies

Trust Territories

Non-members of the United Nations

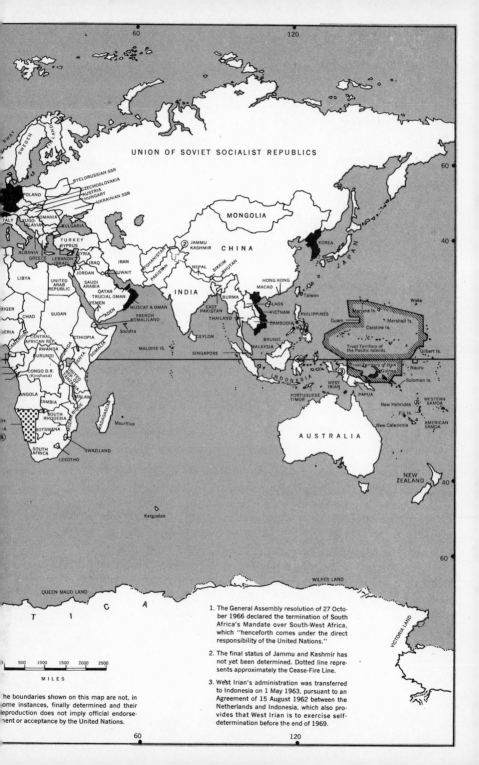

UNION OF SOVIET SOCIALIST REPUBLICS

MONGOLIA

CHINA

JAMMU
KASHMIR

INDIA

KOREA

JAPAN

HONG KONG
MACAO

Taiwan

BURMA

LAOS
VIETNAM

CAMBODIA

PHILIPPINES

Guam

Mariana Is.

Marshall Is.

Caroline Is.

Wake

Wake

Trust Territory of
the Pacific Islands

Gilbert Is.

EAST
PAKISTAN

THAILAND

CEYLON

MALDIVE IS.

SINGAPORE

BRUNEI

MALAYSIA

INDONESIA

Trust Territory of New
Guinea

Nauru

Solomon Is.

WEST
IRIAN

PAPUA

PORTUGUESE
TIMOR

New Hebrides

Fiji Is.

New Caledonia

WESTERN
SAMOA

AMERICAN
SAMOA

AUSTRALIA

NEW
ZEALAND

Kerguelen

QUEEN MAUD LAND

WILKES LAND

VICTORIA LAND

NORWAY
SWEDEN
FINLAND
POLAND
ITALY
YUGO-
SLAVIA
ROMANIA
BULGARIA
ALBANIA
GREECE
TURKEY
CYPRUS
LEBANON
ISRAEL
SYRIA
IRAQ
IRAN
JORDAN
KUWAIT
LIBYA
UNITED
ARAB
REPUBLIC
SAUDI
ARABIA
QATAR
TRUCIAL OMAN
YEMEN
MUSCAT & OMAN
ADEN
FRENCH
SOMALILAND
Socotra
NIGER
CHAD
SUDAN
NIGERIA
CAMEROON
CENTRAL
AFRICAN REP.
RWANDA
BURUNDI
ETHIOPIA
SOMALIA
KENYA
UNITED REP.
OF TANZANIA
CONGO D.R.
(Kinshasa)
ANGOLA
ZAMBIA
MALAWI
SOUTH
RHODESIA
BOTSWANA
SOUTH
AFRICA
LESOTHO
SWAZILAND
MADAGASCAR
Mauritius
BYELORUSSIAN SSR
CZECHOSLOVAKIA
AUSTRIA
HUNGARY
UKRAINIAN SSR
AFGHANISTAN
PAKISTAN
NEPAL
SIKKIM
BHUTAN

① ② ③

500   1000   1500   2000   2500

MILES

he boundaries shown on this map are not, in
ome instances, finally determined and their
eproduction does not imply official endorsement or acceptance by the United Nations.

1. The General Assembly resolution of 27 October 1966 declared the termination of South
Africa's Mandate over South-West Africa,
which "henceforth comes under the direct
responsibility of the United Nations."

2. The final status of Jammu and Kashmir has
not yet been determined. Dotted line represents approximately the Cease-Fire Line.

3. West Irian's administration was transferred
to Indonesia on 1 May 1963, pursuant to an
Agreement of 15 August 1962 between the
Netherlands and Indonesia, which also provides that West Irian is to exercise self-
determination before the end of 1969.

60   120